INDIAN DEMONOLOGY
The Inverted Pantheon

INDIAN DEMONOLOGY
The Inverted Pantheon

N.N. BHATTACHARYYA

MANOHAR
2000

First published 2000

ISBN 81-7304-309-4

Published by

Ajay Kumar Jain for
Manohar Publishers & Distributors
4753/23, Ansari Road, Daryaganj
Delhi 110 002

Typeset at

Kumud Print Service
Boileauganj, Shimla 171 005

Printed at

Replika Press Pvt. Ltd.
A 229, DSIDC Narela Indl. Park
Delhi 110040

To
AMBARISH DATTA

Contents

Preface

The present volume deals at length with the myths and legends pertaining to various kinds of celestial, aerial and terrestrial demons and demoniacal beings: Asuras, Dānavas, Daityas, Rākṣasas, Yātudhānas, Dāsas, Dasyus, Paṇis, Kālakeys, Gandharvas, Yakṣas, Apsarases, Ṛbhus, Bhṛgus, Aṅgirases, Virūpas, Garuḍas, Suparṇas, Kinnaras, Vidyādharas, Nāgas, Pannagas, Kabandhas, Bhūtas, Pretas, Piśācas and Pitṛs, as also mythical apes, beasts, birds, and reptiles, the Pramathas and Gaṇas of Śiva, the blood-consuming Mātṛkās, and so on. All such beings can be called 'demons' in English. In the introductory chapter it has been demonstrated, with references to regions and cultures outside India and to various non-Indian religious systems, that there is no clear-cut demarcation between demons and spirits on the one hand and gods and divine beings on the other. Although gods are supposed to be different from demons, confusion between the two is frequent everywhere and at all times. Indian demonology is vast and complex because India has not less than three hundred surviving tribes, each with mythology of gods, demons and spirits. The latter have been subjected, under diverse historical conditions, to the processes of social, religious and cultural transformation. Thus, we have a stratified demonology in which the characters have upward and downward movement and status in accordance with the upward and downward mobility of the detribalised castes in the social hierarchy. Those who reached the high status and proximity with the Sanskrit culture experienced a modification of their original tribal demonology on to which Brahmanical, Buddhist and Jain elements are also grafted.

The Vedas contain not only various classes of demons which have characterized the 'inverted pantheon' through the ages, but also a number of demons who have attained celebrity in the epics and Purāṇas as well as in Buddhist and Jain literature. In Vedic mythology, belief in the reality of pre-Vedic native deities did not altogether disappear, and those gods whose worshippers had been hostile to the Vedic people or had opposed their deities, so as to be denounced in the texts, were reduced to the rank of demons. Though numerous disembodied spirits and their benevolent and malevolent potentialities pervade the Vedic literature, Vedic demonology is basically anthropomorphic, the characters being recruited from the gods of alien countries, races and religions, indigenous hostile tribes, natural phenomena, and the popular world of spirits. Like the Vedic gods, the demons also belong to three categories—celestial, atmospheric and terrestrial. They are the antitheses of the gods of the three categories, two sets representing respectively the two aspects of the same naturolatry. In the demoniacal hierarchy, in the Vedas as also in subsequent literature, the highest rank is given to the Asuras. The Asuras were historically a collateral branch of the Vedic Aryans, settled in Iran, and both the peoples inherited a common tradition. That is why the Vedic gods also bore the appellation Asura. The general term for demons in the *Avesta* is *daeva*, identical with Sanskrit *deva* which is however the term for gods. This direct opposition between Indian and Iranian terms is evidently due to a great religious schism between the two branches of a community, of which we have historical evidence. Despite hostilities between the Devas and the Asuras, however, the high position of the latter was due to their cultural proximity with the former. The Rākṣasas and other classes of demons were assigned to the lower ranks because they represented the indigenous non-Vedic cultures. The original term *rakṣa*, of which Rākṣasa is a derivative, denotes a 'protector', obviously of the indigenous beliefs, cults and rituals. That is why we find them as destroyers of Vedic sacrifices. But later they imbibed much of the Vedic culture and had an upward mobility in the hierarchy, even making matrimonial alliances with the Asuras. The functioning of this hierarchical process is found in the arrangement of the eight valid forms of marriage in which the Asura form is higher than the Rākṣasa form as the latter is higher than the Piśāca form. The Piśācas though assoicated with the Rākṣasas and often identified with them, belonged to an inferior category owing to their remoteness from the Brahmanical culture.

The figures of the Buddhist and Jain demonology, collected at random from the Vedic and popular sources, are indefinite in outline and vague in character. This is due to the fact that all their evil propensities have been purged. The Buddha himself seems to have taken over from the Brahmanical teachers of his time current belief in gods and demons and held that like all other living things they were impermanent and ultimately subject to endless rebirth. Buddhism, however, required several demons and spirits to prove its superiority and the greatness of its founder. The

Buddhist texts convey the idea that these evil beings causing harm to mankind were originally hostile to the Buddha, but after coming in touch with him, underwent a complete transformation. They became devotees of the Buddha and under his all pervading influence used their special powers for the welfare of mankind.

The first category of Buddhist demons consists of the celestial and aerial beings, often described as gods, serving as the archangels of the Buddha. Here also the Asuras have a special place. Then there are Daityas, Rākṣasas, Gandharvas, Yakṣas, Kumbhaṇḍas, Apsarases, etc. The Nāgas or Mahogras, snake-like or dragon-like beings, resembling clouds, have a very important role in Buddhist demonology. There is also the concept of Māra, the personification of the evil principle and tempter of man, who presents an analogy to the Biblical Satan. Though unknown by that name in the Vedic literature, Māra is manifestly a form of Yama, the god of death. In the chapter dealing with Buddhist demonology, a few demoniacal deites of Tantric Buddhism have been mentioned. Contrary to the general expectation, the Tantras, whether Hindu or Buddhist, have no mythology, hence obviously no demon lore. There are many Tantric rites and concepts associated with the names of Bhūtas, Pretas, Piśācas and other demonic beings, but these are all mental creations. All forms of Tantric worship being symbolic, apart from the mind of the aspirant, neither the gods nor the demons have any separate existence.

Like the Buddha, the Jinas or Tīrthaṃkaras also undertook to reform the demons and spirits, destroying their evil propensities and re-employing them in good works. As a reward for their services to the Jinas, the converted demons and spirits were raised to the rank of gods. All classes of demons are useful in the Jain scheme of the functioning of the universe. In fact it was the demons who repaired and restored the ruined Jain shrines, constructed magnificent statues of the Tīrthaṃkaras and established the Jain faith. Those who had unflinching devotion to the creed were the companions of the Jinas, especially of Lord Mahāvīra, whose entourage consisted not only of the Vedic gods but of the Asuras, Rākṣasas, Yakṣas, Nāgas and others.

That the Vedic gods were subordinated to the Buddha and Mahāvīra and equated with demons did not escape the notice of the Puranic writers who were hostile to Buddhism and Jainism. In order to malign the Buddhists and Jains, the authors of the Purāṇas invented a story. Since the demons became virtuous and steadfast on the principles laid down in the Vedas and hence invincible even to Viṣṇu or Śiva, the gods conspired to weaken their source of strength by tempting them from the path of virtue having sent to them shaven-headed religious teachers who converted them to the apparently attractive doctrines of Buddhism and Jainism. Misled by the philosophical, ethical and eschatological jargon of these systems, they gave up the Vedas and the Vedic ways, their moral strength was lost and they became vulnerable. The Yakṣas and Yakṣiṇīs, along with the Bhūtas, Pretas and Piśācas, have a special place in Jainsim and Buddhism. According to some Jain texts the Bhūtas were marketable commodities. The gods, angels, men, demons and spirits and even animals are conditioned by the fetters of their *karma,* according to which a demon may be reborn as a god and a god as a demon. Although Jainism and Buddhism held that external agencies, either of the gods or of the demons, have nothing to do with human destiny, these systems found it necessary to utilize popular beliefs and sentiments regarding the demons and spirits.

In the two great epics we come across an elaborate demon lore in which the nebulous conceptions found in the Vedic literature and the idealized version tailored to suit the Buddhists and Jains have been greatly modified. It is in the epics that we come across the beginnings of a regular cycle in which the earlier translucent myths have been rendered into understandable and entertaining legends. Epic demonology has two distinct categories. In the first category we have older Vedic demons like Vṛtra, who were slain by the gods. The epics make an attempt to explain the obscure portions of the older myths by grafting on to them new legendary materials. The second category pertains to the demons killed by Rāma, Bhīma, Arjuna or some other hero. The attitude of the epic poets to the demons is rather ambivalent. The higher demons are not exactly evil forces. Many individual Asuras maintain a very high standard of character and morality. Some demons are considered 'fallen angels' in the sense that they were originally gods or human beings or celestial entities, compelled to become demons owing to curses inflicted on them for their misdeeds. In some cases they were friendly to the gods while in others they were hostile. They believed in meditation, prayer and austerities. They were favoured by Brahmā who increased their strength by granting them boons. The demons had matrimonial alliances with human beings and also with gods. Even Indra's wife was the daughter of a demon. The demons did not originally believe in the *varṇa* system, but later owing to their proximity to Brahmanical culture, the higher demons were regarded as of Brāhmaṇa origin. Apart from the Asuras of the Daitya and Dānava categories and the Rākṣasas, the epics, especially the *Mahābhārata,*contains numerous narratives about the Gandharvas, Yakṣas, Apsarases, Nāgas and demoniac beasts and birds. The Bhūtas, Pretas and Piśācas have no specific legends of their own, but their presence in connection with various battles are conspicuous. The Piśācas are described as lower forms of the Rākṣasas, while the Rākṣasas of higher ranks are equated with the Asuras, if not the gods. The epic poets attribute grotesque figures, cannibalism and other repugnant practices to them. Otherwise it would have been difficult for them to distinguish between the Rākṣasas and gods who were also equally power-loving, selfish, cruel, greedy and seducers of women. The *Rāmāyaṇa* is in essence a Rākṣasa lore, and Rākṣasa civilization as described in this epic is worthy of historical consideration.

The epics are the main sources of Puranic demonology. Epic tales pertaining to the fights between the gods and the demons are elaborated and fabricated in the Purāṇas. Certain points are to be kept in mind in this connection. The traditional number of gods is thirty-three, and the same is the traditional number of Asuras. The gods were defeated many times by the Asuras, but they did not die because they had drunk *amṛta*, the nectar of immortality. The Asuras were undoubtedly slain by the gods, but the important Asuras, apart from Hiraṇyakaśipu and his poor imitation Hiraṇyākṣa, did not die for ever. The reason may be that their preceptor Śukra by his special power restored them to life. When one of them became the lord of the Asuras, others, including the great demons of hoary antiquity, fought the gods. The popularity of the Puranic demon lore is attested by scultpure. Varāha, Narasiṃha and Vāmana incarnations of Viṣṇu as separate figures are more common than the others. The Boar incarnation is represented in several ways, the principal modes being theriomorphic and hybrid. The Narasiṃha form in which Viṣṇu killed Hiraṇyakaśipu is always represented as a hybrid form, a lion head and human body. Sculptures representing the Vāmana incarnation in which Viṣṇu subdued Bali, fall under two categories, one the dwarf (*vāmana*) and the other the huge colossus (*virāṭarūpa*) about to take three steps (*trivikrama*). Among images portraying Śiva's terrific nature mention may be made of Gajāsurasaṃhāra-mūrti, Tripurāntaka-mūrti, Andhakāsuravadha-mūrti, Kālāri-mūrtī and Kāmāntaka-mūrti. The first three portray the destruction of demons like Gajāsura, the three Asuras of the three forts (*tripura*) and Andhakāsura. Some of the finest sculptures of the early medieval period represent these motifs and the much-mutilated Ellora and Elephanta panels depicting Tripurāntaka and

Andhakāsuravadha-mūrtis reach sublime heights of artistic creation. Among the demon-slaying forms of the Devī, Mahiṣāsuramardinī images with eight or ten hands are most popular.

Puranic demonology will be discussed below in three chapters. In the Puranic demon lore greatest importance has been laid on demons of the Asura category. The Rākṣasas are less prominent. In fact with the destruction of Rāvaṇa, Rākṣasas began to receive diminishing importance. The Gandharvas, Yakṣas and Nāgas are present in the Purāṇas, but the Puranic authors did not remake their stories because they had other compulsions. The Vaiṣṇavite Purāṇas deal with the exploits of Viṣṇu in his different incarnations, slaying Narakāsura, Hiraṇyākṣa and Hiraṇyakaśipu, and subjugating Bali, Kṛṣṇa's killing of Putanā and subjugation of Kāliya, and slaying of demons such as Pralamba, Ariṣṭa, Keśi, Kaṃsa, Vajranābha, Bāṇa and others. Credit of slaying many demons goes to Balarāma, Pradyumna, Śāmba and Aniruddha in the Vaiṣṇavite Purāṇas. Some of the exploits of Kṛṣṇa have sculptural representations as also the slaying of Dhenuka by Balarāma. Again, in the Śaivite Purāṇas we have the adventures of Śiva. His greatest achievements were the destruction of Tripura and the slaying of Andhakāsura, both themes being well represented in sculputre. The credit of killing Tāraka goes to Kumāra or Skanda-Kārttikeya, but this is mainly a Śaivite story. In the Śaivite legends the Bhūtas, Pretas and Piśācas have joined Śiva, leaving their natural allies, as Śiva had many features in common with the demons. During the fight against the demons Śiva was helped by Viṣṇu as the latter by the former. Sometimes they had confrontations between themselves, as is evident in the case of the Asura Bāṇa. In the Śākta Purāṇas, the Devī or Śakti, variously known as Ambikā, Caṇḍikā, Kauśikī, or Kālikā, born of the collective energy of the gods, is the supreme demon killer. She slays the demons Mahiṣa, Śumbha, Niśumbha, Caṇḍa-Muṇḍa, Dhumralocana, Raktavīja and Durgama.

We have divided the Purāṇas chronologically into three groups treating each group individually. The recurrence of the same characters and deeds in all three chapters could have been a matter of monotony to the readers but, fortunately, so far as the legends are concerned, we come across a progressive multifariousness in the contents. This has helped us determine the chronology of the Purāṇas. For example, the superfluity of the account of the slaying of the demon Mahiṣa as is found in the *Devībhāgavata* proves that this particular Purāṇa is of much later origin than the *Mārkaṇḍeya* in which the slaying of the demon by the Devī was first formulated. That the *Mārkaṇḍeya* again should be placed a few centuries after the *Mahābhārata* is attested by the fact that in the great epic the slayer of Mahiṣa was Skanda-Kārttikeya and not the Devī. In fact the concept of the demon-slaying goddess had not yet developed in the age of the *Mahābhārata.* Even Kālidāsa was probably unaware of this concept.

My thanks are due to Sri Ramesh Jain and Sri Ajay Jain of Manohar Publishers & Distributors for bringing out this volume so nicely. My colleague, pupil and friend Dr. Ranabir Chakravarti has taken keen interest on this work and helped me with his valuable suggestions. My daughter Dr. Parnasabari Bhattacharyya has helped me write this book. Owing to her Asiatic Society connection I was able to handle rare editions of some important texts. As a Visiting Fellow in the Centre of Vedic Studies, Rabindra Bharati University, I could utilize its valuable collection of the Vedic texts, for which I am grateful to its Director, Prof. Samiran Chandra Chakravarti. I am also indebted to Dr. Dipak Chatterjee, Deptt. of Sanskrit, Burdwan University, who has helped me check the references. While I was working on this subject there were some unexpected happenings in my favour which I ought to attribute to the kindness of the demons to me. In spite of my best efforts some mistakes and blemishes must have crept into this book for which I crave the indulgence of my readers. The views expressed in this book are mine, and so are all its errors.

Joraghat
Chinsurah 712101
West Bengal

NARENDRA NATH BHATTACHARYYA

CHAPTER I

Introduction

Demonology is the study of beliefs about demons. Also spelt daemon, the word demon is used today in a variety of senses. Apart from disembodied spirits and ghosts, various classes of superhuman beings, lesser divinities who are to be feared and propitiated, fallen angels, giant-like mythical personalities even capable of terrorising the gods, higher divinities of alien religious systems, imaginary beings who are unseen friends or the enemies of mankind, fiends and monsters, animals or natural objects endowed with supernatural power and function, genii and semi-human creatures born of human, ghostly or even divine parentage and many other undefined entities are included in this category. The original Greek term *daimōn* from which the English word is derived, denoted a semi-divine intermediary between gods and men, a lesser divinity, a super-human being or a deified hero, a tutelary or protective spirit, an attendant, or else an indwelling spirit. In the poetry of Homer and Hesiod a *daimōn* was a powerful, benevolent being or spirit. Later the term *daimōn*, like the Latin *genius*, was commonly employed with reference to lesser spirits or demigods, especially patron or guardian spirits. Eventually, however, the meaning and significance of the word began to change, and *daimonium* or *daemonium* came to denote evil spirits and beings. This change of interpretation found expression in the Greek version of the *Pentateuch*, the New Testament and early Christian writings.

Although a broad division is drawn between demons and spirits, there is no clear-cut line of demarcation between the two. Again, a distinction between spirits and ghosts is easier to make in theory than in practice. Gods are different from demons and spirits, but confusion of the latter with the former is frequent, just as demons and spirits are often confounded with souls or ghosts. Again, we cannot divide up the subject into angelology and demonology because spirits are never good or bad by constitution or in their origin. This aspect is of relatively secondary formation. In the second place, even though the characteristics, powers, attributes, and dwelling places of demons and spirits of the dead are identical with those of other spirits, they belong to a separate category. It must be borne in mind that, while spirits are very frequently believed to inhabit trees, rivers, and rocks there are many spirits to which no specific habitat is assigned. In other cases the abode may be temporary. Not only is the belief in evil spirits almost universal, the veneration of such invisible beings is a common feature of popular or folk religion in all societies including the so-called higher religious systems the world over. This is due to the fact that the human mind is capable of accommodating simultaneously opinions which are not only inconsistent, but even mutually exclusive. A whole-hearted belief in the supremacy of the godhead need not necessarily exclude an acknowledgement of the working of other powers.

The relations of demons and spirits to that phase of primitive belief characterized as animism are particularly close. Animism is a notion that all natural objects are invested with a life-principle akin to the human soul and that the souls of the dead continue to visit the haunts with which they were familiar in life. To the operation of these spiritual powers are ascribed such vicissitudes of life as cannot be explained by visible agencies. Similarly, it is inferred that the soul of a living man may be temporarily detached from its normal habitation in the body, as in sleep or trance, and that the body of the living might be possessed by evil spirits as in epilepsy, lunacy or hysteria. The belief that the whole world is thickly populated by invisible beings who may make their presence felt to man's advantage or disadvantage, has also something to do with the phenomenon of dreams. Ancestor worship is a derivative of animism in which the combination of the concept of life-principle or soul explaining the difference between the living and the dead and the phantoms which appear in dreams and visions has been crystallized in the form of a subtle body or ghost-soul. Various religious beliefs and practices have been based on the fear of ancestors appearing as ghosts who have passed beyond the control of the living.

There is also a close connection of demons and spirits with fetishism which is in essence the doctrine of spirits embodied in, or conveying influence through, certain material objects. A fetish may be described as an object supposed to have been inhabited, for a time at least, by a spirit or some mysterious potency, and worshipped as such, and perhaps carried about for luck. The object is selected not because of its intrinsic value or importance as a natural object, but because of the spirit supposed to dwell within it.

Demons and spirits wield considerable influence not only on tribal or folk religions but also on the so-called higher religions. They also formed an important feature in the social and cultural life of the great ancient civilizations. It has already been stated that angelology forms a part of demonology because many well known demons are fallen angels. Even the great Satan was originally an angel. In the earliest stratum of Hebrew mythology, Jahweh had three classes of attendants—Cherubim or guardians of paradise, Seraphim or the attendants of Jahweh, and spirits serving as his courtiers or messengers. So far as the early Christian writers are concerned, among the Apologists, Justin holds that the angels who had transgressed the Divine appointment and made sinful sexual intercourse with women produced offsprings who were demons. Tatian denies the material nature of demons asserting that they were made of fire or air. Athenagoras identified the giants mentioned by the Greek poets with the illicit offsprings of fallen angels. According to Basil, the sanctity of the angels is due to the activity of the Holy Spirit, but they are liable to sin as is proved by the fall of Lucifer, whose sin was envy and pride. Gregory of Nyssa follows Harmes in the view that every man has a good and bad angel as his constant companion. Among the Latin Fathers, Tertullian alludes to the fall of the angels from whom sprang the race of demons. The earlier Christian writers identified the 'sons of God' with the angels whom the later writers frequently rejected. They held that the angels were capable of sinning, being possessed, like men, of free will. In Islam angels are known as *malak* (in plural *mala'ika*) and servants of Allah. They are created of light and endowed with life, speech, and reason. The four archangels are Jabra'il or Jibril (Gabriel), the angel of revelations; Mika'il (Micheal), the angel of the forces of nature; Israf'il, the angel who will sound the trumpet on the last day; and Azra'il, the angel of death. Besides, there are eight angels who support the throne of God and nineteen who have the charge of hell. Angels could also be subject to temptation, and fall. For example, Harut and Marut, in consequence of their compassion for the frailties of mankind, were sent down to earth to be tempted. They both sinned, and being permitted to choose whether they would be punished instantly or subsequently, chose the former, and hence are still suspended by the feet at Babel in a rocky pit, where they are great teachers of magic.

In India we have no well defined concept of angels, but there are such angel-like beings as Ṛbhus, Apsarases, Gandharvas, Yakṣas, Bhṛgus, Atharvans, Aṅgirases, Virūpas, Navagvas, Daśagvas, and Devarṣis.

Of individual demons, the one who has played the largest part in later thought is Satan, originally a 'son of God' who later turned hostile. Hebrew mythology has preserved the memory of a heavenly court of spirits and kept alive the tradition of how some of these spirits were commissioned in olden times to find out roots of evil leading mankind to destruction, and from this cycle of ideas there was born a belief in an arch-enemy of God, namely Satan. Christianity inherited the demonological tradition from Mesopotamian, Greek and Hebrew mythology but it was in the New Testament that the company of evil spirits was synthesised into a single Satanic figure, leader of the demonic troops of the fallen angels. In fact, Satan was not originally a very bad fellow. In the Slavic tradition, Satan, the lord of the evil spirits, was an intelligent being, who influenced the minds of people by teaching them all sorts of arts and crafts, including reading and writing. According to the early Christian tradition, Satan was sent on a mission to investigate disinterested virtue, in the course of which he transgres-sed his limits and became permanently sceptical. That the concept of Satan also had something to do with the Egyptian sources is attested to by the demonology of the Coptic Christians in which one of his names is Zet, which is a survival of the name of the Egyptian Typhonic god Set, the impersonation of evil and killer of Osiris. In Islam Shaiṭān (in plural Shyātin), i.e. Satan and his horde are those who animate the images of false gods. The term is derived from *shaṭn*, 'opposition'. Another term for devil is Iblis, derived from *balas*, 'the wicked one'. The former expression occurs fifty-two times in the Koran and the latter only nine times, while in some verses the two terms occur for the same personality. Iblis has five sons—Dasim, Tir, al A'war, Sūt and Zalambur—who are the source of all disasters and delude mankind to all forms of vice.

While the Semitic Satan is not a free agent, his Iranian counterpart Ahriman is. The creator of the demons and evil spirits is Ahriman who has brought them forth to wage war against heaven and earth, as is told in the Pahlavi *Bundahisn*. He has six commanders known as Aka Manah, Indra, Sauru, Nāoṅhaithya, Taurvi and Zoicha. According to Zarathustra, the opposing forces of evil and good, represented by Ahriman and Ahura Mazda respectively, shall be in constant war until the last millennial cycle of the world when the power of evil (*druj*) will be finally overcome yielding place to righteousness (*aśa*).

Satan has no parallel in Indian tradition. The Buddhist concept of Māra is his nearest approximation so far as the external similarities are concerned. The Vedic counterpart of the Avestan *druj* is *nirṛti* and that of *aśa* is *ṛta*.

The demonology of the Babylonians and Assyrians who took over from the Sumerians much of their folklore has a triad called Lilu, Lilitu and Ardat Lili. The last was probably the prototype of the Hebrew Lilith, who was the second wife of Adam during the period of Eve's separation. In later Jewish mythology Adam is said to have married Lilith in addition to Eve and filled the world with *shedim* or demons of every description which she bore him. Then, seized with jealousy of Eve's children she attempted to slay the newly born infants. Mesopotamian mythology has also another female demon, Labartu, daughter of Anu, whose target of attack were children. So did the Greek Mormo. The Buddhist goddess Hārītī was originally an ogre causing harm to children who was later transformed into their protector owing to the Buddha's influence. The story of Lilith recalls that of Latona's anger against the children of Niobe. Its Hindu Puranic equivalent is found in the legend of rivalry between the two wives of Kaśyapa—Aditi, the mother of the gods and Diti, the mother of the demons. This has also a parallel in Celtic mythology. The divine dynasty of goddess Danu comprised famous gods like Nuada, Dagda, Brijit, Engas, and Ogma, while her rival Damnu gave birth to Fomors or demons, prominent among whom were the one-eyed Balor, Indech, Elayan, and Brace. Perhaps Lilith is a personification of perils which beset women in childbirth.

In the mythology of the Old Testament, the belief in the reality of native deities did not altogether disappear and those gods whose worshippers had been hostile to Israel, or had opposed the prophets, so as to be denounced in the sacred books, were reduced to the rank of demons. A good number of them had Mesopotamian or Cannanite origins, such as Bel or Leviathan. Tiamat (cf: Taimāta of the *Atharvaveda*), the Deep, was personified in Babylonia as a dragon who appears in post-exile Hebrew literature as Rahab. The latter was a female demon who rose against Jahweh but was overcome by him, the God obviously being here the substitute for Marduk. In *Job* (3.8) Leviathan was evidently a mythical dragon capable of darkening the day. In *Psalms* (74.14-17) Jahweh is said to have broken the head of Leviathan in pieces and created the sun, fixed the earth's bounds and made the summer and winter, in which we have a clear reference to the Babylonian Creation Epic. Azazel was a wilderness-demon and the name signifies 'entire removal'. In the ritual of the Day of Atonement a goat was offered to him since he was supposed to carry the sins which people confessed. In *Deuteronomy* (32.17) Hebrews are said to have sacrificed to Shēdim, a synonym for demons and evil spirits which orthodox writers related to the pagan gods.

Among the embodied spirits, the cuneiform tablets refer to Utukku whose single glance was sufficient to cause harm to people, Gallu (apparently sexless), Rabisu who set the hair on the body, Aḫḫazu (apparently combated in the medical texts), Labaṣu, Sedu and Lamasu. Throughout the New Testament demonic spirits are regarded as a source of both physical and psychological infirmities. The *Book of Revelation* contains a rich and complicated demonology informed of Jewish Apocalyptic, Babylonian and Persian sources. In the historic period of Egypt, inscriptions from the temple of Abydos show that the priesthood frankly admitted the existence of demons, most of whom are provided with material bodies, and like gods they have theriomorphic forms as well, often with mixed forms like winged-lions with hawk's heads, or wild beasts with serpents' heads, or winged heads placed on their backs, or a lion's tail on a monkey's body with a human face, and so on. None of the numerous paintings of the demons makes them larger than worldly men or beasts, except in the case of certain serpent-demons. Their names are far oftener functional epithets, like 'the Archer,' 'the Lancer', or 'the Lady of Terror' than true proper names. Often it is difficult to draw the line of demarcation between a god and a demon. A demon possessing a name is clearly a god. Gods like Sarku or Ririt were originally demons. Naprit, demon of the harvests, Ranninit, Maskhonit, the 'Seven Hathors' and many others of this type are deities rather than demons. The organization of the incoherent spirits around multiple gods of early polytheism has been partly reconstructed by scholars with the help of the texts of the Memphite and proto-Theban coffins.

Homer employed the term *daimōn* as virtually synonymous with *theos* meaning 'god' except that *theos* refers to the personality of a god and *daimōn* to the nature of divine activity. Hesiod identified the demons with the souls of those who lived in the Golden Age. Greek demonology, like the Indian, is vast and varied. The Titans of Greek mythology were the sons and daughters of Uranus, but the whole brood revolted against their father for having cast his other children, the Hecatoncheires or hundred-handed monsters, and the Cyclops, gigantic being with a single eye in the centre of the forehead, into Tartarus. There were also Cerberus with three or fifty heads, the watchdog of Hades; Chimaera, the triple-bodied monster at once she-goat, lion and serpent; Scylla, the sea-monster; Sphinx, a female monster with a human head and body of lion; and Typhon, the hundred-headed monster who was the father of Cerberus. The giants were known by the generic name Gigantes who attacked Olympus, while the Gorgons were three winged females of terrifying appearance with enormous teeth and serpents for hair. Among them Medusa was slain by Perseus and from her blood sprang the winged horse Pegasus. The Laestrygones are described as a race of cannibal giants encountered by Odysseus in his wanderings. Hecate appeared as a goddess of the magic arts and was associated with the ghost-world, haunted spots and crossroads. It was also believed that the demons were capable of entering into and possessing human bodies. In the *Agamemnon* of Aeschylus, after the murder of her husband, Clytemnestra boasted that she herself was the incarnate demon of the Pelopides. In the Olympian religion of the classical age the demons came to be transformed into gods which may be exemplified with reference to the nymphs. Other demons have taken subaltern rank in the celestial hierarchy, as when the Corybantes were classed as the attendants of Rhea and the Satyri attached themselves to Dionysus. The latter was attended by Akratos, the potent spirit of wine and Aphrodite by Tychon. The Harpies were a composite notion in the evolution of which wind-demons and death-angels had taken part. They were related to the Erinyes and the Sirens, both infernal agencies. The Gorgons mentioned in the legends of Perseus were also underworld powers and storm spirits. Besides these, there were lesser beings, rarely dignified in connection with a heroic tale, such as Empusa, a female who had the power of continually changing her shape, Mormo and Lamia who caused harm to children, Acco, Alphito, and Ephialtes.

Plutarch said that in Boeotia a sacrifice to the good demon was made on the occasion of the first testing of the new wine, and at Athens it was the custom after dinner to pour out a small libation of unmixed wine in his honour. Thales, Plato and the Stoics joined Pythagoras in holding that demons and heroes were spiritual substances, or souls separated from the bodies, and that there were good and bad demons corresponding to the same varieties of soul. Empedocles spoke of the wandering of wicked demons cast out of the abode of the blest. The pantheism of the Stoics enabled them without difficulty to find a place for the demons within their system. In the writings of a later period, such as in those of Maximus Tyrius, Apuleius and Philostratus, the maxims of demonology had come to be commonplace, partly owing to the influence of the tradition and partly by contact with Asian cultures, which had become continually more intimate since the beginning of the Hellenistic epoch.

The indigenous Romans appear to have possessed but little in the nature of mythology or folklore before they passed under the spell of the Hellenic culture. Their conceptions of the *genius* will be discussed below. Under the influence of the neo-Pythagorian and neo-Platonic schools, the belief in beings who were more than men and less than gods became universal in Rome. The world was supposed to abound in demons of limited powers for good or evil, the testimony of which is scattered over the literature and art of the Roman empire. The later Jewish or Rabbinic demonology was a legacy of Babylonian, Assyrian and Hebrew demonology. What Chaldea, Arabia and Egypt gave to Cannan underwent substantial change, and received additions from internal and external sources. The ever-growing intercourse with the Greek and Roman world would scarcely have failed to make the Jews acquainted with many new forms of demons and spirits. Although the Judaean teachers were indifferent to demonology, it was popular with Galilaean Rabbis and those who came from Mesopotamia.

As stated, demons are not delinked with gods, many of them being of divine parentage. Apart from spirits, various kinds of superhuman beings, lesser gods and higher divinities of alien pantheons are included in the category of demons. Their connotation was changed in Europe when Christianity condemned the deities of paganism—a change analogous to that by which the Avestan *daeva*, 'demon', is the precise etymological equivalent of the Sanskrit *deva*, 'god'. The term *pagan* generally denotes pre-Christian polytheistic religion and culture. In a wider sense the term denotes any culture which is opposed to Christianity. In course of the prolonged confrontation between Christianity and the pagan cultures, the former had to accept many pagan deities, make room for them in its own spiritual hierarchy as saints, and fabricate their original myths and legends with Christian colour. Others were stigmatized as demons incarnating evil forces. The myths relating to pagan deities not only refer to natural phenomena behind their anthropomorphic forms but also to tribal, racial and cultural conflicts among their worshippers. For example among the Teutons, there were two rival groups of deities, *asa* and *vana*, each group representing a particular branch. Various demons and monsters, their kingdoms and territories, were symbols of enemy tribes, though at different periods they had social intercourse and blood relations. It is also possible that the demons of the Teutonic mythology were modelled after the mythologies of the anterior people. The legends of the fight between the Greek Olympians or Titans, or that between the Irish Danans and Fomors, might have influenced them. Again the conflict between good and evil, light and darkness, summer and winter, was represented on a cosmic plane. This is a common feature of all ancient religions. In Greek mythology Harmes, the god of dawn, kills Argos, the representative of night. In Celtic mythology, the sun-god Lugh defeats Balor, the symbol of night. In Teutonic mythology virtue is overpowered by vice, light is enveloped by darkness, the summer god Balder is killed by mistletoe, the parasitic shrub of winter. The gods are destroyed by the Scandinavian Mephistopheles Loki. Then comes the dusk of the gods, the *ragnarok,* the day of a great battle between gods and demons, when both are destroyed.

Ancient Babylonians and Assyrians believed in the return of disembodied spirits or ghosts (*edimmu*) of a man or woman to this world for some reason or other. In the epic of Gilgamesh it is said that when the spirit of Ea-bani was raised from Hades his shade rose like the wind through an opening in the earth made by the god Nergal. This belief in the return of a disembodied spirit to the world is universal, though in different regions its application in relation to demonology varies in extent and degree. This is because not all spirits that populate the world are the souls of mortal beings. This belief persisted widely in ancient Egypt, but the uniqueness of the Egyptian conception is that demons and spirits were regarded as prototypes of deities and as such they had nothing to do with the spirits of the dead in their essential nature. The same holds good in the case of the Greeks and Romans. Spirits of the Celtic, Teutonic and Slavic worlds may be regarded as legacies of earlier inhabitants of their regions: those which are ancient spirits of their own cultural tradition that accommodates the former category as well, those beings imaginatively considered as dwellers in a hypothetical other world and those which are exclusively regarded as the souls of the departed human beings. The Celts believed in the existence of spirits of human beings, which were, in some mysterious way, connected with the breath, the name and shadow denoted by the Welsh terms *ysgawd or enaid*. The Irish *spiorad* (older *spirut)* bore the same sense. According to the Chinese etymology, the word *kuei,* demon, is connected with a word of similar sound meaning 'to return', and a *kuei* is accordingly defined as a spirit of a man who has returned from this visible world to the invisible. While a *kuei* is strictly speaking a departed spirit, it is hardly to be supposed that all the innumerable *kuei* imagined to be active in this world or that retributive executioners in the infernal regions are of this origin. In Japan there is a class of disembodied spirits known as *kishim* or *kami* which dwell in the dark region of *yomi.* In India the spirits of the departed ones are denoted by three terms—*bhūta, preta* and *piśāca*—the first name being ordinarily applied to all the classes.

A distinction is generally made between good and evil spirits. The former was known to the most ancient Egyptians as *biu* and the latter *khuu.* The *rokhitu* were also a class of good spirits. Numerous representations of *biu* and *rokhitu* in statues, bas-reliefs, and frescos are found. Several other good spirits have left material traces of their former role in parts of sacred furniture. The *hunmamit* which figure in a number of representations seem to have been swarms of spirits of a beneficent character. The Islamic *jann* and *jinn* are also of two kinds, good or believers, and bad or unbelievers. It is said that God created the *jinn* out of fire without smoke long before Adam, and their race inhabited all the spheres of earth. The good *jinn*, when they come to man, are resplendently handsome. The Roman *genius* (when they guarded women had the title *juno)* were at first imagined not only to come into existence along with the human beings to whom they were linked, but also to go out of existence with them. Horace does not hesitate to call the *genius* a god. Later *genii* of the great gods were invented, and shrines were erected to the genius of Jupiter and others. Even *a genius publicus* was worshipped at Rome. The *lares* were household spirits. Originally each house possessed one *lar familiaris* and the worship connected with it was joyous in character, not funereal. To the *manes*, 'good' or 'kindly' is euphemistic, its application to disembodied man being secondary. Among the Teutons, an elf origin has been ascribed to the household spirits who protected homes and were known under many names such *as cofgodar, kobolds, butze, hütchen, gardsvor, tomte, nisse,* etc. Guardian spirits of ships were known as *klabautermann.* Miners likewise had the guardian spirit *schachtmandl.* Supernatural beings like *the bacucei, casloecoe, dusii, ifles, nervini, lugove, matronoe, proximoe,* etc., mentioned in Celtic inscriptions are mostly beneficent or neutral, though a few of them appear to be malevolent. Among the Slavic people the *dolja* is a family heirloom who descends to a person from his parents. The domestic spirits were known as *domovojs* or *domoviks.* Every house had its *domovojs* who had also a wife and even a family. In China, besides the *kuei,* there are *hsien,* which name is applied not only to the fairy-like beings but also to those who have raised themselves to the rank of immortals. Moreover, sages and worthies are worshipped as tutelary spirits. The Japanese hold that the spiritual world lies as near to the material and is as closely interwoven with it, as the spirit of man is with his body. The line of connection is never broken, and the Japanese ghost feels the same keen interest in the welfare of his family, province or country as he felt when alive.

Evil spirits are of a bewildering variety. The passing allusions in a few chapters of the Egyptian Book of the Dead seem to indicate that they were conceived under the forms of devouring spirits, troops of monkeys, jackals, lizards and hawks. *Azhi dahākā* is the special serpent demon of the Iranian Ahriman. In Islamic demonology, besides the evil *jinn,* there are *shyātin* (troops of Shaiṭān), *ifrits* (powerful evil genius) and *marids* (the most powerful ones). The evil *jinn,* who are unbelievers, are said to appear to mankind most commonly in the shapes of serpents, dogs, cats or horribly hideous human beings. Among the Teutons, evil spirits sometimes appeared as animals, sometimes as *incubus* (goblin, mare, troll) and other disfigured beings. In this way arose the ideas of the *werewolf,* the *fylgja,* and the witch. Among those who could cause their souls to pass out of their bodies and injure others were the *hexe* of the Western Teutons and the Scandinavian *trold* who was a witch. The male counterpart of the witch was the *werewolf,* i.e. man-wolf, a human soul who roamed in the shape of a wolf inflicting cruelties upon human beings. There were giants, personified as *fornjot,* 'the old giant' whose descendants were *hler,* the boisterous sea, *logi* the wild fire, *kari,* the tempest, *jokull,* the glacier, and *frosti,* the cold. Hostile spirits were known to various Teutonic people by variants of the name *nix.* Like the Teutons, the Slavic people also had the conception of the *werewolf.* The vampire is the soul of a dead man that comes out of the grave to injure the living. The Serbs believe that impious people, especially witches, become *vukodlaks* after death and drink the blood of sleeping persons. A term for a Celtic supernatural being which is always of maleficent import is *siabroe.* The Chinese evil spirits known as *shā* move in straight lines. In China it is believed that, of living creatures, the birds and animals, especially the fox, have the potential to represent evil spirits. In Japan spiritual beings were known as *mono, mononoka* or *bakemono* and were supposed to be essentially evil in nature.

Female spirits also have a very important role in ancient demonology. We have already had the occasion to refer to the female demons mentioned in Mesopotamian cuneiform tablets, Lilith, the night-monster lurking in desolate places, and whose character became more prominent in Hebrew mythology; the Egyptian Lady of Terror; Greek female demons and so on. In Iranian mythology there is a large class of she-devils or female fiends known as *drujis*. Their leader is the feminine embodiment of deceit or falsehood, who draws in her train a ribald crew of followers known as *dregvants* or *drvants*. Foremost among them is *druj-nasu*, the veritable incarnation of pollution arising from the decomposition of the dead body. Another fiend is *jāhi*, 'harlot', who embodies the spirit of whoredom destructive to mankind. Little better are the seductive *pairikās* 'enchanters' and their male partners *yātus* (sorcerers). In Celtic demonology, the Welsh term for fairy and magic is *hud, hudol* signifying a male fairy and *hudoles* for a female. The Norse *völves* were sorcerers with magical powers. The *Eddas* often tell of men and gods who visited the grave of a *völva* for obtaining knowledge of the future. Even Odin rode to such a grave to know from her the interpretation of Balder's dream. The *fylgja* referred to above when attending a person as a soul took the form of an animal and as a tutelary spirit assumed the female form. The *valkyrs*, the battle-maidens of Odin of Teutonic mythology, appeared in groups of nine, armed with helmet, shield and lance, riding through the air and sea. The female *nixies* were noted for their singing which lured human beings into their toils. Among the Slavic people, a powerful female being is *baba-jaga* (in Russian, *jedza* in Polish, *jazibaba* in Slovak) whose children are evil spirits. Analogous to the *mora* (equivalent to German *mahr* and English *mare*, cf. nightmare) is the nocturnal demon who is known among the Slovaks, Poles, Serbs and Russians as the *nocnitsa* or night-hag. In some localities they are supposed to form a group of twelve sisters. The demon of fever is believed to be one of the three, seven, or twenty-seven so-called *lichoradka* sisters. The *morovajapanna* is the Slavic demon of pestilence who appears mostly in the figure of a woman. Certain traditional forms of the Japanese spirits are mostly of the female sex, clad in white flowing robes which conceal the absence of legs, and are commonly seen in the twilight or at dead of night in lonely and solitary places or in houses recently visited by death or deserted, in shrines, temples, graveyards, or among the shadows of willow trees.

In China, besides the *kuei*, there are *hsien*, which name is applied not only to the fairy-like beings but also to those who have raised themselves to the rank of immortals. Moreover, sages and worthies are worshipped as tutelary spirits. Mention should be made of demon-possession causing disease or madness, of spirit mediums inspired by an idol-spirit and one who utters an oracle. The Japanese ghost has a spiritual sword and is thought of as being surrounded by ghostly counterparts of all the objects that surround him in the material and spiritual worlds which are looked upon as being very closely connected. A certain class of beings of hideous aspect and immense strength that assume the human form with the addition of a pair of bull's horns, and a tiger's skin, is known as *oni*. There are many types of *oni*, and some of them, unable to rest in the dull peace of Elysium, turn to more active employments. Another class of mysterious beings is known as *tengu* which was later explained by the Buddhists as the operator of light and darkness, of enlightenment and error. Shintoist and Confucian writers do not hesitate to denounce the *tengu* as invented by a crafty priesthood. Both Chinese and Japanese demonologies are influenced by Hindu and Buddhist concepts of demons and spirits. This also holds good in the case of Tibetan beliefs which we shall deal with in connection with Buddhist demonology in a separate chapter. To Hinduism is certainly due the Japanese idea which makes the *oni* the attendants of the god of Hell, Yama. *Oni* is sometimes conceived of as playing the part of Māra, the Tempter, vanquished by the Buddha, who was the enemy of truth. More frequently he is the Yakṣa or Rakṣasa of Hindu demonology.

There are numerous regional varieties of demons and spirits pertaining to different countries and people. Various provinces of ancient Egypt had different sets of demons and spirits, each with a distinct tribal origin, that were amalgamated with one another during the formation of the Egyptian state under which process the characters and attributes of many a spirit or demon underwent complete change. This is true also in the case of Greek city states and the countries of Asia Minor under Greek colonial and cultural influence. It is also to be noted that many Egyptian deities and demons came to Graeco-Roman mythology, and the reverse process also had taken place. Roman demonology had a basic Italian core and a Hellenic superstructure, but with the extension of the Roman empire indigenous Asian and North African elements made their way into it. Religious systems like Judaism, Christianity and Islam remodelled the ancient demonologies in accordance with their own theoretical viewpoints. The same holds good in the case of Iranian demonology in which Zarathustra had converted even certain abstract concepts into the forms of demon such as *tarōmaiti* (arrogance), *methaoxta* (false speech), *āzi* (greed), *būsyāstā* (inordinate sleep or sloth), *asto-vidātu* (divider of bones at death), *apāoša* (drought), *zemaka* (winter), etc. The Celtic people comprised the highland Scots, Welsh, Cornish and Irish as occupying the outlying edge of the British Isles, though their original homeland was the Iberian peninsula. The Slavs belong to the Slavonic Linguistic group inhabiting large parts of eastern and central Europe—the Russians, Poles, Czechs, Bulgarians, Serbo-Croats, Slovens, etc. The early Teutons belonged to Germany, Scandinevia, and the Netherlands, being speakers of German, English, Frisian, Swedish, Danish, Norwegian, Icelandic, Gothic, etc. The herolegends among these people contains interesting lore in which we come across demons of a higher type, manly in nature, with human excellences and frailties, acting as friends or foes of the heroes or the gods. Christian influence on their conceptualization is also noticeable.

It is against this background that we are to deal with the complexities of Indian demonology. India has no less than three hundred surviving tribes, each of them with its own mythology of gods, demons and spirits. Besides, through the ages numerous tribes were converted into castes of various rank and status within the larger fold of Hindu society. This has been facilitated by the adaptability of the caste system which allows the converted tribes to retain their original beliefs and rituals, cultural traits, customs and social norms, deities and demons. Thus we have a stratified demonology of various grades in which the characters have upward and downward movement and attainments in accordance with the upward and downward mobility of the detribalized castes in the social hierarchy. As a consequence those who have reached the higher ranks owing to their proximity with the Sanskrit culture modified their tribal demonology in which Brahmanical, Buddhist and Jain elements are also grafted. The simultaneous working of these processes may be traced, identified and documented with reference to the personalities of certain well known demons. Leaving aside the disembodied spirits, the characteristics of which are more or less the same in all parts of the world, the higher demons of India may be divided into three groups—transparent, translucent, and opaque. Another threefold classification is also possible—those who have found a place in the Sanskrit literary tradition, those who are known in the literature of regional languages, and those who exist only in oral traditions. For our convenience, however, we prefer to make three broad categories, the lower, the middling and the higher.

The second and third categories are to be dealt with in subsequent chapters in historical outline. In this introductory chapter we shall concentrate on the third category, which is primarily based upon the animistic beliefs found in folk and oral traditions among people all over India. This lower demonology is also vast and enormously complicated and can be worked out in detail in a big volume on the basis of information provided by the anthropological literature. Here we shall give only a summary account. Tribals and simple villagers who form the majority of the Indian masses, are oppressed with the belief that they are haunted by evil spirits of all kinds, some malignant fiends, some mischievous elves, to which agency are attributed all forms of sickness and misfortune. The most well known class of the evil spirits, however, is that of ghosts of human beings, the *bhūta.* In contradistinction to fiends or non-human spirits, these are malignant spirits of men, who for various reasons are hostile to the human race. The *bhūtas* originate from the souls of those who have died untimely or had violent deaths, or have been deformed, idotic or insane, or who have been robbers, notorious evil-doers or dreaded for cruelty. *Preta* is simply the spirit or soul of a dead person who roams about. They are vagabonds of the other world who have a prospect of being reborn in this world. But a *bhūta* has no future prospect: once a *bhūta* is always a *bhūta.* The *piśācas* are supposed to emanate from mad men, habitual drunkards, and the debauched. They were originally a human tribe despised by others for some peculiar habits and practices. Later they merged with other people but their tribal designation remained a term of opprobrium and abuse. There are other types of evil beings such as *niśi,* the personification of night as a she-demon who comes at midnight, calls the housemaster or any member of the household and forces him to follow her. She drags her victims into the forest, drops him among the thorns or atop a high tree, or makes him insane. Her victims may be females as well. It is dangerous to answer her call. In north India, the most dreaded spirit is *churel (churail, chuḍel, chuḍail),* one who has left the world with unsatisfied desires.

Spirits of Brāhmaṇas who lost their lives in a tragic way are known as *brahmadaitya, brahmarākṣasa, brahmapuruṣa* or *brahmḍeo.* Ordinarily this spirit appears in the form of a Brāhmaṇa wearing a sacred thread, and his presence is known by the sound of his stepping wooden sandal. He is an object of reverence to other spirits who salute him by touching his feet, uttering *goḍ-lāgi brahmdeoji.* In the caste hierarchy of ghosts he belongs to the highest. He is mostly self-restrained and philosophical and acts as moral guardian of the lesser spirits. In the Deccan the *brahmasamandh*, the spirit of a married Brāhmaṇa, haunts empty houses, cremation grounds, and river-banks, but seldom attacks people. In the same region the *brahmapuruṣa* is the spirit of a miser Brāhmaṇa who zealously guards his wealth even after his death. Likewise, Muslim ghosts are known as *mamdoh* and *raji*, the latter being of a lower category. They wear Muslim dress and carry branches of a tree. The spirits of *pīrs* are benevolent, but sometimes they become hostile to those who unguardedly sit on their tombs, spit at them, or in other ways annoy them. In fact, Indian Muslims have appropriated much of the demonology of their Hindu neighbours. It is also to be noted that there is no communalism in the case of demons and spirits among Hindus, Muslims, and other communities.

Evil spirits are believed to lurk everywhere, on top of palmyra trees, in caves and rocks, in ravines and chasms, or in the air ready to pounce on an unprotected victim. They are endowed with superhuman powers, and possess bodies of various kinds which they can change at will. They are believed to take possession of a corpse and speak through its mouth. They appear in the form possessed when living; enter a living man and cause him to speak as they please; afflict him with fever or other disease; appear as animals and frighten people; remain sometimes invisible and speak only in whispers. They have disabilities as well. As a rule, they are helpless by day, but most powerful at midnight. So villagers turn for protection to the guardian deities of the villages, whose function is to ward off these spirits and protect the villagers from epidemics, cattle-disease, failure of crops, childlessness, fire and other disasters. The village deities or *grāmadevatās* are generally non-human spirits, mostly female, since women are generally supposed to be more susceptible than men to spirit influence. Then there are guardian spirits who have a protective role. In south India the chief of these is Aiyanar, 'honourable father' who rides a horse or elephant, sword in hand, to clear the land from evil spirits. In the *Vetāla-pañcaviṃśati* we have the conception of *vetāla*, who appears as goblin tenanting a dead body. The *vetālas* are guardian spirits. They are often represented in human form, but their hands and feet are turned backwards. Śiva has a host of demons, spirits and ghosts who protect innocent persons from the evil spirits. His attendant Bhairava, popularly called Bhairon, also has the same function. 'Insiders' are the spirits of the departed members of the family or the clan who are easily conciliated if the funeral rites are performed properly. But 'outsiders' are dangerous.

Possession by evil spirits provides an explanation of the phenomena of morbid exaltation and derangement, especially as connected with abnormal utterance and disease. Possessed persons, mostly females, generally have unnatural characteristics. The women most liable to spirit attacks are girls, young women who have lately come of age, young widows, prostitutes, brooders on the unknowable, and also irregular eaters. Spirit possession accounts for various abnormal states of mind including hysteria. Attempts are often made to conciliate spirits on such occasions by placing food for them by the roadside or in the house. In some cases expulsion of spirits are made by flagellation. Especially in the case of attacks of the hysterical kind, the patient is soundly beaten until the demon speaks through him or her, and promises to depart. The spirits of disease are often expelled by transference, the spirit being compelled or induced to remove to another village or to a distant place. A very common method is to remove the evil spirit by means of an animal serving as a scapegoat from the infected area. The exorcism of evil spirits by professional exorcists prevails widely in all parts of India. He does not undergo any special training, but works through the inspiration of a familiar spirit or guardian, which enters him when he works himself up into the proper state of ecstasy. The exorcist is subject to numerous taboos. He uses various methods to identify the evil spirit, such as dropping grains, creating smoke, spreading leaves, tying a charmed thread around the house, and driving iron nails into the ground. Often the demon is appeased by blood-sacrifice and wild dances. In special cases the exorcist drinks the blood of a sacrificial victim in order to bring himself into communion with its spirit. The periodic and occasional expulsion of evil spirits is also common, especially at the close of the harvest season.

NOTES AND REFERENCES

See articles on demonology by J. Bruce Long and Alfred Ribi in *The Encyclopaedia of Religion*, edited by Mircea Eliade, New York: Macmillan, 1987, vol. IV, pp. 282-92. The entry 'Demons and Spirits' in *The Encyclopaedia of Religion Ethics*, edited by James Hastings, Edinburgh, 1911, vol. IV, pp. 565-636, is a series of twenty articles pertaining to demonology in various cultures which has been especially consulted for the present introductory chapter. Also valuable as a general reference is the *Larousse World Mythology*, edited by Pierre Grimal and translated by Patricia Beardsworth, New York, 1965. Gustav Davidson's *Dictionary of Angels including the Fallen Angels*, New York, 1967, is very informative. Lutz Röhrich gives a concise survey of demons in legends and fairy tales, including a psychological section under 'Dāmon', in *Enzyklopadie des Märchens*, vol. III, Berlin, 1979. Material from the standpoint of the history of Christianity is collected in Otto Böcher's article 'Dāmonen' in *Theologische Realenzyklopadie*, vol. VIII, Berlin, 1981. Among other works mention should be made of Moncure D. Conway, *Demonology and Devil Lore*, 3rd edn., 2 vols., London, 1889; Edward Langton, *Essentials of Demonology: A Study of Jewish and Christian Doctrines, Its Origin and Development*, London, 1949; 'Demonology', in the *Encyclopaedia of Jewish Religion*, edited by R.J. Zwi Werblowsky and Geoffrey Wigoder, New York, 1966; Eric Maple, *The Dark World of Witches*, London, 1962. Among anthropological classics are E.B. Tylor, *Primitive Culture*, 2 vols., 3rd edn., London, 1891; F.B. Jevons, *Introduction to the History of Religion*, Methuen, 1896; R.R. Marett, *The Threshold of Religion*, London, 1914; Emile Durkheim, *Elementary Forms of Religious Life*, London, 1915; James G. Frazer, *The Golden Bough*, abridged edition, London, 1923. Lists of works on Indian Demonology are given at the end of the subsequent chapters.

CHAPTER II

Vedic Demonology

The roots of Indian demonology, like those of all other branches of Indian wisdom, can be traced to the Vedas which mention several demons who have characterized the 'inverted pantheon' through the ages, and also several who have attained celebrity in the epics and Purāṇas and in the Buddhist and Jain literature. Vedic demonology is basically anthropomorphic, its personae being recruited from the gods of alien countries, races and religions, indigenous hostile tribes, and natural phenomena. Like the Vedic gods, the demons also belong to four categories: celestial, such as the Asuras who are described as regular adversaries of gods, atmospheric, such as the Paṇis, and Vṛtra; terrestrial, such as the Rākṣasas, Dāsas, and Dasyus; and abstract, such as Manyu, Nirṛti, and Arāti. Although there are no angels in the strict sense, there is a class of superhuman beings like the Ṛbhus, Apsarases, Gandharvas, Bhṛgus, Aṅgirases, Virūpas, Navagvas, Daśagvas, and Saptarṣi, whose functions resemble those of the angels. There are a few demons of divine parentage. The forms of the demons are either anthropomorphic or theriomorphic and in some cases both forms are compounded. They are enumerated in groups, but the distinction between the groups is not carefully drawn. They are named by their activity or appearance, or take the names of real enemies. The spirits which surround the everyday life of people act in all sorts of malevolent ways, and their particular kind of evil is usually indicated by their names. They are as a whole unconnected with phenomena or forces of nature, seeming partly as least to be derived from the spirits of the enemies. Less personal are the hostile powers that are conceived as a kind of impalpable substance of disease, childbirth, or guilt, which, flying about in the air, produce infection, and to deflect which to enemies is one of the chief tasks of sorcery (*RV* 10.103.12; *KS* 14.22). Some terrestrial spirits are not injurious, and instead help at the harvest or weave long life for a bride, while others assist in battle by striking terror in the foe (*AV* 3.24.25; 11.9.12; 14.1.45).

Among the lower kinds of demons are various kinds of goblins, usually conceived as forming an infinite crowd, but sometimes forming pairs. The latter constitute a class named Kimīdin (*RV* 7.104.23; 10.87.24). According to some scholars, the Kimīdin occur, contrary to the more normal practice of grouping in sets, perhaps as a pair under the influence of the dual deities. Names of such Kimīdins, Mroka and Anumroka, Sarpa and Anusarpa, however, show their distinction from the dual deities which have distinct personalities and quite different appellations (cf. *AV* 2.24). The Arātis, who occur about a dozen times in the *RV* and frequently later, are clearly abstract demons of illiberality but clothed with quite real life in the imagination of the indignant Vedic poet who asks the gods to overthrow them. They are always feminine as the name suggests. Arbudi (*AV* 11.9.12; 14.1.45) is a helping demon who assists tribesmen in war. The Druhs are a group of injurious spirits, both male and female, who are frequently mentioned in the *RV*. They are of Indo-Iranian origin, their name occurring in the *Avesta* as Druj. But the Avestan Druj as the symbol of the power of evil is far more comprehensive than the Vedic Druh. In the *Avesta* the special cohort of fiends (*drujes*) is headed by the Druj-paramount, or the feminine embodiment of deceit and falsehood who has a host of corporeal and incorporeal followers known as *dregvants* or *drvants*. Foremost among these agents in pernicious activity is the Druj Nasu, the incarnation of pollution and contagion. Conceptually, the Iranian Druj is closer to the Vedic Nirṛti, the antithesis of Ṛta, the law-governed universe. Druh has parallels also in Norse Draug and Old English Dréag, meaning 'malignant spirit'.

The most common forms of disembodied spirits—the Bhūtas, Pretas and Piśācas—which are dreaded all over India today, occur also in the Vedic texts. Bhūtas are hostile spirits. In modern usage the term has come to denote a malevolent spirit of the dead, but this is palpably not its early meaning. So while dealing with the Bhūtas it is necessary to say something about the Vedic conception of the spirit of departed beings. This is based on the belief that the soul is capable of separation from the body, even during unconsciousness, and of continued existence after death. In a whole hymn (10.58) the soul (*manas*) of one who is lying apparently dead is beseeched to return from its wandering. Besides *prāṇa* (respiration) and *ātman* (breath), the usual terms denoting the animating principle are *asu* (spirit), expressing physical vitality (*RV* 1.113.16; 1.140.8), and *manas* (soul), the seat of thought and emotion (*RV* 8.89.5). Many passages show that life and death depend on the continuance or departure of *asu* or *manas*. The term *asunīti* or *asunītā* (spirit-leading) refers to the conduct by Agni on the souls of the dead on the path between this and the other world (*RV* 10.154; 10.16.2). The souls or spirits of the deceased go to the abode of Yama, where they are transformed into Pitṛs, or else they go to heaven or hell or elsewhere. The doctrine of transmigration is indicated in a passage (*ŚB* 10.4.3.10) in which those who do not perform rites correctly are born again and repeatedly become the food of death. Elsewhere in the same text (1.9.3.2.) it is more categorically stated that the dead leaving this world pass between two fires which burn the wicked but let the good pass. The good spirits proceed either by a path leading to the Fathers or by that leading to the sun. In the Upaniṣads there is no problem for those who have realised the *brahman*. An average good spirit goes to heaven, whence, after the fruit of good works has been exhausted, it returns to earth for rebirth. Those who are devoid of virtue go to the dark world of evil spirits or are reborn on earth in an inferior position.

Although the idea of the hostile spirits of the dead, which are demons of disease and bringers of misfortune, is abundantly reflected in the Vedic literature, the term Bhūta, by which such spirits are denoted in later times, is used there in a somewhat different sense. The ordinary meaning of Bhūta is 'that which is past'. In the philosophical texts the term stands for 'elements'. In the *Ṛgveda* and later Saṃhitās and Brāhmaṇas the term Bhūta denotes 'being'; 'becoming', 'past', or 'what actually happened'. Eventually the verbal 'being' came to be used as a noun meaning any animate or inanimate, visible or invisible existence. In this sense in the Gṛhya texts (*ŚGS* 4.9, *AGS* 3.4, *PGS* 2.12) the Vedic deities, sacrifice, heaven and earth, the constellations, the atmosphere, day and night, the numbers, the twilights, the oceans, rivers, mountains, fields, herbs, trees, Gandharvas and Apsarases, serpents, birds, Siddhas, Sādhyas, Vipras, Yakṣas, Rākṣasas—all are classed as Bhūtas. The term *bhūtavidyā* used to denote one of the sciences as enumerated in the *CU* (7.1.2; 7.1.4; 7.2.1; 7.7.1.) has been explained by Macdonell as the 'science of creatures that trouble men and the means of warding them off', or 'demonology' (*VI*, 2, 107), but the explanation is doubtful. The term *bhūtayajña*, sacrifice to the Bhūtas (*SGS* 2.14; 4.9, *AGS* 1.2.3; 3.41, *GGS* 1.4, *KhGS* 1.5. 20ff) is generic and there is nothing to prove that it was originally meant for propitiating evil spirits. According to the *AGS* (1.2.3-11), the deities to whom offerings are to be presented in the *bhūtayajña* are the same deities to whom the *devayajña* is offered. Other recipients of the offerings are waters, herbs and trees, the houses, domestic deities, deities of the ground, Indra and his men, Yama and his men, Varuṇa and his men, Soma and his men, the *brahman*, Viśvadevas,

Rākṣasas and Pitṛs. The existence of beings of the last two categories as recipients of offerings in the *bhūtayajña* does not prove that the sacrifice has any connection with the Bhūtas in the sense of evil spirits. However, the later tradition of Śiva's overlordship of a host of demonic beings called Bhūtas are foreshadowed in the Brāhmaṇa literature. According to a legend found in the *AB* (3.33-34), in order to punish Prajāpati for establishing an illicit sexual relationship with his own daughter, the gods out of their most fearful forms fashioned a divine being called Bhūtavat who pierced Prajāpati with his shaft. This Bhūtavat is none other than Rudra, for in the *ŚB* (1,7.4.1-8) version of the same legend the task of piercing Prajāpati was assigned by the gods to Rudra. This legend later developed into the well known story of the destruction of the sacrifice of Dakṣa-Prajāpati by Śiva, also called Rudra. Both legends are the same in outline. In the legend found in the Brāhmaṇa literature Prajāpati did the vile act of incest with his daugher. In the epico-puranic tradition he was base and insulted his own daughter publicly at the sacrificial hall. In both cases he was punished by Rudra-Śiva. In the first case he did it himself in the form of Rudra or Bhūtavat. In the second case he got it done by his attendants led by Vīrabhadra. These attendants, neither gods nor men, later multiplied as obedient Bhūtas of Śiva. These Bhūtas comprised various kinds of demons and spirits, but had a special respectability owing to their association with Śiva.

The term Preta denoting 'departed spirit' is found in *ŚB*(10.5.2.13) and the *BU*(5.11.1) as also in the Gṛhya texts (*SGS* 4.2.7, *PGS* 3.10. 49ff). Pretas are souls-in-waiting. The spirits of the departed ones have different careers. In the earlier conceptions, they go to the abode of Yama and live a life of eternal happiness among their Pitṛs or ancestors. The blessed dead who dwell in the third heaven are called Pitṛs or Fathers. This term originally meant the early or first ancestors (*RV*10.15.8-10). Later there was an increase in their number. Two hymns of the *RV* (10.15; 10.54) are devoted to their praise. In the *AV*(6.41.3) the Fathers are immortal and are even spoken of as gods (16.56.4). But they are not gods, though godlike they regulate the life of their descendants by remote control. Hence they are to be worshipped or propitiated with monthly or yearly offerings. They thirst for the libations prepared for them on earth and are invited to come with the gods (*RV*10.15.8-11). But a man does not become Pitṛ immediately after his death. He has a period of probation during which he travels as a ghost and is known as a Preta. The period of probation generally lasts for one year. In the first period, for a year after death, the monthly *śrāddha* offerings are not paid to the Preta or newly dead in the usual form of offerings to father, grandfather and great grandfather. A separate offering is given to him. In this the Preta is not invoked to come because he is supposed to be near at hand. In the Gṛhya texts the distinction between the Pretas and the Pitṛs is clearly drawn. They also state how a Preta becomes a Pitṛ in course of time. The concept of Preta may be regarded as a sort of compromise between the idea of soul in heaven and the soul on earth.

In later traditions, the Piśācas are classed with the Bhūtas and the Pretas as disembodied spirits. In the Vedas, however, they are treated in a different light. The name occurs only once in the *RV*(1.133. 5.) as a singular in the form of *piśāci.* Indra is here invoked to crush the yellow-peaked (*piśaṅgabhṛstim*) watery (*anbhṛṇam*) *piśāci* and to strike down every *rakṣas.* In the later Saṃhitās they figure in the plural, and they are decsribed as opposed to the Pitṛs, as the Asuras to the gods and the Rākṣasas to men, but not consistently (*TS* 2.4.1.1). The Piśācas are frequently spoken of as *kravyād* or eaters of raw flesh (*AV*5.29.9). Agni is asked to heal the sick man whose flesh has been eaten by the Piśācas (*AV*5.29.5). They are also spoken of as shining in water (*AV*4.20.9; 4.37.10) or infesting human dwellings and villages (*AV*4.36.8). The *PB* (13.3.11-13) and *JB* (3.94-6) tell the story of a Piśācī who married the Ikṣvāku king Tṛyaruṇa and dulled his fire, until the priest Vṛśa by a rite had her burned up. They are looked upon as the originators of disease. Numerous are the incantations directed against them. In *AV*(4.36.6-8) the wizard proclaims that he is a pest to the Piśācas, who cause disease, like a tiger to the oxen or a lion to the dogs.

While the concept of the Pretas is based on speculations with regard to the spirits of the dead, and that of the Bhūtas of the Vedas does not accord with their later characteristics, the Piśācas have an actual base. They were undoubtedly a people or tribe who were hostile to the Vedic groups. The language known as *paiśācī-prakrit* in which Guṇādya's *Bṛhatkathā* was composed must have been their original language. The *paiśāca* form of marriage though despised in the Dharmaśāstras, is one of the eight traditional forms of marriage. Since they are said to be *kravyād* or eaters of raw flesh, which was not approved by the Vedic people notwithstading the fact that raw flesh of certain animals is quite edible and not tasteless though rather salty and tough, they were regarded as scornful cannibals. It should be remembered in this connection that the Sabarai (*Śabaras*) living in central and south-eastern India are mentioned by Ptolemy (7.1.80) as eaters of raw flesh. The same habit of the Poulindai (Pulindas) living in the Deccan is also recorded by him (6.1.64). The

Kirrhadae (Kirātas) of Dosarene (Puri-Cuttack region of Orissa) have been desribed by the author of *Periplus* (Sec. 62) as eaters of raw meat. The Piśācas might have been the ancestors of these people.

In *AV* (5.22) Takman or fever itself is imagined as a demon who is asked to go to the Mujavans or to the Bāhlikas or to seek for itself a lascivious Śūdra woman. Even worms that infect a person with various kinds of disease are regarded as demonic beings. All morbid and abnormal states of body and mind, to which no special reason was assignable, were thought to be caused by the attack of demons. In the Gṛhya texts, in order to protect a woman in childbirth, spirits are banned under the names of Śaṇḍa and Marka, Upavīra, Śauṇḍikeya, Utūkhala, Upaśruti, Haryakṣa, Kumbhin, Śatrū, Pātrapāṇi, Nṛmaṇi, Hantrimukha, Sarṣapāruṇa, Cyavana, Pramṛśant, Kūṭadanta, Vikleśa, Lambastana and Urapeśa (*PGS* 1.16.23, *APGS* 18.1; *HGS* 2.3.7). Their identity, position and character are not precisely known to us, though a few of them occur in later Puranic literature. For example, Śaṇḍa and Marka became Ṣaṇḍa and Amarka, sons of Śukrācārya, the preceptor of the Asuras, and acted as the rouguish and godless teachers of Prahlāda. The compound of their names means a very obstinate and robust rogue, a rowdy, a ruffian. Kurkura is the cough-demon conceived in the form of a dog. Viśīrṣṇī, and Gṛdhraśirṣṇī and others are mentioned in the *TA* (1.28) as evil spirits to be driven away from the place of the sacrifice with rites. A demon slain by Indra and described as having ninety nine arms, modelled in the form of a spider, known by the name Uraṇa is mentioned in the *RV* (2.14.4). The Kālakañjas live in inanimate objects (*TB* 1.1.2.4-6). Nejameṣa, who later came to be known as Naigameṣa, occurs in the Gṛhya texts (*SGS* 1.22.7; *AGS* 1.14.3) . The *MGS* (2.14) refers to a rite prescribed for one who suffers from possession by the Vināyakas, Sālakaṭankaṭa, Kuṣmāṇḍarājaputra, Usmita and Devayajana in which a strange variety of deities with dual identity (implying that they are endowed with demoniac attributes) are invoked. Among these, Mahādeva is no doubt the great Rudra whose closeness with demons and spirits is well known. The Vināyakas probably emanated from the earlier conception of the *gaṇas*, who formed Rudra's entourage (*TS* 4.5.4). Later in singular form Vināyaka was identified with Gaṇeśa, crystallization of the said *gaṇas*, the lord of *vighnas* or obstacles. Mahāsena later became an epithet of Skanda-Kārttikeya. Mahārāja cannot be identified properly, but in the Buddhist *Niddesa* commentary there is mention of a cult of Mahārāja. The term Yakṣa which occurs in the list and also in the *JB* (3.203, 272) in connection with the tortoise Akupārā, is better known in the Buddhist tradition. Vaiśravaṇa is Kubera, later the lord of wealth, who is described in the later Saṃhitās and Brāhmaṇas as a Rākṣasa and leader of robbers and evil-doers (*AV*8.10.28, *ŚB*13.4.3.10), while in the Gṛhya texts (*SGS* 1.11.7, *HGS* 2.1.3.7) he is invoked in marriage rituals and his hosts are described as damaging children.

We now turn our attention to the higher demonology in the Vedas. By far the most frequent generic name in the *RV* for terrestrial and often aerial demons, enemies of mankind is Rākṣasa. The correct form of the term is *rakṣa,* in anglicised plural *rākṣases* or *rākṣasas.* They occur in the *RV* more than fifty times nearly always in connection with a god who is desired to deal with them. All forms of misdeeds are attributed to them. They appear as animals and birds (*RV* 7.104.18-22) and assuming the form of human beings molest women and hurt their children (*RV* 10.162.5), wait for women in the form of dogs or apes (*AV*4.37.11), disturb pregnancy and childbirth (*AV*8.6), suck blood by entering the body of a person (*AV*5.29.6-8; 8.6.3), eat human flesh and cause disease (*RV*10.87.16-17; 8.7.20; *AV* 7.74.4), bring about madness and destroy the power of speech (*AV*6.11-1, 3; *HGS*1.15.5), invade human dwellings (*Kau.Su* 135.9), dance about houses, make noise, pray or laugh aloud and drink out of skull cups (*AV* 7.6.10-14, *HGS*2.3.7). In the *KS*(10.5) they are described as disease demons. In *AV*(4.37.2,12) it is said that by using the smell of the fragrant *ajaśṛṅgī* plant the Apsarases, Gandharvas and Rākṣasas, who cause disease, can be driven away. The sacrifice especially is vulnerable to their attacks. In order to obtain the advantage of sacrifices, they often assume the form of souls of ancestors (*AV* 18.2.28). They injure not only spontaneously but also at the instigation of men (*RV*6.62.9). They are haters of prayers (*RV*10.182.3). Like most evil spirits they love the night (*RV*7.104.18), especially the night when there is no moon. Blue, yellow and green are their colours (*AV*19.22.4-5). Mostly human in form, they also sport monstrous deformities, being three-headed, two-mouthed, bear-necked, four eyed, five-footed, fingerless, with feet turned backwards, or with horns on their heads (*AV* 8.6).

The question is, who are these horrible beings? That they were originally human neither evil spirits of the hostile dead, nor products of pure imagination, is attested by sources of the later period. Even in the Vedic texts we find they are mortal beings, with wives, and families under a state system headed by the king (*AV*5.22.12; 6.32.2, *HGS*2.3.7).

The original term *rakṣa*, of which the later Rākṣasa is a derivative, denotes a 'protector'. Were they the protectors of indigenous beliefs, cults and rituals from the encroaching hands of an alien culture? Data on their material culture and social institutions, reigious beliefs, practices, and moral values, and the favours and privileges they used to obtain from Śiva and Devī, obviously lead us to this conclusion. The most striking fact about their activities is that they were opposed to the sacrificial religion of the Vedas. In every case we find them destroying the Vedic sacrifice and creating havoc among its participants. They did not hesitate to kill sages. The *RV* (7.104.18, 21) speaks of Rākṣasas who polluted the divine sacrifice. Agni is blessed to burn them in order to protect the sacrifice (*RV* 1.76.3). In the *Mbh* (7.156.25-28) we find that, when Ghaṭotkaca, son of Bhīma by a Rākṣasī, sacrificed his life in favour of the Pāṇḍavas during the Bhārata war, Kṛṣṇa, did not hide his joy. He began to dance like an irresponsible person, although Ghaṭotkaca was the son of his esteemed friend Bhīma. Asked why, he replied that he was happy because Ghaṭotkaca, though begotten by his friend, was basically a Rākṣasa, hence an enemy of the Vedic way of life and the sacrificial cult. It is therefore evident that such declared enemies of the Vedic cults received an honourable position in Buddhism and Jainism which were opposed to the authoritativeness of the Vedas.

In two hymns of the *RV*(7.104;10.87), the Rākṣasas seem to be more precisely defined as *yātus* or *yātudhānas* (sorcerers or wizards according to the *Avesta*). They are a subdivision of the Rākṣasas, which shows how important was the belief even in the *RV* that such beings were real men. The *yātudhānas* eat the flesh of men and horses and drink the milk of cows (*RV* 10.87.16-17). The *yātus* create confusion at sacrifices (*RV*7.104.18, 21). The *AV*(7.70.2) contains a spell meant to nullify the sacrifice of an enemy through the wiles of *yātudhānas* and of the *rakṣas*. The *RV* (6.6.29) speaks of the 'yoker of the Rākṣasas, *rakṣoyuj* and refers to the *rakṣas* and the *yātus* or sorcerers (RV 7.104.23; 8.60.20). Other characteristics of the Rākṣasas (*rakṣases*) are that in the east they have no power because they are dispersed by the rising sun (*TS* 2.6.6.3). A falling meteor is an embodiment of *rakṣas* (*KS* 126.9). Agni, the dispeller of the darkness, is the god who is directly opposed to them and is frequently invoked to burn them (*RV* 10.87.3.6, etc.). In this capacity he receives the epithet of *rakṣahan*. One suffering from hostile sorcery drives away the Rākṣasas by offering to Agni Yaviṣṭa (*TS* 2.2.3.2).

The Paṇis are regarded as atmospheric demons and enemies of Indra, Soma, Agni, Bṛhaspati and Aṅgirases (*RV* 6.20.1; 6.39.2). They were undoubtedly human beings belonging to a tribe hostile to the Vedic people. In nearly all the passages in which these demons are named, their cows are expressly mentioned (*RV*10.108; 6.39.2), and so too their treasures (*RV*2.24.6; 9.111.2). Agni is said to have opened the doors of the Paṇis (*RV*7.9.2). Capture of the cows of the Paṇis by Indra is described in a single hymn of the *RV*(10.108) in which it is stated that the Paṇis possessed herds of cows which they kept hidden in a cave far beyond the river Rasā, that Saramā, Indra's messenger, went to their country to locate the hidden place and notwithstanding the repeated entreaties of the Paṇis, refused to betray the cause of the gods. In another passage (*RV*6.39.2) Indra, desiring the cows around the rock, is said to have pierced Vala's unbroken ridge and to have overcome the Paṇis. In a third passage (*RV*4.58.4) the gods are described as having found in the cow the clarified butter hidden by the Paṇis. There are also other references to the capture of their cows by Indra or Agni-Soma (*RV*1.93.4; 10.67.6). The Paṇis are surpassed in might by Indra (*RV*7.56.10) and do not attain the greatness of Mitra-Varuṇa (*RV*1.151.9). The Paṇis are named in the *RV* about sixteen times in the plural and four times in the singular. Soma is invoked to strike down the voracious Paṇi who is a wolf (*RV*6.51.14). The Paṇis play no great part in literature after the *RV*. Undoubtedly the Paṇis were an enemy tribe who did not sacrifice to the Vedic gods or bestow gifts on the priests. But the identification of this historical tribe, conceived as a group of demons, is not certain. The words *paṇik* or *vaṇik*, *paṇya* and *vipaṇi* suggest that the Paṇis were merchants. They have been variously identified by scholars as Phoenicians, Babylonians (on the strength of the word *bekanāṭa*), Parnians, the Dahae and other Iranian tribes, non-Vedic caravan traders and so forth. But the uncertainty remains.

Among the individual atmospheric demons the most important is Vṛtra. The name is derived from the root *vṛ*, signifying 'to cover or encompass'. He is said to have encompassed the waters (*apo varivāṃsam* in *RV* 2.14.2, etc., *vṛtvi* in *RV* 1.52.6) and the rivers in *RV*1.52.2; 8.12.26, *paridhi* or encloser in *RV*3.33.6). He is a serpent (Ahi) with power over lightning, mist, hail and thunder (*RV*1.32.13; 1.80.12). His head, jaws and hissing are sometimes mentioned (*RV*1.52.6, 10; 1.61.10; 5.29.4; 6.17.10; 8.6.6; 8.85.7) and he is often described as being without feet or hand (*RV*1.32.7; 3.30.8). From the single Vṛtra, the Vedic conception has produced his multiplication in plural (*RV*3.49.1; 4.42.7; 6.29.6; 7.19.4; 7.34.3; 8.85.18; 10.49.6). With the bones of Dadhyañc Indra is said to have slain ninety-nine Vṛtras (*RV*1.84.13) just as he is said to have shattered ninety-nine forts of Vṛtra (*RV* 7.19.5: cf. 8.82.2;10.89.7). Vṛtra's mother is Danu, and so he is a Dānava, the term being used five times to denote him indirectly (*RV* 2.11.10; 2.12.11; 4.30.7; 5.29.4; 5.32.1). The same term has also been applied to the demon Aruṇavābha (*RV* 2.11.18) and to seven other demons slain by Indra (*RV* 10. 120.6). In later tradition Vṛtra is called Asura. He has a hidden abode, whence the waters released by Indra escape flowing him (*RV* 1.32.10). He is also said to be enveloped by waters (*RV* 1.121.11; 2.11.19), at the aerial space (*RV* 1.152.6), and lying on a summit or lofty height when Indra made the waters flow (*RV* 1.80.5; 8.3.19). Indra was destined to slay Vṛtra (*RV* 8.78.5; 10.55), which he accomplished accompanied by the Maruts and exhilarated by Soma. Hence the most distinctive epithet of Indra is *vṛtrahan* (*RV* 8.17.9; 8.78.3). Some scholars look upon Vṛtra as the demon of drought, holding back water within the clouds. Others hold that as the waters released by Indra are described as running like horses in a race, rain water could not be meant, as it does not flow horizontally. They hold that Vṛtra was originally a frost and winter demon from whose grasp the waters has to be wrenched free every year and that the description of the Vṛtra fight originated not in India but in a land where the hideous winter lies on land and water. The Avestan concept of *verethraghna* should also be taken into account. It is often held that in the Indo-Iranian epoch there were two different gods, Indra and Vṛtrahan and they combined into the personality of Indra in the Vedic texts, while in Iran Indra was dropped from the pantheon and made a demon. Verethraghna, the resistance-breaking god who personified the *vṛtrahan* aspect of the Vedic Indra, continued his career in the Iranian pantheon.

Now we come to the Dāsas and Dasyus who are also regarded as lords of water (*RV* 1.32.11) and having seven aerial forts. The Dasyus seek to scale heaven (*RV* 1.33.7; 8.14.4). Indra vanquishes them from birth (*RV* 1.51.6, 8.77.1-3) and wins the sun and waters after defeating them (*RV* 1.00.18;10.73.5). Although they are described as demons, they were basically indigenous tribes opposed to the Aryans. The Dāsas lived in fortified towns (*āyasiḥ puraḥ*) and were divided into clans (*viśaḥ*). *Dāsavarṇa* has been alluded to a number of times, and the Dāsas are said to be black-skinned (*kṛṣṇatvac*), noseless or flat-nosed (*anās*), and evil tongued (*mṛdhravāc*), some of these epithets being shared with the Dasyus who are rite-less (*akarman*), indifferent to gods (*adevayu*), without devotion (*abrahman*), not sacrificing (*ayajvan*), lawless (*avrata*), following strange ordinances (*anyavrata*), and revilers of the gods (*devapiyu*) (*RV* 2.11.4; 2.12.4; 2.20.8; 5.29.10; 8.70.11; 10.22.8, etc., *AV* 12.1.37). The Dāsas are frequently identified with the Iranian Dahae. Greek writers mention the Dahai people inhabiting south-east of the Caspian Sea, and Dāha is but the Iranian modification of Dāsa. In Iranian, the word *dahyu* (whence modern Persian *dih*), 'country' or 'countryside', would appear to have been originally a tribal name, the Iranian equivalent of the Indo-Aryan Dasyu generalised to mean only the 'country'. In South Asia the words *dāsa* and *dasyu* changed their meaning, as names of the enemies of the Aryans offering them resistance, who were frequently enough conquered and enslaved, and these words came respectively to mean 'slave' and 'robber'. Thus the original meaning of Dasyu (and Dāsa) was 'enemy' which later developed into 'hostile country' with the Iranians, while the Indians extended the original significance of 'enemy' to include demon foes.

Among the individual Dāsas, Śuṣna is mentioned about forty times in the *RV*. He was the chief enemy of Kutsa and was vanquished by Indra (*RV* 4.16.12; 5.29.9). He is a horned being (*RV* 1.33.12) and of serpent form as is indicated by his description as a brood (*RV* 8.40.10-11; 10.22.11) and as a hissing one (*RV* 1.54.5). Shattering his moving forts Indra released the waters (*RV* 1.51.11; 4.30.13; 8.1.28). Indra also fought against him over cattle (*RV* 8.85.17). A demon of drought, Śuṣna has some characteristics of Vṛtra. He is called the 'son of mist' (*mihonapāt*) and a Dānava (*RV* 5.32.4). Among other demons of the Dāsa category, Śambara is mentioned along with Śuṣna, Pipru and Varcin (*RV* 1.101.2; 1.103.8; 2.19.6; 6.18.8). He was smashed by Indra (*RV* 3.47.4) in his mountain abode (*RV* 1.54.4; 1.130.7; 2.12.11; 6.26.5). Śambara was the son of Kulitara and thought himself to be a god (*RV* 4.30.14; 7.18.20). He is often said to have ninety, ninety-nine or a hundred forts (1.30.7; 2.14.6; 2.19.6). Indra vanquished him for the sake of Atithigva Divodāsa (1.51.6; 1.130.7; 2.19.6; 4.126.3). Pipru is styled a wild beast, an Asura and a Dāsa, and is defeated by Indra in the interest of Ṛjiśvan (*RV* 1.101.1-2; 4.16.13; 5.29.11; 10.99.11; 10.138.3). He has the wiles of Ahi and possesses forts shattered by Indra (*RV* 10.138.3). Namuci is both an Asura and a Dāsa (*RV* 5.30.7-8; 10.131.4; *ŚB* 12.7.1.10). He was vanquished by Indra, who, for his favourite Nami Sāpya, destroyed his hundred forts and cut off his head while slaying Vṛtra (*RV* 1.53.7; 2.14.5; 5.30.7-8; 6.20.6; 7.19.5; 8.14.13). The Dāsa Cumuri is mentioned along with Dhuni, their names once appearing as a dual compound (*RV* 6.20.13). Along with Śambara, Pipru and Śuṣna they were crushed by Indra in their forts. They were sent to sleep or put to sleep by Indra in favour of Dabhīti who pressed *soma* for him (*RV* 6.20.13; 10.113.9). Cumuri seems to be a borrowed non-Vedic name, while Dhuni means 'roarer'. Varcin, who is always mentioned with Śambara, is called both a Dāsa and an Asura (*RV* 6.47.21; 7.99.5). Indra is said to have slain 1,00,000 warriors of Varcin during his destruction of the forts of Śambara (*RV* 2.14.6; 4.30.15). Several others whose names occur only once in the *RV* are Dṛbhika, Rudhikrā, Anarśani, Sṛbinda and Ilibisa (1.13.12; 4.14.3-5). They probably preserve a memory of the prominent terrestrial foes of the Vedic tribes.

The chief enemies of the gods throughout the Vedic literature are the Asuras. This term occurs only a few times in the *RV* in the sense of demon. The word occurs three times as the designation of individual demons. As we have seen, Indra is said to have shattered the forts of the crafty Asura Pipru (10.138.3) and slain a multitude of heroes of the Asura Varcin (7.99.5). Bṛhaspati is asked to pierce with a burning stone the heroes of an unnamed, wolf-like Asura (2.30.4). In other places Asuras are mentioned always as opposed to the gods in general. Gods are said to have crushed them (10.157.4) and Agni promises to formulate a hymn by which the gods may vanquish them (10.53.4). The sense of demon is found in the epithet *asurahan*, or Asura-slayer, which occurs three times with reference to Indra (6.22.4), Agni (7.13.1) and the Sun (10.180.2). In one place (10.151.3) gods are even said to have placed faith in the formidable Asuras. On three occasions the term *asura* is applied in the *RV* (5.40.5; 5.40.9; 10.131.4) to Namuci and Svarbhānu. In the *AV* the singular Asura is used in a hostile sense three times and the plural thirty times. They are regarded as the regular adversaries of the gods in their mythical conflicts and rarely appear as the foes of men (*AV* 8.6.5; *KS* 87.10; 88.1). In the Brāhmaṇa literature the Asuras are associated with darkness (*ŚB* 2.4.2.8). Day belongs to the gods and night to the Asuras (*TS* 1.5.9.2). In the *AB* (1.1; 8.4) it is stated that during the fights between the Asuras and the gods, the latter were repeatedly defeated for lack of leadership. Later the gods elected Indra as their war leader which eventually brought about their success. Who, then, were the Asuras?

The answer cannot ignore the evidence of the Iranian *Avesta*. There the term Asura or Ahura is applied to the highest gods, but the general term for the demons is *daeva*, as the later Iranian *div*, 'devil'. The latter is etymologically identical with Sanskrit *deva* 'god', although diametrically opposed in meaning. This contrast is generally ascribed to a great religious schism between the two branches of the Indo-Iranian community. The *devāsura* conflict, which is narrated in the Vedic texts and further elaborated in subsequent literature is the legacy of an earlier cultural conflict between the *daiva*-worshipping Indic groups and the Asura worshipping Iranians. Probably owing to the influence of the Asura civilization (Assyrian) of the neighbouring Tigro-Euphrates valley the ancient Iranians developed new abstract and ethical deities, and applied the term *asura* to denote them instead of the older term *daiva* by which the nature gods were designated. Varuṇa was the chief of the *asura* deities, just as Indra was the chief of the older *daiva* nature-gods. Even as early as in 1400 BC antagonism between the *daiva* and *asura* worshippers had not broken out, as is indicated by the existence of the *daiva* gods Indra and Nāsatyas side by side with the asura gods Varuṇa and Mitra in the Boghaz-köi inscription. In Iran there were followers of the *daiva* cults as in India there were those of the *asura* cults. The *daiva* inscription of Xerxes clearly shows that as late as the fifth centrury BC *daiva* worship had to be forcibly suppressed within the Achaemenian empire. And in India we meet the curious situation that in the oldest period all the great gods received the title *asura* as an epithet, though later it came to be used exclusively as a term of abuse.

That the term *asura* originally denoted a superior kind of deity in the Vedic literature is proved by the fact that most of the important Vedic deities had it as their epithets. It is connected with Varuṇa, (alone or accompanied by Mitra), more often than Indra or Agni. Mitra and Varuṇa are *asura-ārya* among the gods (*RV* 7.65.2). Dyaus is sometimes called *asura* (*RV* 1.122.1; 1.131.1; 8.20.17), so also Savitṛ (*RV* 4.53.1), Puṣan (*RV* 5.51.11), Indra (*RV* 1.174.1; 8.79.6), Rudra (*RV* 2.1.6; 5.42.11), the Maruts (*RV* 1.64.2,12), Parjanya (*RV* 5.63.3-7) and Agni (*RV* 3.3.4). Tvaṣṭṛ had formed a new cup which contained the food of *asura* (*RV* 1.20.6; 1.110.3). In numerous passages of the Brāhmaṇas the Asuras have been represented as superior to the Devas in the art of civilized life, and both in the Vedic and Puranic tradition they are regarded as the elder brothers of the gods. They are constantly spoken of as being the offsprings of Prajāpati. *Māyā* meaning 'craft' and magical power was a special property of the Asuras. It is hardly an accident that in Hindu mythology the architect of gods is an Asura whose name is Maya. To the Vedic poets *asura* must therefore have meant 'possessor of magical powers'. The superiority of the Asuras was acknowledged in the matters of arts and crafts and various aspects of material culture.

It should, however, be noted in this conetext that the Asura region in the Vedic texts meant not only Iran, but also western Asia and parts of

Egypt. This is attested by the legend of Prajāpati and Indra-Virocana as found in the *CU*(8.7.8). According to this legend, Virocana, the king of the Asuras, and Indra, the king of gods, went to Prajāpati to study the doctrine of *brahman.* Virocana did not rightly understand the real significance of Prajāpati's teachings and went back with the misconception that the human body was identical with *brahman.* Since then, the Asuras, believing that the human body is the same as the *brahman,* ceased to burn or bury their dead. They preserved the dead with medicines and various other artificial means. This refers to mummification which was prevalent in ancient Egypt.

In the Brāhmaṇa literature there are many legends regarding the contest between the Devas and Asuras in connection with various sacrifices. In *ŚB*(3.2.3.15) it is said that since speech or Vāc could not be treated properly by the Asuras, they and other barbarians talk badly. Over the question of immortality, the gods had desperate struggles with the Asuras. In one case the gods were being steadily killed because Śuṣṇa, the Asura, had in his mouth the ambrosia, that Indra as an eagle stole from him, thus depriving his breath of the power to revive the smitten Asuras (*KS* 37.14). This is the nucleus of the later elaborate legend of the churning of the ocean by the gods and Asuras. More famous is the use of Viṣṇu as a dwarf to accomplish the winning of the earth from the Asuras (*MS* 3.8.3; *ŚB* 1.2.5.1-7); this legend is the precursor of the exploits of Viṣṇu in his Vāmana incarnation in which he took advantage of the pride and honesty of Asura Bali and pushed him into the underworld. It is also said that the three citadels of the Asuras, of iron, silver and gold (*tripura*), in the three worlds were obtained by the performance of the Upasad ceremonies (*TS* 6.2.3.1; *MS* 3.8.1; *ŚB* 3.4.4.3-5; *KB* 8.4). The gods by the use of the new- and full-moon sacrifices forced the Asuras to abandon the half month of waning moon which they had occupied (*ŚB* 1.7.2.22-24; *TB* 1.5.6.3-4). The Asuras are said to have been defeated by the gods because they did not follow the correct method of sacrifice (*MS* 2.5.9; 3.2.7; *TB* 1.5.6.1). The gods detached the Rākṣasas (*rakṣases*) from the Asuras by promise of equal shares of the spoil, and later cheated them (*TS* 6.41.0.1; *PB* 7.5.20; *TB* 1.8.3.3.). In one case the defeat of the Asuras was due to their inability to find a feminine gender for the number five (*ŚB* 1.5.4.6-11). According to one story, when the Asuras sought to build a fire altar to reach heaven it was destroyed by Indra in disguise (*TB* 1.1.2.4-6; *MS* 1.6.9; *KS* 8.1; *SB* 2.1.2.13-17). Danger from the Asuras united the gods: they deposited their bodies with Varuṇa on the understanding that he who violated it would not be reunited with his form (*TS* 6.2.2.1-2; *MS* 3.7.10; *ŚB* 3.4.2.4-5).

Among the individual Asuras Svarbhānu, whom Indra vanquished, mentioned in a hymn of the *RV* (5.40), causes an eclipse of the sun. In later mythology his place is taken by Rāhu. Among the names of other minor Asuras we have Kirāta, Ākuli, Araru, Aru, Kusta, Etadu, Dābhi, Puru, Vibhiṇḍuka and Viṣād (*PB* 13.12.5; *ŚB* 1.1.4.16; 13.4.3.11; *TS* 2.4.3; *MS* 2.1.11; 4.2.3; *JB* 3.168ff). Demons opposed to Indra include Vala, mentioned in the myth of the Paṇis. Bṛhaspati or Indra took from his forts a number of cows. His fences were broken by Indra who had opened his cave and cast out the best beast from it, a thousand others following (*RV* 6.18.15; 6.39.2; 10.67.6; 10.68.10; *TS* 2.1.5.1). In *RV* (3.30.10), Vala is spoken of as a stable. In post-Vedic mythology he appears in the epithet of Indra (*vala-vṛtra-han*) and is a brother of Vṛtra. Arbuda is a wily beast. Indra drove out his cows (*RV* 8.3.19), cast him away (2.11.20; 2.14.4; 8.32.3), trod him down with his feet (1.51.45), pierced him with ice (8.32.2), and struck off his head (10.67.12). He is mentioned with Vṛtra or Ahi and appears to be cognate in nature to him. Viśvarūpa, the son of Tvaṣṭṛ, is a three-headed demon slain by both Trita and Indra who seize his cows (*RV* 2.11.19). He is rich in horses and cattle (*RV* 10.76.3). In the *TS* (2.5.1.1) Viśvarūpa, though related to the Asuras, is the priest of the gods.

The concept of angles or fallen angels is not found in the Vedic texts though there are a number of mythical beings not fully divine, and in some cases malevolent though their benevolent nature is more pronounced. The most important of these are the Ṛbhus. They form a triad, Ṛbhu or less commonly Ṛbhukṣan (chief of the Ṛbhus), Vāja and Vibhan. The Ṛbhus are often called Saudhanvana, or good archer. They are also collectively addressed as sons of Indra (*RV* 4.37.4). They are frequently invoked to come to the sacrifice and drink *soma* (*RV* 3.34.1-4; 4.36.2; 4.37.1; 7.48.1). They are said to resemble the Sun (*RV* 1.110.1), a bright car (*RV* 11.61.7), metal helmets and necklaces (*RV* 4.37.4). They were originally mortals, children of Manu, who by their industry acquired immortality (*RV* 3.6.1;1.110.4). The *AB* (3.30) speaks of them as men who by austerity obtained the right to drink *soma*. Like the gods, they are asked for prosperity and wealth (*RV* 4.33.8; 4.34.10; 4.37.5). They made a car for the Aśvins (*RV* 1.20.3; 1.161.6; 10.39.12), two bay steeds for Indra (4.33.10), and a nectar-yielding cow (1.20.3). They rejuvenated their parents (*RV* 1.20.4; 1.11.1; 4.35.5). As rivals of Tvaṣṭṛ, they made one cup into four (1.20.6; 1.110.1; 4.35.2; 4.36.4). The skill of the Ṛbhus is exemplified by the statement that they fashioned prayer (*RV*10.80.7), sacrifice (3.54.12), and the two worlds (4.34.9). The word *ṛbhu* is apparently derived from the root *rabh*, 'to grasp', thus meaning 'handy' or 'dexterous'. Vāja means the 'vigorous one' and Vibhan 'the eminent artist'. Thus the essential character of this triad is that of skilful artificers. They are generally taken to be the genii of the three seasons, which are at a standstill during the twelve days of the winter solstice. The cup of Tvaṣṭṛ probably represents the moon, and the four into which it was trasformed by the Rbhus, its four phases. It seems probable that the Ṛbhus were originally terrestrial or celestial elves, whose dexterity gradually attracted to them various myths.

The Apsarases were nymphs of a sort, one of them the mother of Vasiṣṭha (*RV*7.33.12). The Apsarases of the sea flow to *soma* (*RV*9.84.3). Their abode is in the waters (*RV*10.10.4, AV 2.2.3). They are the wives of the Gandharvas (*AV*2.2.5), and their association with the latter has assumed the character of a formula in the later Saṃhitās (*VS* 30.8; *AV* 8.9.9). In the *ŚB* (11.5.1.4) the Apsarases are described as transforming themselves into a kind of aquatic bird (cf. *RV*9.5.9). The sphere of the Apsarases extends from the heavens to the earth, particularly to trees, along with the Gandharvas, which anticipates the subsequent concept of Yakṣiṇīs and Yakṣas (*AV*4.34.7; *TS* 3.4.8.1). The Gandharvas and Apsarases in such trees are entreated to be propitious to a passing wedding procession (*AV*14.2.9). In *ŚB* (11.6.1) they are described as engaged in dance, song and play. The *AV* says that the Apsarases are fond of dice and bestow luck on players; they are feared as bringers of mental derangement (2.2.5; 2.3.5). It is dangerous for a person to fall in love with an Apsaras, but there are instances of such affairs. The *VS* (15.15-19) speaks of Urvaśī and Menakā. The *ŚB* (3.4.1.22; 11.5.1.1; 13.5.4.13) also speaks of them with reference to Śakuntalā, the ancestress of the royal family of the Bharatas. In the *RV*, Urvaśī is said to be the mother of Vasiṣṭha, and in another she is invoked with streams (5.41.19; 7.33.11-12). The dialogue of Urvaśī and her mortal lover Purūravas as found in a hymn of the *RV* (10.95) which indicates that the latter was sacrificed after ceremonial intercourse with Urvaśī has been elaborated in the Brāhmaṇa literature and has become the source of Kālidāsa's *Vikramorvaśī*.

With the Apsarases are associated male beings known as the Gandharvas. The name occurs occasionally in the *Avesta* as *gandarewa*, a kind of dragon. Of the twenty occurrences of the word in the *RV* only three are in the plural. In the *RV*, Gandharva seems to be localized in the high region of air as the measurer of space, heavenly, lover of Apsaras, messenger of Varuṇa and associated with rainbow, Soma and other gods (1.63.1; 8.66.5; 10.123; 9.83.4; 9.85.12; 9.113.3; 10.139.4). They are wind-haired, wearing fragrant garments and using brilliant weapons (*RV* 3.38.6; 10.123.7). In the later Saṃhitās they are spoken of as forming a group distinct from the gods, fathers and Asuras (*AV* 11.5.2; *TS* 7.8.25.2). Their number is fixed at twenty-seven, probably because they are connected with twenty seven stars (*VS* 9.7) and particulary with Rohinī (*AV* 13.1.2), though elsewhere we find that their number is 6333. The epithet *viśvāvasu* is atributed to them which is suggestive of 'possessing all gods' (*RV* 9.86.36; 10.139.4-5; *AV* 2.2.4; *VS* 2.3). Yet the Gandharvas are often thought of as disease-demons. In various forms of animals and human beings they cause dementia to women (*AV* 4.37.11). We often meet with the expression *kumārī gandharvagṛhita* 'a maiden seized by the Gandharva' (*AB* 5.29; *KB* 2.9). They are sometimes connected with the waters (*RV* 9.86.36; 10.10.4; *AV* 2.2.3; 4.37.12) [in the *Avesta* also Gandarewa is a lord of the abyss who dwells in the waters (*YT* 15.28)], and with the wedding ceremony, supposed to possess unmarried maidens and rival of the husband (*RV* 10.85.22, 40-41). Their love of women is prominent in later texts (cf. *MS* 3.7.8). The Gandharvas and Apsarases preside over fertility and those who desire offspring pray to them (*PB* 10.9.3.2). In the *AV* 4.37; 8.6.1ff) they are said to be shaggy with half-animal forms and in many ways dangerous to men.

Among other angelic beings, Manu, the father of mankind, who has been equated by Dara Sukoh with Adam, has been raised to the level of gods. His brother is Yama who was the first man to die. Hence in the *ŚB* (13.4.3.3-5) Manu Vaivasvata is described as ruler of men and Yama Vaivasvata, the ruler of the Manes, the king of the dead in the other world. The Bhṛgus are also an angelic race of mythical beings who are chiefly connected with the communication of fire to men (*RV* 1.60.1; 2.4.2; 3.2.4; 4.7.1; 6.15.2; 10.46.9, etc.). In one passage (*RV* 9.101.13) they are connected with an unintelligible myth, when worshippers express a wish to drive away niggardly persons, just as the Bhṛgus drove the demons. To the same category belong the Atharvans who are enumerated as Fathers along with the Aṅgirases, Navagvas and Bhṛgus (*RV* 10.14.6). They destroy goblins with a magical herb. The oldest name of the *AV* is *atharvāṅgirasaḥ*, that is 'the Atharvans and the Aṅgirasaḥ'. The two words denote two different species of magic formulae: *atharvan* is 'holy magic bringing happiness' and *aṅgiras* is 'hostile or black magic'. Of more than sixty occurrences of the Aṅgirases in the *RV*, about two-thirds are in the plural. A whole hymn (*RV* 10.62) is devoted to their praise as a group. Dadhyañc is the son of Atharvan (*RV* 1.116.12; 1.117.22; 6.16.14) who is mentioned with Atharvan, Aṅgiras, Manu and other ancient sacrificers (*RV* 1.80.16; 1.139.9). The Aśvins gave him a horse's head (*RV* 1.116.12; 1.117.22; 1.119.9). Like the Aṅgirases he was also connected with the release of cows from the demons for the sake of Indra. In post-Vedic literature the name generally occurs in the form of Dadhīca, and the thunderbolt for slaying Vṛtra is said to have been fashioned out of his bones.

Closely connected with the Aṅgirases are the Virūpas who are described as the sons of heaven (*RV* 3.53.7) and born of Agni (*RV* 10.62.5-6). The Navagvas and Daśagvas are mythical beings mentioned in association with the Aṅgirases who are connected with Indra in fights against demons and the recovery of cows from the Paṇis (*RV* 1.62.3-4; 3.39.5; 5.29.12; 10.108.8, etc.). A group of seven *ṛṣis* are mentioned as angel-like beings in *the RV* (2.1.2; 4.42.8; 10.109.4; 10.130.7). In the *ŚB* (14.5.2.6) they become individualized, each receiving a name, and are regarded as the seven stars in the constellation of the Great Bear (*ŚB* 2.1.2.4; 8.1.10).

Benevolent spirits of the forest, trees and plants in the Vedic texts combat successfully against demons and evil spirts. A long hymn in the *RV* (10.97) is devoted to the deification of plants with healing properties. The *AV* (6.136.1) poetically describes a plant as a goddess. The *TS* (2.1.5.3) says that plants have the power to hinder childbirth. Forest trees, Vanaspati, are lauded in the *RV* (7.34.23; 10.64.8). The *TS* (3.4.8.4) assigns to the Gandharvas and Apsarases as their homes Aśvattha, Nyagrodha, Udumbara and Plakṣa trees. The hymn dedicated to the forest-goddess Araṇyānī (*RV* 10.146) shows that spirits of dangerous character abound in the forest. The spirits of the furrow occuring in the Gṛhya texts (*GGS* 4.2.27; *PGS* 2.17.13ff) cannot properly in any sense be classed with abstract deities. They are not personifications of human activities. They live simply on the growth of the crop. The spirits of the mountains (*RV* 6.49.14; 7.34.23; *TS* 3.12.2.9; 6.2.4.3) are described as rejoicing in sacrificial offerings and abiding securely. Reference should also be made in this connection to the horses Dadhikrāvan, Tārkṣya and Paidva who are endowed with supernatural abilities. The goat which draws the car of Puṣan, the ass drawing the car of Aśvins, boar which is the form of the Maruts, Rudra and Vṛtra, the brindled dogs, Śabala and Śyāma (*RV* 10.14.11), attendants of Yama, the male ape Vṛṣākapi

(*RV* 10.86) who caused trouble between Indra and Indrāṇī, the theriomorphic tortoise appearing as Kaśyapa (*AV* 19.53.10, *AB* 8.21), the serpent Ahi, not merely identified with Vṛtra, but occasionally as encompassing or swallowing waters, the bird Garutmant, etc., all exhibit certain incipient conceptions which were later conserved and crystallized into various forms of divine, semi-divine and demoniac entities.

NOTES AND REFERENCES

For the original texts referred to in this chapter with the initial letters of their names see the *Abbreviations* in which the complete titles, editions and translations, and publication details are given. The secondary sources comprise A. Hillebrandt, *Vedische Mythologie*, Breslau, 1891-1902, Eng. trans., *Vedic Mythology* by S.R. Sarma, Delhi, 1980; A.A. Macdonell, *Vedic Mythology*, Strassburg, 1897, rpt. Delhi, 1981; A.A. Macdonell and A.B. Keith, *Vedic Index*, 2 vols., London, 1912, rpt. Delhi, 1982; H. Oldenberg, *Die Religion des Veda*, Berlin, 1894; M. Bloomfield, *The Religion of the Veda*, New York, 1908; A.B. Keith, *Religion and Philosophy of the Veda and the Upanisads*, Cambridge Mass., 1925, rpt. New Delhi, 1989; M. Winternitz, *A History of Indian Literature*, vol. I, Calcutta University, 1927, rpt. New Delhi, 1972; A. Banerji Sastri, *Asura India*, Patna, 1926; A.K. Coomaraswamy, *A New Apporach to the Vedas*, London, 1933; L. Renou, *Vṛtra and Verethraghna*, Paris, 1935; R.C. Majumdar (ed.), *The Vedic Age*, London, 1951; S.A. Dange, *Vedic Concept of Field and Divine Fructification*, Delhi, 1971; K.P. Chattopadhyay, *Studies in Vedic and Indo-Iranian Religion and Literature*, ed. by V.N. Misra, Delhi, 1976, 1978; R.N. Dandekar, *Vedic Mythological Tracts*, Delhi, 1979; J.R. Joshi, *Some Minor Deities in Vedic Mythology and Ritual*, Pune, 1977; G.U. Thite, *Medicine: Its Magico-Religious Aspects According to the Vedic and Later Literature*, Poona, 1982; A.K. Lahiri, *Vedic Vṛtra*, Delhi, 1984; W.E. Hale, *Asura in Early Vedic Religion*, New Delhi, 1986.

CHAPTER III

Buddhist Demonology

Buddhism has an elaborate mythology in which early conceptions of the cosmos, heavens and hells, gods and goddesses, semi-divine beings, demons and spirits have all been retained, even as the omniscient and omnipotent Buddha is projected over and above all of them. Buddhism from its very commencement accepted Vedic mythology, with its evil and good spirits, as part of its theory of the universe. The Buddha himself seems to have taken over from the Brahmanical teachers of his time, the current belief in the gods and demons, and held that like all other living things they were impermanent and ultimately subject to endless rebirth. In course of time, the Buddhist pantheon became one of the largest in the world, especially in its array of demons and spirits. The distinctively Buddhist demons and spirits, while generally modelled on the early Vedic types, are different from the latter in appearance and in their outward symbols. Some of the Buddhist demons, besides the Asuras, Piśācas, Rākṣasas, etc., of the earlier tradition, are recruited from sources other than the Vedic. As Buddhism extended its range outside the monastic order it gave greater prominence to new supernatural beings which were figured in special conventional attitudes with characteristic symbols, at once distinguished from the earlier ones. The demons and spirits are not classed in any definite systematic order in the Buddhist texts. Many of them are good genii and friendly to their human votaries. Others are evil. The exorcising or coercing of the actively harmful amongst these evil spirits and demons by means of certain *sūtras* spoken by the Buddha (or stereotyped sentences collected therefrom) have been practised from very early times. Maudgalyāyana (Moggalāna), one of the chief disciples of the Buddha, is generally credited with having exorcised evil spirits in this way. With the development of the of the Mahāyāna and its offshoots, new dimensions were added to Buddhist demonolatry.

A kind of angelology is also found in Buddhism. The earlier texts agree in ascribing to the Buddha the statement that he descended from the heaven of the thirty-three gods in order to save mankind. In the

Jātakas he claims to have been one or other of the gods in his previous births, mentioning himself four times as Brahmā, twenty times as Śakra or Indra, forty-three times as a tree-god, and once as a fairy. Some of the major Vedic gods are described in Pali Buddhist texts as attendants or angels of the Buddha. Thus Vedic Indra is a companion of the Buddha. While in the Vedas, Śakra is a title of Indra, in Pali literature Indra (Inda) is a title of Śakra (Sakka) who is always spoken of as *devānāṃ indo*, the king of the gods (*DN* 1.216-17, 2.221, 275; *AN* 4.89; *SN* 1.219). Owing to the importance of the Vṛtra myth, the chief and specific epithet of Indra is Vṛtrahan, or the Vṛtra-slayer. In Buddhist mythology he is called Vatrabhū, because he had slain Vṛtra (Vatra), the Asura chief (com. on *SN* 1.104; *Jāt.* 5.153). He is also known as Indavajira and Vajirahattha, the god with the thunderbolt in his hand (*Jāt.* 3.146; 5.33, 115, 409-12, 568), Tidivapuṟavara, king of heaven (*DN* 3.176), Pākaśāsana (*CV* 82.186), Maghavā, bountiful (com. on *DN* 3.710ff., on *SN* 1.267; *Jāt.* 1.201ff.). Vasudevatā (*Sum. Vil* 690) and other epithets such as Sahassākkha, Vāsava and Purandara. The Vedic concept of Indra as the shatterer of the forts of the aerial demons finds expression in Buddhist Purindada or Purandara (*SN* 1.230). In Buddhist mythology although Varuṇa is spoken of as the king of the gods and the gods of theTāvatiṃsa heaven are asked to look to the banner of Varuṇa for regaining their courage when in combat with the Asuras (*SN* 1.219), he has not been given that exalted position which Sakka was able to acquire. Among other Vedic gods Agni, Sūrya, Viṣṇu, Yama, Soma, Parjanya, Prajāpati, Brahmā, Viśvakarman, Rudra-Śiva (Śiva and Īśāna), Śrī, Śraddhā, Lakṣmī, etc., occur in Buddhist mythology as attendants of the Buddha.

Among the Vedic gods of the Buddhist pantheon mentioned above, Yama has a good connection with demons and spirits by virtue of his profession. He is the god of death whose abode is Ussadaniraya beyond the Vetaraṇī (*Jāt.* 1.21; 2.318; 3.472; 4.273, 405; 5.268, 274, 304). His assistants are the Nirayapālas who take the sinners and throw them into different hells (*MN* 3.179ff.). The weapon of Yama is his eye, a glance of which can destroy many thousands of Kumbhaṇḍas (*Suttani*, com. 1.225). Buddhaghoṣa refers to two or four Yamas as the guardians of four gates of Nirayas or hells (*DN* com. 2.690; *AN*, com. 2.228). Yama is also described as Vemānika Petarāja, the lord of the ghosts. The Buddhist Sūrya is seized by Asura Rāhu, but when he takes refuge with the Buddha, the Asura disappears. When the gods fight against the Asuras, Īśāna is the commander whose banner indicates fearlessness (*SN* 1.219). The Cātummahārājika heaven has four archangels of the Buddha for its four quarters—Dhataraṭṭha to the east, Viruḷhaka to the south, Virupākkha to the west, and Vessavaṇa or Kubera to the north. Their retinues are the Gandhabbas, Kumbhaṇḍas, Nāgas and Yakkhas respectively. The Tāvatiṃsa is above the Cātummahārājika heaven, described as the world of thirty-three, probably borrowed from the Vedic conception of thirty-three gods. The early Iranian conception of thirty-three gods may also have something to do with this world because it is said that it was originally the abode of the Asuras. It was Sakka or Indra who drove the Asuras out of this heaven, and later built their city, Asurabhavana, on the foot of the mount Sineru. To defend this heaven from the attack of the Asuras, Sakka built walls around it. This heaven is guarded by the Nāgas, Supaṇṇas, Kumbhaṇḍas, Yakkhas and Catummahārājikadevas. There are four other worlds known in ascending order as Yama, Tuṣita, Nimmānarati and Paranimmitavasavatti. These are inhabited by better persons, higher gods, Bodhisattvas and beings of higher spiritual plane.

In the Vedas, as we have seen in the preceding chapter, there are a number of mythical beings, benevolent or malevolent, whose position varied according to their proximity to the higher gods. The Ṛbhus, for example, were such beings who had attained elevated status due to their association with Indra, Agni and Ādityas. The same has happened also in the Buddhist texts. In the *RV* the Gandharvas seem to be localized in the higher region of the sky and are often associated with some form of celestial light, or 'golden-winged bird, the messenger of Varuṇa' (*RV* 10.123.6), or the stars of moon's orbit, especially Rohiṇī (*VS* 9.7; *AV* 13.1.23) or the rainbow (*RV* 10.123) and water (*AV* 10.10.4; 10.86.36; *AV* 4.37.12, etc.). The Gandharvas' love for women and their proficiency in music are prominent in the later texts. The conception of the Gandharva was somehow related to that of the Yakṣas who gradually acquired prominence. The Vedic idea that the Gandharvas and Apsarases live in the trees may have some bearing on the characteristics of the Yakṣas who were also regarded as tree- spirits. Originally both the Gandharvas and the Yakṣas who made their way into Hindu and Buddhist mythology probably belonged to the group of tribal divinities who held power over life and death, were hoarders of unspent wealth and had a beautiful earthly form.

Kubera, who is regarded both as the king of the Gandharvas and that of the Yakṣas in Hindu mythology, is extolled in the early Buddhist literature as Vessavaṇa (Vaiśravaṇa). He is one of the four regent gods or archangels of the Buddha, and rules the northern quarter (*DN* 2.207), often called as Uttarakuru. It should be mentioned in this connection that even today there are people in north India living close to the Himalayas who are known as Gandharvas, their chief occupation being music. A devout follower of the Buddha and a *sotāpanna* as Kubera is (*Suttani* 379, *AN* com. 4.36), he is the leader of ten thousand crore Yakkhas (*DN* 2.207), the god of wealth with nine treasures (*CV* 37), ten messengers (known as Tatolā, Tattolā, Tatotalā, Ojasi, Tejasi, Tatojasi, Sūra, Rāja, Ariṭṭha and Nemi) and a life of ninety thousand years (*DN* 3.201-2; *CV* 37). Kubera is the name of his previous birth (*Jāt.* 6.201; *DN* com. 3.966). He is the constant companion of Buddha, his spokesman (*DN* com. 3.962, *Suttani*, com. 1.370) who attends the meetings of the gods (*DN* 3.207), and skilled in conversation (*DN* 2.194). Yakkha Puṇṇaka is his minister (*Jāt.* 6.30.325), Bhuñjali is his wife (*DN* 2.207f), and Latā, Sajjā, Pavarā, Accimati and Sutā are his daughters (*Vim.* 4). His chariot runs through space like that of his Hindu counterpart (*Suttani.* com.1.370). He is worshipped by those who desire children and is also invoked to avert earthquakes (*Thera* com. 1.49, 409). The character of Kubera underwent significant changes in subsequent mythologies.

According to the Buddhist mythology the Gandharvas (Gandhabbas) are the lowest of all gods (*DN* 2.12). People who earn little merit in their life are reborn in the world of the Gandharvas (*DN* 2.12, 271-4). Their association with fragrance is recorded in the Vedic texts, and this tradition is also maintained in Buddhist literature in which it is said that they dwell in the fragrance of root-wood and sap-wood and their flowers (*SN* 3.250-51). In some texts the Gandharvas are classed with the Asuras and Nāgas, regarded as heavenly musicians waiting on Sakka capable of going through the air (*AN* 2.39; 4.200, 204, 207). Sometimes they are malevolent causing trouble to monks and nuns (*DN* 3.203-4). They are ruled by Dhataraṭṭha (Dhṛtarāṣṭra), king of the eastern quarter, whose sons bear the generic epithet Inda, and whose daughter is Siri. He attends the sermons of the Buddha (*DN* 2.253-62). Among other Gandharva chiefs the Pāli texts refer to Panāda, Opamañña, Mātali, Cittasena, Nala, Janesabha, etc. (*DN* 2.258; 3.204).

The Gandharva Pañcaśikha was a musician *par excellence* for whom Suriyavaccasā, daughter of the Gandharva Timbarū left her lover Śikhaṇḍi, son or Mātali, with the blessing of Sakka. When the latter wanted to meet the Buddha he sent Pañcaśikha in advance as his envoy, the latter pleased the master with a song composed by himself (*DN* 2.263ff. com. 3.699). The gods imitated his form in their assembly meetings, the proceedings of which were conveyed to the Buddha by him. Pañcaśikha acted as a reporter of the good deeds of human beings. When the Buddha descended from the Tāvatiṃsa heaven he was there to honour him. In his human birth he was a pious and generous person wearing his hair in five knots, which accounts for his name. In the Catummahārājika world he has immense riches which he is to enjoy for ninety thousand years (*DN* com. 2.647-50, *Dhamma*, com. 3.225, *Vis* 392). Some of the Gandharvas are also mentioned as Yakṣas who are invoked by the followers of the Buddha in times of need (*DN* 3.204).

The Apsarases are likewise regarded in the Buddhist mythology as female counterparts of the Gandharvas. They are celestial nymphs and in Pāli are termed Accharā. They live in the Nandana, the celestial park in the Tāvatiṃsa heaven where they play the lute and awake the gods and goddesses in the morning and delight them with dance and song (*SN* 1.33). The garden of Nandana has an important role in the epics and Purāṇas. Like Indra of the Hindu tradition, Sakka often sends them to earth to seduce ascetics who with their austerities threaten his suzerainty in heaven (*Jāt.* 5.152). Often they are employed to serve good purposes (*Jāt.* 2.253). Among the important Apsarases mention may be made of Nandā, Sunandā, Sokatiṇṇā, Alambuṣā, Mirśakesī, Hundarikā, Enipassā, Suphassā and Subhaddā (*Vim.* 16). Some of these names are also found in Hindu mythology. Alambuṣā was sent by Sakka to destroy the virtue of Isisimga, dwelling in the Himalaya and controlling all his senses (*Jāt.* 5.152). This legend is an adaptation of the *Rāmāyaṇa* story of Ṛṣyaśṛṅga, the innocent ascetic who knew no woman and was brought to Aṅga at the behest of the king Lomapāda with the help of beautiful courtesans so that he could bring rain to the drought-stricken country.

There are several stories of Nandā in Pali texts. According to one legend in her previous birth she was one of the four wives of Magha. Owing to her meritorious act of excavating a pond (Nandāpokkharaṇī) she was reborn as the mate of Sakka (*Jāt.* 1.201; 204-5; *Dhamma* com. 1.269ff.). This Nandā may not be the same as the nymph Nandā. According to another legend, the Vejayanta palace, which was built by Sakka in the Tāvatiṃsa heaven after his victory over the Asuras had seven storeys, each of which was waited on by seven nymphs. The crimson-footed (*kakaṭapādiniyo*) nymphs of Sakka came forward to greet the Buddha who visited the Tāvatiṃsa with Nandā. The nymphs had massaged the feet of Kassapa Buddha with scented oil (*DN* 2.296: *SN* 1.234-6; *MN* 1.253 f.; *Jāt.* 1.203; *DN,* com. 3.698; *Dhamma*, com. 1.273; *Suttani*, com. 1.274).

Closely allied with the Gandharvas and Apsarases were the Yakṣas and Yakṣiṇīs. In Pali they are spoken of as Yakkhas and Yakkhinis. They are often described as non-human beings and mentioned along with the Devas, Rākṣasas, Dānavas, Gandharvas, Kinnaras and Mahogras (*Jāt.* 5.4.20). The term Yakkha applies also to *purisa* and *pudgala* (soul), *sattva* and *jīva* (animated beings), *nara* and *mānava* (man), *posa* and *jantu* (animals), *jagu, indagu* and *manuja* (other classes of beings). Sometimes they are spoken of as beings belonging to a category between human beings and the Gandharvas (*AN* 5.4.20). In other places they are described as humanized Pretas or departed souls (*Peta*, com. 2.38). Generally, the Yakṣas are semi-divine beings with supernatural power that brings good or bad to people. Sometimes they are described as equal to gods (cf. *SN* 1.205). There is no doubt that the Yakṣas were pre-Buddhist divine or semi-divine beings who were objects of an extensive cult. The Buddhist texts record the existence of an elaborate Yakṣa worship and speak of certain important Yakṣas such as Nighaṇḍu, Puṇṇaka, Kāmaseṭṭha, Kinnaghaṇḍu, Koratiya, Gula, and Cara, who were also worshipped by the followers of the Buddha (*DN* 3.204-5). Vessavaṇa is their king who rules with the help of Yakkha-senāpati and presides over the courts and is waited on by servants, messengers and Yakṣiṇīs (*DN* 2.267, 3.201-2; *Jāt.* 4.492; 6.270; *DN* com. 2.270; *Suttani*, com. 1.197; *Peta.* com. 145.274). Prajāpati is described as Mahā Yakkha, apparently a saviour of the followers of the Buddha in times of distress (*DN* 3.204). Kakuddha and four other regent gods are also known as Yakkha (*SN* 1.54; *Vim* com. 333). Two kinds of Yakṣas are frequently mentioned, *rukkha* and *bhauma*, the first associated with trees and the second with the earth (*Peta.* com. 2.5.55; *Jāt.* 3.309, 345). Although some of the Yakṣas do no believe in the teachings of the Buddha and often molest his followers, most of them are sympathetic (*DN* 2.236, 257; 3.194-5; *AN* 4.63; *Udāna* 4.4.). Yakṣas such as Indakuṭa and Suciloma can ask intelligent questions on metaphysics and ethics. Some of them acted as messengers to warn prospective sinners (*Peta* 45-6). They are the guardians of underground riches and hidden treasures (*Peta*, com. 2.145.274).

The Yakkhas possess supernatural power. They can assume any disguise and go to any place, are more active at night, and are carnivorous. (*Jāt.* 1.129; 4.191; 5.91; 6.303). They are of different categories, the highest among them being very nearly gods, while the lowest resemble ghosts (*Jāt.* 4.492). Often they are described as red-eyed and possessing horrific and uncanny qualities (*DN* 2.344-5, *Jāt.* 1.103; 5.34). They neither wink nor cast a shadow (*Jāt.* 1.492; 5.34; 6.331-7). Though most of them are suspended in the air and dwell in trees or ponds, some of them live on earth and even have cities of their own, such as Alakamandā. The female Yakṣas or Yakṣiṇīs are described as being more frightening and evil-minded and full of spite than the males (*Jāt.* 1.205; 2.15ff. 128; 3.200; 4.549, 5.21, 34; 6.336). Although sex with a Yakṣiṇī is generally forbidden, sometimes they marry human beings. For example, Kuveṇī, the Yakṣa princess of Śrīlaṅkā, married Vijaya and bore him two children (*Vinaya* 3.27; 4.20). Cetiyā lived with Puṇḍukābhaya for four years and gave him counsel in battle. The latter took Yakkha Cettarāja with him to festivities (*MV* 7.87). Yakkha Vajirapāni is represented as a kind of mentor hovering in the air and chastising the non-believers (*DN* 1.95). They have the epithet *mahiddhikā* and owing to their enjoyment of all kinds of luxury they are called *kāmakāmi* (*Peta* 2.9; *Jāt.* 6.118). The Yakṣiṇīs entice ship-wrecked men, drink their blood, and eat their flesh (*Jāt.* 1.265; 2.15ff., 128; 4.549; 5.34). They eat babies as well (*Jāt.* 5.21; 6.336). They put down poisoned food on roads and in the forest for the travellers to eat (*Jāt.* 3.200). In some cases the Yakṣas have been identified in the Buddhist texts with Piśācas, Rākṣasas and Asuras and branded as demons, while in other cases they are regarded as fallen angels who came eagerly to listen to the discourses of the Buddha. Historically, however, the Yakṣas were primitive popular divinities with a wide following among the masses, the influence of which could not be ignored, and hence, notwithstanding a basic apathy to the Yakṣa cult, Buddhism had to make compromise with it.

This ambivalence is also found in animistic and zoomorphic cults of Nāgas, Garuḍas, Kinnaras and others mentioned in Buddhist literature. The Nāgas play a prominent part in Buddhism. Those who live beneath the surface of the earth are called *sthalaja* Nāgas and those who live in water are called *jalaja* Nāgas (*Jāt.* 6.160). Often described as snakes, they are nevertheless able to assume human form at will. Four royal families of Nāgas are mentioned, Virupākkha, Erapatha, Chābyāputtā, and Kanhāgotamaka (*Vinaya* 2.109). Several Nāga dwellings are mentioned, such as Mañjerika in Sineru, Darddara under the mountain of the same name, the river Yamunā and the lake Nabhasa; and there are references to Nāga settlements in Vaisali, Tacchaka and Prayāga (*DN* 2.258). The *Bhuridatta Jātaka* speaks of a Nāga woman who married a human prince and bore him children (*Jāt.* 6.160). In Hindu mythology also the Nāgas, despite their basic snake-like characteristics, are regarded as having human form. Historically it appears that the Nāgas were snake-worshipping tribes of ancient India, or those who had the snake as their totem, and that certain features of their cults and rituals and some legends pertaining to them were accommodated in Vedic, Buddhist, Jain and Puraṇic mythologies. The story that a Nāga king protected the Buddha by spreading his hood like umbrella over his head reminds us of the same service done by the serpent-king to the newly-born Kṛṣṇa, whom his father shifted from the prison of Kaṃsa to the house of Nandagopa on a rainy night. They were not only followers of the Buddha, but the word Nāga was often used as an epithet of the Buddha and Arhants (*MV* 31.27-8; *MBV* 153-4; *MNid* 201). The Bodhisattava was born several times as the king of the Nāgas under the names of Atula, Bhuridatta, Mahadaddara, and so on. They are watery, delicate, passionate and easily angered. Their breath is poisonous and glance deadly (*Jāt*. 6.164). They are carnivorous, surviving mostly on frogs (*Jāt*. 3.361; 6.159). They sleep on ant-hills (*Jāt*. 6.170). When worshipped as human beings they are offered milk, rice, fish, meat and strong drink (*Jāt*. 1.497-8). Celestial Nāgas live in the Cātummahārājika world, occupying its western quarter under the kingly rule of Virupākkha (*DN* 3.199). The jewel of their head is wish-fulfilling to its possessor (*Jāt*. 6.179-80).

The counterforce of the Nāgas in Buddhist mythology is a kind of heavenly bird known as the Garuḍa, sometimes identified with the Suparṇas (*Vim*. com. 9). While in Puranic mythology Garuḍa and Suparṇa are proper names, in Buddhist mythology they are a class living in the Simbali grove which is regarded as a special tree of the Garuḍa world (*Jāt*. 3.397, *Visuddhi* 1.206). In Pali Garuḍa is written Garuḷa. The Garuḷas are huge, sometimes 150 *yojanas* from wing to wing, capable of raising a storm and plunging a whole city into darkness (*Jāt*. 3.188, 397; *Dhamma*, com. 3.135). They are eternal enemies of the Nāgas. They can assume human form, mix with men and even seduce their wives (*Jāt*. 3.91, 187; 4.177, 463; 6.178, 184). They are frequently devotees of the Buddha (*Jāt*. 3.187, 400; 6.261-2). The Garuḍas can carry off a whole banyan tree, tearing it up from its roots (*Jāt*. 4.177). Their plumage is so thick that a man can hide in it (*Jāt*. 3.91). Two Garuḍa kings played dice with the princes of Vārāṇasī and abducted their queens, Sussoṇḍi and Kākātī (*Jāt*. 3.91; 6.175-6). They learnt the *ālambāyana* spell from the ascetic Karambiya by means of which they caught the Nāgas (*Jāt*. 6.178, 184). Some of their kings were virtuous. A son of Vinatā visited the park of Dhanañjaya Koravya and presented him a golden necklace after hearing Vidhurapaṇḍita's teachings. The associates of the Buddha were sometimes born as Garuḍa kings (*Jāt*. 3.187, 400; 6.178, 184, 261-2).

Apart from the Garuḍas or Garuḷas, the Suparṇas or Supaṇṇas are mentioned along with the Nāgas, Kumbhaṇḍas, Yakṣas and

Catummahārājika-devas as guards of the Tāvatiṃsa heaven who are often equated with the Garuḍas. They are called Karoṭi probably because of the same name of their diet, and live in the Simbali grove also inhabited by the Garuḍas (*Jāt*. 1.204, 3.397). The Kumbhaṇḍas are a class of supernatural beings, mentioned with Garuḷas and Supaṇṇas who have huge stomachs and very big procreative organs. They live in the south under their king Virulha. Kumbhīra is the name of one of their chiefs (*DN* 2.257; *DN*, com. 3.964; *Jāt*. 6.272).

Compared with the Nāgas and Garuḍas, the Kinnaras of the Buddhist tradition, like their Puranic counterparts, are of mild temperament. They are human faced birds generally found on the mountains and banks of rivers, and often fall in love with human beings. They are devoted to the Buddha. Some Bodhisattvas also are born as Kinnaras. Their feminine form is Kinnarī (*Jāt*. 4.106, 254, 262ff., 282ff., 5.47, 456; 6.422; *Milinda* 267).

The Petas or Pretas are spirits of the departed ones. They are the subject-matter of a text of the *Khuddaka Nikāya* known as the *Petavatthu*, which contains stories with a moral flavour for lay-listeners. In a story the spirit of a dead person is asked about the action which has brought about his unhappy lot. In reply he says that for doing evil acts in his mundane existence he has received the mouth of a pig. The Buddhist conception of the Pretas is not different from that in the Vedas and popular tradition. The world of the Pretas is known as Pretaloka (Pali, Petaloka), which is situated above the animal kingdom and is regarded as a kind of hell where the spirits suffer severe pain for the misdeeds of their previous births (*Jāt*. 6.595). They dwell in the kingdom of Yama consisting of 36 provinces, situated five hundred *yojanas* below *Jambudvīpa*. The span of their life is five hundred years, each day of the year being equal to a human month (*KV* 20.3). The departed spirits of good persons who receive heavenly mansions for their noble deeds performed on earth are known as Vimāna-devatā. They are reborn in Tāvatiṃsa, in exceptional cases in Nimmānrati and Brahma worlds. Spirits of the second grade are called Vimāna-Petas. Since in their worldly life their good deeds outweighed their bad deeds they also have their *vimānas* or dwellings, not very uncomfortable, in desert, sea, or forest. Spirits of the third grade, whose good and evil deeds are more or less equal, suffer pain during the day and pleasure during the night. But ordinary Petas who were in their worldly life backbiters, murderers, brigands, rogues, thiefs or cheats (*DN* 3.197-8, *Jāt*. 5.1-3) have to undergo endless suffering in the Petaloka. The female Peta is known as Peti (Pretinī in Sanskrit) who were selfish, greedy, unfaithful, quarrelsome and miserly in their worldly life. Both Peta and Peti have flimsy anthropomorphic form, voice, feeling, and sentiment and roam near their worldly habitat or at the crossroads. Even as spirits, the male and female ones want the company of each other. But their power to harm makind is limited, because according to Buddhism fortune or misforutne of an individual depends on his/her own *karma* and not on external agency. As the Petas have no means of livelihood, they subsist on food offered by friends and relatives (*AN* 5.269ff.). Householders perform *pubbapetabali,* a ceremony of offering which establishes a bond between the living and the dead (*DN*3.66; *AN* 3.46). There is no compulsion to make such offerings because if people earn merit for their good actions that merit goes to their forefathers as well. Gifts to the Bhikkhu and the Saṅgha produce the highest merit which has the power to alleviate suffering of Petas and Petis.

The Asuras are described in Buddhist mythology as a class of evil beings usually in conflict with the Devas (*AN*2.91). They are higher in ranking than commonplace demons, the Piśācas, Yakkhas and Rākkhasas. The Buddhist conception of the Asuras is in striking agreement with the Vedic. In the preceding chapter we have seen that in the older substratum of the Vedas, the Asuras are highly exalted divine beings, but later the Asura worshippers, probably owing to their Iranian connection, began to be treated with diminishing importance, and the meaning of the term Asura changed. But even in the Purāṇas and epics, which give details of the never-ending battles between the Devas and the Asuras, they are held in high esteem, and are stated also to be well-versed in the Vedas. They are often favoured by Brahmā who grants them the boon of invincibility. Might, generosity, virtue, and other noble qualities of some Asura kings are recognised in the Purāṇas, though the general tendency is to defame them as hostile to goodness and virtue. The same double standard in the treatment of the Asuras is found in Buddhist mythology which holds that they were originally Devas because Sakka refers to them as the 'older Devas', or Pubbadeva (*SN*1.222; *Suttani,* com. 2.484). They are also regarded as the brethren of Sakka or Vāsava (*Jāt.* 5.139). When Sakka was born among the Asuras, they received him cordially. It is also said that the Asuras dwelt in the Tāvatiṃsa heaven from which they were dislodged by newcomer gods (*Suttani,* com. 2.484-5). The older Devas fell from Deva-hood losing their morality and became Asuras. In some texts the Asuras have a connection with *surā* or wine. When Sakka and his followers were born in the Asura world, the Asuras prepared a drink for them. Sakka and his followers did not drink it but the Asuras did in consequence of which they became unconscious and were thrown to the bottom of Sineru. When they gained consciousness, they made a vow never to drink *surā* hence they were called Asuras (*SN*, com. 1.338). The story does not end here. The expelled Asuras thereupon made a city of their own at the bottom of Sineru. It was known as Asurabhavana and was 10,000 *yojanas* in extent (*Suttani*, com. 2.485). Then wanting to regain their old region, the Asuras invaded the Deva kingdom. This is the Buddhist version of the Puranic Deva-Asura conflict. Sakka tried to resist the Asura invasion, but was worsted in the fight and his Vaijayanta chariot took him to the realm of the Garuḍas. Ultimately he was able to reconquer his heavenly abode from the Asuras.

The Asuras are called Dānavas because they are the descendants of Danu (*Milinda* 153). In another tradition as recorded by Buddhaghoṣa, they are regarded as descendants of an Asura maiden named Sujātā. This Sujātā, however, cannot be the same as her namesake the daughter of Vepacitti, a celebrated Asura, whom Sakka married (*Jāt.* 1.205-6). The Asura-world is sometimes described as one of the four evil destinies (*Jāt.* 5.186, 6.595; *ITV* 92). Elsewhere the Asuras are called *bibhaccha*, aweful and vile, who use a drum called the *ālambara*, made of a crab's claw (*AN*, com. 2.526). It was left behind in the Tāvatiṃsa when the Asuras had to leave this world, and Sakka took possession of it. Its sound resembled a peal of thunder (*Jāt.* 2.344).

The Kālakañjakas are a special class of Asuras of fearful shape. They resemble the Petas not only in shape but also in sex-life, diet, and longevity. There is intermarriage between Petas and Kālakañjakas. They belong to the lowest category of the Asuras. They suffer from excessive thirst which they cannot quench even by immersing themselves in the Ganges. Korakkhatiya was reborn among them after his death from epilepsy (*DN* 3.7-8; *DN* , com. 3.789, 820; *KV* 360; *Jāt.* 1.389; *Vibh.*, com. 5). Dānavaghasās are another class of Asuras who were present during the preaching of the Buddha's sermons (*DN* 2.259). They are described as archers (*DN*, com. 2.689). Asura Sucitti belongs to this class (*DN* 2.259). The king of the Asuras is called Asurinda, the Indra (Inda) of the Asuras. It is not a personal name. Sakka is also called Asurinda and Asurādhipa (*Jāt.* 1.66; 5.245). This epithet is probably due to his conquest of the Asuras or to the fact that the Asuras and the Devas are of common origin. In the Vedas and the Purāṇas the Asuras are described as having *māyā*, i.e. magical or miraculous power to their credit. The same is echoed in the Buddhist tradition as well.

The Buddhist texts mention a good number of Asura chiefs, prominent among them is Vepacitti (*SN* 1.22; 4.201ff; *Jāt.*1.205). His Puranic counterpart is Vipracitti, founder of an Asura lineage. It is also said that the original name of Vepacitti was Śambara, the Asura of Vedic and Puranic fame (*SN*1.227). Once when Vepacitti was ill on account of a curse of the sages, Sakka visited him and offered to cure him if he would teach him Śambari-māyā or the magic art of Śambara (*SN*, 1.237-9). According to the legend when Śambara refused the request of the sages for guarantee of safety they cursed him in consequence of which he slept badly and was plagued by nightmares. This deranged his mind and he was called Vepacitti or 'crazy-nerve' (*cittam vepati*). Although Vepacitti was always in conflict with the Devas and was eventually defeated by Sakka (*SN* 1.221-5; 4.201), there was a family relation between the two, since Sakka had married his daughter Sujā (*Jāt.* 1.205-6; *Dhamma* com.1.278-9). Vepacitti was present with Namuci at the preaching of a special Sutta (*DN*2.259). Though identified with Śambara, Vepacitti might have been a different personality, because in one place (*SN* 1.237-8, *SN* com.1.355) the latter told Sakka that Śambara was suffering for a long time in purgatory for practising magic. Śambara is often described as the wily chieftain of the Asuras (*Jāt.* 5.452, 454). On one occasion it is said that when the Asuras were defeated in a fight with the Devas, Vepacitti was bound hand and foot and brought to Sakka in the Sudhammā-hall. The Asura king reviled Sakka with abuse, but Sakka remained silent. The bondage caused him no harm so long as he remained with the Devas, but the moment he desired to rejoin the Asuras he felt himself bound (*SN*1.221-2; 4.201; *Thera*749). Sakka said to Mātali that he won a two-fold victory because he defeated Vepacitti in battle and did not revile him. As a result both the Devas and the Asuras declared victory in favour of Sakka (*SN*1.222-3). Later Sakka permitted Vepacitti to go free (*SN* 1.225). Other members of Vepacittii's family married Devas, in consequence of which a troop of Asuras belonging to the retinue of Vepacitti was rescued from the four-fold plane of misery.

Among other important Asuras the Buddhist texts mention the Puranic Rāhu who devours the sun and the moon but fails to digest them because they are worshippers of the Buddha. Rāhu is described as one of the four 'stains' on the sun and the moon and one of the five causes of drought. He is also associated with the ocean. Orginially he was hostile to the Buddha, but later he understood his folly and became his disciple. According to Buddhaghoṣa (*DN*, com. 2.285) Rāhu did not visit the Buddha because he thought the latter would fail to see him on account of his height. The Buddha read his thought and made himself so high that

Rāhu was in comparison a dwarf. Rāhu has a self-expressive personality (*attābhāva*). He is said to be 4800 *yojanas* in height. His hands and feet are 200 *yojanas* in length, his face 100 *yojanas*. He hides the sun and moon in his mouth. He is described as one of the five causes of drought. He holds water in his hand and it spills into the ocean. When he steps into the ocean the waters of even the deepest part reach only his knees. It is impossible to bring him down from the sky. The texts mention *rāhu-mukha* as a kind of torture in which the victim's mouth is forced open and fire or spikes are sent through the orifice of the ear into the mouth. He is also called Rāhubhadda and Veroca. He is the uncle of the hundred sons of Bali. Veroca is Verocana (Vairocana), the lord of the Asuras who went with Sakka to meet the Buddha (*AN* 2.17, 35, 53, 295, 488; 3.243; *DN* 2.259; *DN*, com. 2.285, *SN* 1.225-6; *MN* 1.67; 3.164; *MN* com. 2.790-1, *Jāt.* 3.365, etc.). Prahlāda (Prahārada) of the epic-Purāṇa tradition also occurs in Buddhist mythology as one of the three leaders of the Asuras who conceived an idea of visiting the Buddha on the day of his enlightenment (*AN* com. 2.758). Elsewhere Vepacitti, Rāhu and Prahārada are described as distinguished Asura chiefs (*SN*, com. 1.342).

In view of what has been stated above, demonology, as of the early Buddhist Pali texts, can be classified under the following categories. The first category consists of the celestial beings, often described as gods serving as the archangels of the Buddha. Then come the Nāgas or Mahogras, snake-like or dragon-like beings resembling clouds who live in the sky, on earth and under water. Often their maidens assume siren-like shapes. The Nāga Mucilinda shielded the Buddha under the *bodhi* tree. There are Gandharvas and Yakṣas, who though sometimes malevolent, are friendly to the Buddha's family and tribe at Kapilavāstu. To this class belong the Apsarases or nymphs. The Asuras are Titanic demons headed by Vepacitti, Śambara, Rāhu, Verocana, or Prahārada and are related to the gods and have interesting role in subsequent mythologies. The Rākṣasas, Daityas and Piśācas are ogre-fiends capable of assuming siren-like and other forms who are mentioned along with Asuras, Gandharvas, Yakṣas, Kumbhaṇḍas, Pretas and others in a general way and are not treated in detail. The Pretas are starving ghosts, spectres, and ghouls, basically malignant in character.

To these classes maybe added a few other types unknown to the early Brahmanical texts. They may be local spirits of popular imagination like the famous she-devil Hāritī. She and her consort Pañcika have been represented in Indian art from the Gandhara sculptures owards. According to the Buddhist legends, she was the guardian deity of Magadha who was in the habit of stealing and devouring children. But under the influence of the Buddha she was converted into a protector of children. She is easily recognized in sculptures by her association with children. She is sometimes represented as holding a pomegranate which the Buddha gave her as food as a substitute for human flesh.

We come to Māra, the personification of the evil principle and tempter of man. The culminating episode of the Buddha's career—the attainment of Buddhahood—is universally represented as his personal struggle with Māra and his daughters Desire, Unrest and Pleasure. This event is regarded by the Buddhists not as an allegory, but as actual bodily temptation and a conflict with manifested evil spirits. Māra presents an analogy to the Satan of the Bible, although he is not a fallen angel in the literal sense; nor is he, like Ahriman of the Iranians, a foe of equal power. Though unknown by that name in the Vedic literature, Māra is manifestly a form of Yama, the god of death. After his enlightenment the Buddha addressed Māra, saying 'you are evercome, O Death'. In other aspects Māra resembles Kāma, the god of sensuous desire. The Pali texts often refer to Māra as a Yakṣa. It is said that Māra attacked the Buddha with a ten-fold army comprising lust; aversion; hunger and thirst; craving; sloth and indolence; cowardice; doubt; hypocricy and stupidity; gain; fame; honour; and glory; and lauding of oneself while condemning others. This, however, suggests that Māra is an abstract principle comprising all the evil propensities found in people to a greater or lesser degree. Māra's three daughters—Tanhā, Arati and Rāga—are personifications of desire or craving, unrest or insatiety and pleasure or lust. Māra's other names are Kanha, Adhipati, Antaka, Namuci and Pamattabandhu. His usual epithet is Pāpimā. The term Māra is applied to the whole of the evil of wordly existence, the five aggregates of existence, as opposed to *nirvāṇa* (*SN* 3.74, 189, 195, 198; 4.91, 202 *Suttani*, com. 2.506). From a single Māra, the conception has multiplied. Thus we have Khanda-Māra, Kilesa-Māra, Abhisaṅkhāra-Māra, Maccu-Māra and Devaputta-Māra (*Vis.* 1.211). Among these, Devaputta-Māra is supposed to be the head of the Kāmavacra world (*AN* 2.17). It was he who attacked the Buddha with his forces but failed to conquer him. When his ten-fold army was shattered he hurled at the Buddha his last weapon, the *cakkāyudha,* but it stood on him like a canopy of flowers. Then he claimed that the seat of the Buddha was his own. Since the Buddha had no witness, he asked the earth to be his witness and the earth roared in response. Māra was thus completely defeated. The Buddha's touching the earth to proclaim his victory is represented by the *bhūmisparśa-mudrā* in images (*SN* 1.103ff;

Jāt. 1.73ff.). Even though Māra was defeated, he followed the Buddha for seven years to find his weakness (*SN* 1.122; *Suttani*, com.2.391-3). He tried to misinterpret his teachings. In the assemblies held by the Buddha he influenced some of his listeners and made them utter heretical doctrines. He often assumed the guise of a bullock and broke the bowls of the monks (*SN* 1.567, 103ff; *DN* 3.58; *Dhamma*, com. 3.195-6). The Buddha and his monks experienced difficulty in obtaining food because of Māra's machinations (*Vinaya*, com. 1.178-9). He misguided the monks with apparently attractive sermons assuming the form of an old and very learned Brāhmaṇa (*DN* 2.261; *DN*, com. 3.864). He assumed various forms and tempted the *bhikṣuṇīs* in lonely spots. His temptations were not confined only to monks and nuns, but also extended to lay men and women. He tried to lure them from the path of goodness (*SN* 1.129-34; *Jāt.* 1.131-2; *Therī* 57-9).

The mythology of the Mahāyāna Buddhists is different from that of the followers of the Hīnayāna. But the two are not essentially delinked. Mahāyāna Buddhism differs fundamentally from the Hīnayāna in its conception of the Buddha as all-pervasive world-principle with three *kāyas* or forms; the Bodhisattvas; and a host of divinities adopted from various sources, and the new-fangled doctrine of vacuity as its philosophical basis. It has a demonology of a different kind. But the residues of the earlier Hīnayānic tradition have not completely sunk into oblivion. In the Mahāyāna texts, the four guardians or Lokapālas of the Catummahārājika world, given Sanskritized names, are Dhṛtarāṣṭra, Virudhaka, Virupākṣa, and Vaiáravaṇa. Likewise Śakra (Sakka) of the Tāvatiṃsa world, Suyāma of the Yama world, Santuṣita of the Tuṣita world, Sunirmita of the Nirmāṇarati world, and Vaśavartī of the Parinirvāṇavaśavartī world are mentioned (*Gaṇḍavyūha* 117, 119, 216; *Saddharma* 46f.; *Samādhi* 62, *Lalita*, 217-18, etc.). The Vedic gods like Indra, Varuṇa, Prajāpati, Viṣṇu, Yama, Āditya, etc., regarded in the Pali texts as archangels of the Buddha, are retained in the Mahāyāna texts. Hīnayāna and Mahāyāna have the same conception of the spirits of departed persons who are reborn in different worlds in accordance with their earned merits and demerits. Those spirits who earn merit are reborn in Devaloka and Brahmaloka and those earning demerits are born in four Apāyalokas, i.e. they are reborn among the animals, Asuras, Pretas or ghosts and inhabitants of hell (*Mahāvastu* 1.30-1). The region of the Pretas is regarded as a kind of hell, because the spirits of the dead suffer here from severe pain owing to their misdeeds of previous births (ibid. 2.324).

Supernatural beings are regarded in the Mahāyāna as spirits who are sometimes visible and are frequently conceived of as good or hostile to mankind. The spirits that dwell in the gardens, houses, hills, rivers, seas, royal umbrellas, waters, etc., are generally treated as semi-divine. The evil spirits are troublesome and terrifying demons such as the Asuras, Yakṣas, Rākṣasas, Piśācas, and Māras. The struggles between the gods and the Asuras recorded in the Vedic literature and reaffirmed in the Pali texts (cf. *SN* 1.222; 4.201ff., *Jāt.* 1.205) also find expression in the later Buddhist works which place Rāhu and Vemacitri (Vaimacitra, Pali Vepacitti) in the list of Asura kings (*Mahāvastu*, 3.138, 254; *Lalita* 241; *Divyā* 126, 182; *Saddharma* 5; *Ganda* 250; *Avadāna* 1.108). Four archangels of the Cāturmahārājika world are the guardian spirits of the four quarters, who rule respectively over the Gandharvas, Kumbhaṇḍas, Nāgas, and Yakṣas (*Divyā* 126, 182). The Gandharvas are treated alike in the Hīnayāna and Mahāyāna texts. The legends of Pañcaśikha Gandharva are also included (*Mahāvastu* 3.197, 215; *Avadāna* 1.95; *Samādhi* 19.37). The Yakṣas, though occasionally malevolent, are described as devotees of the Buddha (*Saddharma* 1). Nāgas, Garuḍas and Kinnaras are described as minor deities. The legend of Mucilinḍa occurs in the Mahāyāna texts, according to which Māra began to disturb the Buddha's meditation and the serpent king unfolded his coils and spread his hood over the head of the Buddha to protect him (*Lalita* 379). The conflict between Māra and the Buddha is recorded in the pro-Mahāyāna and Mahāyāna texts. He is the personification of evil who tried to prevent the Buddha from the attainment of perfection by threats and temptations. Māra is often styled Namuci in Hīnayāna and Mahāyāna mythology. The Sanskrit Buddhist texts refer to the five Māras except Abhisaṅkhāra. Devaputra Māra is described as the head of the Kāmavacara world. Māra is often identified with Kāmadeva, the god of desire. The three daughters of Māra are also referred to in the Mahāyāna texts (*Divyā* 393; *Lalita* 261, 302, 311, 328, 357; *Samādhi* 19; *Saddharma* 210).

The story of Māra's defeat is illustrated in Buddhist art. In Cave 26 at Ajanta we have two compositions, one representing the *parinirvāṇa* of the Buddha and the other the assult and temptation of Māra on the eve of the enlightenment. On the dexter of the relief is Māra, mounted on his elephant, with his demon hosts threatening the Buddha with various missiles and weapons to dislodge him from his seat under a *pipal* tree. In the centre the Buddha, challenged by Māra as regards to his right to the seat, calls upon the earth to bear witness by touching the ground with his right hand. On the sinister is the flight of the discomfited Māra along with his retinue. In Cave 11 at Ellora there is a colossal image of the Buddha with his attendants. In front of the throne there are two females, the one on the right being Pṛthivi, who was called by the Buddha to bear witness to his victory, striding over the prostrate Māra. At Goli in the Guntur district, a frieze which depicts scenes from the Buddha's life contains the representation of the assault and temptation of Māra. At Gantasala in the Krishna district, in a mound containing the ruins of the Mahācaitya, a few slabs have been found, one of which contains a relief depicing the assault and temptation of Māra. Individual Buddha images in *bhūmisparśa-mudrā* (touching the earth) are in themselves suggestive of the discomfiture of Māra by the Buddha. The Brahmanical gods who are represented as the archangels of the Buddha are depicted in connection with the theme of the eight great miracles. For example, the relief of the Miracle of Śāṅkāsya on the northern gateway of Stūpa 1 at Sanchi depicts the Buddha's descent from the Tāvatiṃsa heaven to earth at Sāṅkāśya. The top of the panel depicts the heaven with gods seated by the side of the Buddha represented by a seat below a tree at the head of a ladder. The ladder flanked by rows of *devas* signifies the Buddha's descent. Among other aerial and terrestrial beings mentioned above the Buddhist Kubera is found in Cave 2 at Ellora. Among the important loose antiquities found at Paharpur in north Bengal there is a bronze image of the Buddhist Kubera. The caves of Pitalkhora in Maharashtra, which most probably represents the ancient Pītaṅgalya where resided the Yakṣa Sankarin according to the Buddhist text *Māhāmāyūrī*, contain figures of the Yakṣas and winged Kinnaras. The Kinnaras are also found in Cave 7 of Nasik. Individual Yakṣa and Yakṣiṇī images are legion. Among those associated with important Buddhist sites, mention should be made of the posts from Bharhut which depict large-sized standing figures of the Yakṣas and Yakṣiṇīs, the walls of the front porch of the gateway of the monastery at Sirpur in Madhya Pradesh embellished with Yakṣa figures, Cave 6 of Ajanta which has figures of Nāgarāja, Yakṣas, Pañcika and Hāritī, and Cave 6 of Aurangabad which bears the relief of a beautiful *śālabhañjikā* under a blossoming tree above and a pot-bellied Yakṣa below. The ogress-cum-protectress Hāritī had a temple in the Ghositārama monastery complex at Kausambi and another at Nagarjunikonda. The Buddhist sites of Takht-i-Bahi, Sirpur, Aurangabad, Ellora, Sankaram and Ratnagiri, contain the figures of Hāritī engraved on the walls. Nāga figures are also numerous since they serve legendary, cultic and decorative purposes at the same time. In the Bharhut depictions we have representations of Nāga Erāpatha's worship of the Buddha. Particular interest attaches to the depiction of Nāgarāja Mucilinda at the foot of the Buddha's seat on the western gateway of Stūpa 1 at Sanchi. The Buddha spent the sixth week after englightenment in the company of the serpent king Mucilinda who shielded him during a rain-shower by his coils and hoods. On this Sanchi relief, however, Mucilinda with a five-headed hood is seen seated below the seat of the Buddha under a tree, over which is an umbrella. The full retinue of the king consists of his two queens, an attendant, and a troupe of dancers and five musicians, all single-hooded female Nāgas (BM, *passim*).

The Mahāyāna introduced a new type of divinity comprising a multiplication of Dhyānī and mortal Buddhas, their emanations, various Bodhisattvas, and a host of subordinate deifications in which philosophical dogma, ritualistic literature, abstract ideas, human qualities, even desires such as sleeping , yawning and sneezing were given the form of a god. Besides, integral to the pantheon were Hindu deities like Indra, Yama, Varuṇa, Kubera, Īśāna, Agni, Āditya, Nairṛti, Vāyu, Brahmā, Viṣṇu, Maheśvara, Gaṇapati, Kārttikeya, Sarasvatī, Tārā, Vārāhī, Cāmuṇḍā, and Mahākāla; Yakṣas, Kinnaras, Gandharvas and Vidyādharas, mythological beings like Bhṛṅgi and Nandikeśvara; and the nine planets and twenty-eight constellations. It is to be observed that the Mahāyānic gods and goddesses in many cases are conceived in terms of demoniacal attributes, side by side with their normal forms. They are endowed with violent character, terrible appearance, angry looks and deformed bodies. The Mahāyāna argument is that all the deities are the creation of mind and as such they are to be conceived both in gentle and in fierce forms, because the human mind has both these propensities. The purpose is not worship but concentration. The Mahāyāna gods lack the traditional mythological background. Some of them are, however, local or traditional deities who were inducted in Mahāyāna scheme. Just as the Vedic pantheon was ruled by the thunderbolt-bearer Indra, so also the Mahāyāna pantheon was headed by Vajradhara who was the bearer of thunderbolt and the embodiment of the highest reality, Śūnya. Likewise the Dhyānī Buddha Vairocana seems to have been conceptually related to the Asura chief Virocana of the Vedic texts. Nīlakaṇṭha was evidently modelled on Śiva who swallowed the poison that issued from the mouth of Vāsuki, the lord of serpents, while the gods and the demons were churning the ocean together. In the same way, the Hayagrīva or horse-faced form of Viṣṇu was inducted in the Buddhist pantheon. According to the Purāṇas, Hayagrīva was a demon. Viṣṇu assumed the horse-headed form to kill him. Jambhala was a Yakṣa originally of non-Buddhist origin. Vajravārāhī reminds us of Vārāhī, one of the traditional seven Mātṛkās. In the Buddhist texts she is often called a Ḍākinī, or a fiend.

The Tibetans do not differentiate between Mahāyāna and Vajrayāna. They equate the Mahāyāna Sūtras with Tantra. In the *Tattvaratnāvali*, collected in the *Advayavajrasaṃgraha,* Mahāyāna is subdivided into two schools—Pāramitānaya and Mantranaya. The latter is claimed to be a distinctly superior way and is to be adopted only by those who are free from delusions and of high intellectual calibre (*ADV* 21). This Mantranaya or Mantrayāna is the precursor of Vajrayāna and its offshoots, Kālacakrayāna and Sahajayāna. Vajrayāna is described as the cult of the five *kulas* or clans of the Bodhisattavas, each representing a distinct mental state of the aspirant (*GS* 154). It is described as a path of transcendental perfect elightenment, to be achieved through different rites and ceremonies, *mantras* and meditations (*SDM* 1.225; 2.421). Vajrayāna considers Śūnya or nothingness as the ultimate reality and innumerable gods and goddesses as its manifestations. The gods have no real existence; they are born of the mind, issuing from the *bījamantras* uttered by the worshipper. The Śūnya takes the form of a divinity in accordance with the germ-syllable uttered, and exists only as a positive idea in the mind of the aspirant. It takes different forms, even demonic, according to the different functions it has to discharge (for instance, the form of Siṃhanāda when a disease is to be cured, Jāṅguli when there is a snake-bite, and Kurukullā when there is a love affair). The weapons and emblems by which the deities of Vajrayāna are characterized are nothing but the weapons needed by the Bodhicitta (mind bent on attaining perfect enlightenment) to fight the elements obstructing the path of knowledge. For instance, when the darkness of ignorance is to be dispelled the Bodhicitta becomes a sword, when the heart of the wicked is to be pierced it becomes the *aṇkuśa* or goad and when a bad element is to be cut away it becomes a *kartari* or knife.

As has been stated above, many of the deities of the Vajrayāna pantheon are described with demoniac features in the *SDM* and *NSP*. Among them Saptaśatika Hayagrīva, who is really a demon in the Puranic tradition, is of red complexion, three-eyed and brown-bearded. He is angry-looking, with a protruding belly and wears a garland of skulls and ornaments of eight serpents. Clad in tiger-skin, he holds thunderbolt and staff in his two hands. Another form of this god is of red colour, with eight arms and three faces with three eyes in each face. He is clad in a tiger-skin and shows in his four right hands the thunderbolt, staff, *karaṇa* pose and raised arrow. Of his four left hands, one has the raised index finger, the second touches the breast, and the two remaining ones hold the lotus and the bow. Heruka stands on a corpse, clad in human skin with the *vajra* in his right hand and a *kapāla*, full of blood, in the left. From his left shoulder hangs a *khatvaṅga* with a flowing banner. Decked in ornaments of bones, his head is decorated with five skulls. When in embrace with his consort Heruka is known as Hevajra, blue in colour, one- or three- or eight-faced, two- or four- or sixteen-armed. His consorts are Nairātmā, Vijrayoginī and Vajraśrṃkhalā. Vajrayoginī is of yellow or red colour, standing in *ālīḍha* carrying her own severed head in her upraised left hand. One should not fail to recall in this connection the Śākta-Tantric conception or Chinnamastā. In one variety, she is said to be standing *pratyālīḍha* on a corpse and to have two hands. She has a terrifying mien with three frowning round eyes, bare fangs and protruding tongue, and red hair rising up like flames. Śambara, obviously the demon of the Vedic tradition, later transformed into a god in Vajrayāna, is not very different from Heruka/Hevajra since he is also in *yuganaddha* or in union with his consort Vajravārāhī. A rare stone image of this deity of about the ninth century, is in the Indian Museum. It has three heads and twelve arms, of which two are crossed on the breast, holding a thunderbolt and a bell in the attitude known as *vajraparyaṅka*. His heads bear matted hair, the front one having three eyes. In his hands there is magic wand, skull-cup, and a severed head of Brahmā. Above his head appears a four-armed female standing in the same pose as the god and this figure is repeated thrice below, between the legs of the central figure and at the sides. There is no doubt that she is Vajravārāhī (*IBI*, *passim*; *ASIAR*, 1934-5, 80, Pl. XXIV C).

Yamāntaka, also known as Yamāri, has two forms, Rakta and Kṛṣṇa. The former is described in the *SDM* as one-faced, two-armed, standing in *pratyālīḍha* with *kapāla* full of blood in the left hand and a staff in the right, decked in ornaments of snakes, clad in tiger-skin and embraced by his female consort. Kṛṣṇa-Yamāri has three varieties: (1) one-faced, two-armed, staff marked by *vajra* in right hand; raised index finger with noose against the chest in the left; (2) three-faced, four-armed, *mudgara* and sword in the right hands, lotus and jewel in the left; in union with consort; (3) three- or six-faced, six-armed; *vajra,* sword and *musala* in right hands; *vettali* (goblin) axe and noose in the left hands. Though Kubera occurs both in Hīnayāna and in Mahāyāna, his other prototype Jambhala is described in a large number of *sādhanas.* He has many forms, simple as well as demonic. He holds a citron and a mongoose vomitting jewels. He is often represented as surrounded by eight Yakṣas.

Four faced and eight-armed is Trailokyavijaya. The front face is fierce-looking and wrathful, the right imprinted with anger, and the left with disgust, whereas the face behind exhibits heroic disposition. Standing in *pratyālīḍha* pose he tramples the head of Maheśvara with his left leg and with the right leg the bosom of Gaurī. This interesting Buddhist deity shows the superiority and preponderance over Hindu goddesses. The goddess Kurukullā is nice, but Uḍḍīyana Kurukullā is demoniac. She is red in colour, seated upon a corpse. The goddess has five skulls on the head, protruding teeth and tongue, garments of tiger-skin and brown-hair rising above her head in the shape of a flame. The goddess of epidemics, Parṇaśabarī, evidently a tribal adaptation, is three-faced and six-armed, standing in *pratyālīḍha* trampling under her feet the Vighnas (Gaṇeśa). In another conception she has a green complexion, three faces, three eyes and six hands. Here she tramples under her feet various diseases and pestilences.

Chastiser of all wicked beings, Aparājitā is described as trampling upon Gaṇeśa. In *SDM* we come across the description of a three-faced and six-handed goddess under the designation Sitātapatrā Aparājitā. Mārīcī is usually represented with three faces, the left one being that of a sow, with the figure of Vairocana on her crest and riding on a chariot drawn by seven pigs and by the charioteer Asura Rāhu. She is generally accompanied by four other fearful goddesses, Vartālī, Vadāli, Varāli, and Varāhamukhī (*IBI, passim*).

Kālacakrayāna, an offshoot of Vajrayāna, came into vogue in the tenth century and also became popular in Tibet and China. Kālacakra, the principal deity of the Kālacakramaṇḍala of *NSP*, is conceived as dancing on the bodies of Anaṅga and Rudra, blue in colour, wearing a tiger-skin, having twelve eyes, four faces and twelve principal hands on each side. In one of his hands he carries the severed head of Brahmā (*NSP* 83-4). The word *kālacakra* (Tibetan: *dus-kyi-k'or lo*) means wheel of time. According to Abhinavagupta, it is possible to control time by controlling the vital winds in the nerves through yogic practices (*Tantrāloka* 6). This is a system of *yoga* which with all its accessories of *maṇḍala* (magic circle) and concentration (*abhiṣeka*) is explained within the human body, how all the universe with all its objects and localities are situated in the body, and how time with all its varieties (day, night, fortnight, month, etc.) are within the body in the process of the vital wind. From the *Sekoddeśaṭīkā* which is a commentary on the Sekoddeśa section of the *Kālacakratantra* it is known that by *kāla* is denoted the ultimate immutable and unchanging reality remaining in all the elements, and by *cakra* is meant the unity of the three kinds of existence. In the *Laghū-kālacakraṭīkā*, entitled the *Vimalaprabhā*, Kālacakra is conceived of as the nature of Śūnyatā and Karuṇā. In principle there is, therefore, no difference between Vajrayāna and Kālacakrayāna. Lord Śrī Kālacakra is not basically different from Ādi Buddha or Vajrasattva or Vajradhara.

But in practice a kind of demonolatry characterized the Kālacakra system. Waddell writes: 'In the tenth century AD, the Tantric phase developed in Northern India, Kashmir and Nepal, into a monstrous and poly-demonist doctrine, the Kālacakra, with its demoniacal Buddhas, which incorporated the Mantrayāna practices and called itself Vajrayāna or the "Thunderbolt vehicle", and its followers were named Vajrācārya or followers of the thunderbolt. . . . . The extreme development of the Tantric phase was reached with the Kalacakra which, although unworthy of being considered as a philosophy, must be referred to here as a doctrinal basis. It is merely a coarse Tantric development of the Ādi-Buddha theory combined with the puerile mysticism of Mantrayāna and it attempts to explain creation and the secret powers of nature, by the union of the terrible Kālī, not only with the Dhyānī Buddhas, but even with Buddha himself. In this way Ādi Buddha, by meditation evolves a procreative energy by which the aweful Śambara and other dreadful Ḍākinī fiendesses, all of the Kālī type, obtain spouses as fearful as themselves, yet spouses who are regarded as reflexes of Ādi Buddha and the Dhyānī Buddhas. And these demoniacal "Buddhas" under the name Kālacakra, Heruka, Acala, Vajrabhairava, etc., are credited with powers and inferior to those of celestial Buddhas themselves, and withal ferocious and blood-thirsty; and only to be conciliated by constant worship of themselves and their female energies, with offerings and sacrifices, magic circles, special *mantra*-charms, etc.' (*BT*15.131).

Admitting Waddell's great contribution to the study of Tibetan Buddhism, it may be said that since he has viewed Vajrayāna and Kālacakrayāna from the Lamaistic standpoint, his approach is one-sided. The deities of Vajrayāna and Kālacakrayāna are in many cases demon-like, but they are gods and not demons. According to the theoretical point of view, which is most clearly recorded in the Hindu and Buddhist Tantras, deities are creations of the mind and have no external existence apart from the mind of the aspirant. They are conceptual and subjective. Historically, however, what ought to have remained purely in the domain of conception, an introspective imagery, assumed in course of time a concrete form leading to the development of iconism. When the deities, benign or demoniac, thus became conserved and crystallized in their iconic forms, what was the object of mental concentration in its formative stage came to be the object of a specialized cult. From this point of view it may be said that the cultic aspects of Vajrayāna and Kālacakrayāna, as opposed to their meditational aspects, had created certain conditions leading to demonolatry. This explains Waddell's standpoint. The process was reversed in the case of Tibetan Buddhism in which an elaborate pre-existing demonolatry was amalgamated with the tenets of Buddhism. The great majority of the Tibetan demons were of pre-Buddhist Bon origin. Known as *lha* and *rDud*, they were mostly personified natural forces, tribal gods supposed to live in the sky, evil genii, or malignant fiends. Later these terms were extended to the gods and demons of Brahmanical and Buddhist mythology. Even Māra was regarded as a *rDud*. The pre-Buddhist demonology of Tibet included good spirits, rural gods, and fairy guardians who are defenders of Lamaism; ghosts and goblins sprung from discontended disembodied priests haunting the vicinity of temples; devils male and female who were persecutors of Lamaism; planet-fiends producing diseases among which fifteen great ones are recongnized; bloated fiends, dark purple in colour; ghouls and vampires, raw-flesh-coloured and bloodthirsty; kind fiends who are the treasure masters and apotheosized heroes; and she-devils who are disease-mistresses. Many of the above are local genii, of which numerous are 'earth-owners' (*sa-bdag*). At every temple or monastery the local spirit is represented as an idol or fresco within the outer gateway, usually to the right of the door. The selected ones, either individually or by class, are identified with the Hindu Bhūtas (*'byung-po*), Pretas (*yi-dyag*), Piśācas (*sā-za*), Kumbhaṇḍas (*sGrul-'bum*), Rakṣas (*srin-po*), etc. With the introduction of Mahāyāna Buddhism in Tibet certain demons and spirits of the earlier tradition were mixed with Mahāyāna deities. Just as the pre-Buddhist demons and spirits of India had found a place in the Buddhist system having been eliminated of their malignancy through the grace of the Buddha, so also in Tibet many earlier spirits had a reformed character in Buddhism and became objects of meditation and worship as deities, notwithstanding their demonic garb.

NOTES AND REFERENCES

For the original texts referred to in this chapter with the initial letters of their names see the *Abbreviations* in which the complete titles, their editions and translations, place and date of publication are given. The secondary sources comprise R.S. Hardy, *Manual of Buddhism,* London, 1860; *Legends and Theories of the Buddhists,*

London, 1866; W.W. Rockhill, *Life of the Buddha,* London, 1884; M. Monier-Williams, *Buddhism,* London, 1890: L.A. Waddell, *The Buddhism of Tibet,* London, 1895; H. Kern, *Manual of Indian Buddhism,* Strassburg, 1896; A Grünwedel, *Mythologie des Buddhismus,* Leipzig, 1900; *Buddhist Art of India,* translated from the *Handbuch* of the author, *Buddhistische Kunst in Indien,* by Agnes C. Gibson, revised and enlarged by J. Burgess, London, 1901; A. Fourcher, *L'Iconographie bouddhique de l'Inde,* Paris, 1900-5; A Getty, *The Gods of Northern Buddhism,* Oxford, 1914; A.B. Keith, *Mythology of all Races,* vol. VI, Boston, 1917; W. Mc Govern, *A Manual of Buddhist Philosopy,* Calcutta, 1925; *Buddhist Conception of Spirits,* 2nd edn., London, 1936; A.K. Coomaraswamy, *Yakṣas,* 2 vols., Washington, 1928, 1931, rpt. New Delhi, 1971; *Elements of Buddhist Iconography,* London, 1935; M. Winternitz, *History of Indian Literature,* vol. II, Calcutta, 1933; rpt. New Delhi, 1972; E. Clark, *Two Lamaistic Pantheon,* Cambridge Mass., 1934; G.P. Malalasekera, *A Dictionary of Pali Names,* 2 vols., London, 1937-8, A.K. Gordon, *Iconogrphy of Tibetan Lamaism,* New Delhi, 1939; T.O. Ling, *Buddhism, and the Mythology of the Evil,* London, 1962; B.T. Bhattacharyya, *Indian Buddhist Iconography,* Calcutta, 1968; J.W. Boyd, *Satan and Māra: Christian and Buddhist Symbols of Evil,* Leiden, 1975; J.R. Haldar, *Early Buddhist Mythology,* New Delhi, 1977; N.N. Bhattacharyya, *History of Researches on Indian Buddhism,* New Delhi, 1981; *Buddhism in the History of Indian Ideas,* New Delhi, 1993; *Indian Religious Historiography,* vol. I, New Delhi, 1996.

CHAPTER IV

Jain Demonology

Although demonolatry was not directly encouraged in Buddhism, it required several demons and spirits to prove its superiority. The Buddhist texts convey the idea that these evil beings causing harm to mankind were originally hostile to the Buddha and that after coming in contact with him they underwent a complete character transformation. They became devotees of the Buddha and under his all-pervading influence they used their special power for the welfare of mankind. Since the Buddha was a super-divine entity he had an entourage of gods and angels. Apart from the Vedic gods, early Buddhism created a variety of new divinities as attendants of the Buddha, the important among them being Aruṇā, Ariṭṭhakā, Āpa, Ummāpupphā, Odātagayhā, Khiḍḍāpadosikā, Manopadosikā and other thirty-one classes (*DN* 2.253-62); the Valāhakāyika class comprising Sitāvalāhaka, Unhavalāhaka, Abbhavalāhaka, and Vātavalāhaka deities including those of the Satullapakāyaikā category (*SN* 1.16-22; 3.254ff., *Milinda* 191); the Samacitta class comprising Parisuddhābhā, Saṃkiliṭṭhābhā and Abhibhu deities (*MIV* 3.102, 147) those belonging to the categories of Pabbata, Sayaṃpabha and Nārada (*Suttani* 404, 543); the Varavāraṇa (*Sumaṅgala* 2.76-7), Lokavyūha (*Visuddhi* 415-16) and Bhavya (*Jāt.* 5.171) classes. But interestingly none of these were able to leave its mark on the subsequent history of Buddhism. These deities were sudden products of the imagination with no popular traditional base. But the Vedic deities continued to survive as associates of the Buddha even during the Mahayanic period because they were originally nature gods quite consistent with the spirit of primitive naturolatry. They became anthropomorphised under diverse socio-religious situations through the ages. The same held good also in the case of the inverted pantheon of the demons and spirits. They were no less powerful than the gods. The Asuras, Rākṣasas, Dānavas, Yakṣas, Nāgas, etc., had a more powerful base in the mind of the people who believed in their destructive power. The benevolence of the gods was a matter of inference whereas the malevolence of demons was an observed fact, because worldly life is full of sufferings and obstacles. The dread of evil happenings in life, supposedly caused by malevolent demons and spirits, is stronger than the appreciation of the benevolence of the gods which, as men knew from their personal experience, was rarely showered upon them. That is why in Buddhism, as also in Jainism, demons and spirits of the earlier sources were taken into account.

Like the Buddha, the Jinas or Tīrthaṃkaras also had taken up the noble job of reforming the demons and spirits, destroying their evil propensities and re-employing them in good works. As the reward of their services to the Jinas, the converted demons and spirits were raised nearly to the rank of the gods. Those who had unflinching devotion to the creed became the companions of the Jinas and especially Mahāvīra, whose entourage consisted not only of the Vedic gods but of the refined Asuras, Rakṣas, Yakṣas, Nāgas and others. But while in Buddhism, notwithstanding living in the 'ocean of impermanence' their position as companions of the Buddha is more or less secure and permanent, this was not so in Jainism. In Jainism gods, angels, men, demons, spirits and even animals are conditioned by the fetters of their *karma* according to which a demon may be reborn as a god and a god may be reborn as a demon. They are all, including men and animals, destined to be reborn in different categories of existence according to their actions. Though theoretically both Buddhism and Jainism admit that all the happenings in a man's life, whether good or bad, are dependent on his own *karma* and that no external agency, either of the gods or of the demons, has anything to do with his destiny, the exponents of these systems found it necessary to utilize popular beliefs and sentiments regarding the demons and spirits in their favour.

Another factor had also contributed to the development of a new kind of demonology in Buddhism and Jainism. Both systems have drawn much from the Vedas. Not only have they incorporated the Vedic gods in their own pantheon, but they have formulated their views on cosmology, epistemology, ethics, eschatology and other ingredients of their philosophical doctrines on the basis of the Vedic texts, especially those connected with transmigration and rebirth. But they were not ready to accept the Vedas as *apauruṣeya* (not composed by any human being) or absolutely authoritative. They were also opposed to the sacrificial religion of the Vedas, not because it required animal sacrifice (the Buddhists and the Jains have their own views of sacrifice, which is meritorious acts) but because it was rather 'alien' to the indigenous culture. They were intelligent enough to understand that beings like the Rakṣas, Yakṣas, Nāgas etc., were originally the objects of important folk cults and so depicted by the Vedic poets with demoniacal attributes. Naturally these beings, as we have discussed earlier, were treated with sympathy by the Buddhists and the Jains.

According to the Jains, the entire cosmos is composed of substances of different kinds which are possessed of some unchanged essential characters (*guṇas*) and changing modes (*paryāyas*)—the former being a body (*astikāya*) having extension (*DS* 24; *Uttara* 28, 36). *Astikāya* substances are again subdivided into two kinds—*jīva* or living and *ajīva* or non-living (*SDS* 3.33; *PTSMS* 129-32). *Ekendriya* or one-sensed *jīvas* possess only the sense of touch and are subdivided into earth-bodies, water-bodies, fire-bodies, air-bodies and vegetative bodies. *Dvīndriya* or two-sensed *jīvas* possess the organs of taste and touch to which category belong the animalcule, worms, things living in shells, leeches, earthworms, etc. *Trīndriya* or three-sensed *jīvas* possess the senses of touch, taste and smell to which category belong various kinds of ants, moths, etc. *Caturindriya-jīvas* are possessed of the four senses of touch, taste, smell and sight. To this class belong the wasps, scorpions, mosquitoes, flies, locusts, butterflies, etc. *Pañcendriya-jīvas* have an extra sense, that of hearing. In this category are included the bipeds and quadrupeds. The five-sensed beings are again of two kinds, those that originate by generatio acquivoca (*samucchāna*, coagulation) and those that are born from the womb. Each of these are again of three kinds—aquatic, terrestrial and aerial. Fish, tortoises, crocodiles, *makaras* and the Gangetic porpoises are the five kinds of aquatic animals. Quadrupeds and reptiles are the two kinds of terrestrial animals. The former are of four kinds—solidungular animals, as horses, etc., biungular like cows, etc., multiungular like elephants, etc., and animals having toes and nails such as lions, tigers, etc. The reptiles are of two kinds—those that walk on their arms, like lizards, and those which move on their breast, like snakes. Both are again of many kinds. Winged animals are of four kinds—those with membranous wings, those with feathered wings, those with wings in the shape of a box and those which sit on outspread wings. Men are of two kinds—originated by coagulation to which category belong gods and other supernatural beings—and those who are born from the womb. Those who are born from the womb are of three kinds those living in the *karmabhūmi*, those living in the *akarmabhūmi* and those living in minor continents (*Uttara* 36).

The aforesaid classification is based on direct observation and a scientific approach. Later on, however, owing to dogmatic influence, and especially as a means to explain and justify the theory of *karma,* we come across different types of classification, the artificial character of which can be easily detected. The five-sensed *jīvas* were classified into four divisions—hell beings, lower animals, human beings and demi-gods. Other modes of classification led to the following division. (1) Siddha and Saṃsārī (male, female, neuter); (2) Nāraka or Nārakī (born in hell), Tiryak (lower animals), Manuṣya (human beings), and Devatā (spirits, demons, gods); (3) hell-beings, male lower animals, female lower animals; (4) the five subdivisions of the one-sensed *jīvas* as well as the two-sensed, three-sensed, four-sensed and five-sensed *jīvas,* thus making a total of nine classes; (5) the old aforesaid five divisions of one-sensed, etc., sub-divided into two groups, *paryāpta* and *aparyāpta,* thus making a total of ten classes; (6) first four orders of the sensed *jīvas,* three subdivisions of the five-sensed *jīvas* (Nāraka, Tiryak and Manuṣya) and four subdivisions of gods (Bhavanapati, Vyantara, Jyotiṣka and Vaimānika), making a total of eleven classes; and (7) combination of all these in different ways making a total of twelve, thirteen and fourteen classes (*Uttara* 36). There is another classification based upon the concept of *lesyā.* By the term *lesyā* is understood the different conditions produced in the *jīva* by the influence of different *karmas.* The *lesyās* are six in number, the first three of which are bad and the remaining good. An individual is always a *saleśi* because he is swayed by any of the three good or three bad *lesyās.* Only the Siddhas are free from their influence and are called *āleśi.* In between the two there are six classes of *jīvas,* each being swayed respectively by the influence of black, blue, grey, red, yellow and white *lesyās.* Black is the worst of all under the influence of which a *jīva* becomes ill-tempered, cruel, and violent. Under the influence of the blue *lesyā* a *jīva* becomes envious of others, lazy, gluttonous, selfish and wanting in modesty. Under the influence of the grey *lesyā,* a *jīva* becomes a thief, a liar, an intriguer who likes to expose the bad qualities of others and conceal his own. *Tejaḥ* or red *lesyā* removes all evil thoughts from the *jīva.* Under the influence of *padma* or yellows *lesyā* a *jīva* controls anger, pride, deceit, and avarice. Under the influence of *śukla* or white l*esyā* a *jīva* becomes completely stainless (*Uttara* 34).

Superhuman beings fall into two categories—the denizens of hell (Nārakas, Nārakīs) and the gods (Devas). Gods in Jainism have an inferior position and mortals can easily excel them in merit. The good gods are described as Daivī and Āsurī while the evil ones are known as Kudevas or Kadamaras. Demons and ghosts are also indicated by the term Kudeva.

Neither the state of a god or that of a demon is permanent. Whether they would continue as gods or demons depends on their *karma*. The Nārakas or hell-beings have a demoniacal nature, but cannot leave the place where they are commissioned to stay or cause harm to any one except their fellow Nārakas. The souls of those who have committed grave sins are removed to one of the seven nether worlds which contain different hells. There the soul of the condemned is fitted out with an enormous ugly body. They possess superhuman power which they waste by fighting amongst themselves. In addition to the pains produced by the wounds they inflict on one another and by the tortures they have to undergo, they continually suffer from extreme heat or cold, intolerable smells, and horrid sounds. Other demons and ghosts reside in the two lowest classes of the former gods, the *bhavanavāsins* and *vyantaras*. The lowest class of the former gods are the Asurakumāras or simply Asuras. They reside in the upper half of Ratnaprabhā, the highest of the seven nether worlds. The Asuras may be good or bad, but there are fifteen extremely wicked Asuras, such as Ambariṣa and others who administer tortures in the three uppermost hells. The Nāgas are also included in the *bhavanavāsin* category who are reformed demons and have received the postion of demi-gods. The *vyantaras* include demons, goblins, ghosts and spirits living above or below the earth who are divided into Kinnaras, Kiṃpuruṣas, Mahogras, Gandharvas, Rākṣasas, Bhūtas, and Piśācas. The last four classes are not always bad. There are even among the Rākṣasas good ones who have been converted to Jainism. The evil ones are often called *duṣṭavyantaras* (*TTDS* 3-4).

The position of the superhuman beings has been altered by the Jains to introduce order into the mythological conceptions current at the time when their religious teachings crystallized into a definite form. According to the Jain conception, below the earth-disc are seven lower regions, one below the other. These are Ratnaprabhā, Śarkarāprabhā, Valukāprabhā, Paṅkaprabhā, Dhumraprabhā, Tamaḥprabhā and Mahātamaḥprabhā. Above these seven regions is the disc of the earth, with its numerous continents in concentric circles separated by rings of oceans. Above the earth are situated the heavenly regions styled *vimānas*, consisting of twelve *kalpas*, Saudharma, Aiśāna, Sanatkumāra, Mahendra, Brahmaloka, Lantaka, Mahāsukra, Sahasrāra, Ānata, Praṇata, Āraṇa, and Acyuta, the nine *graiveyakas* or the heavens forming the neck of the human-shaped universe, and five *anuttaras*, Vijaya, Vaijayanta, Jayanta, Aparājita and Sarvārthasiddha. Above the highest heaven called Sarvārthasiddha is situated Iṣatpragbhāra, the place which is the final resort of all souls (*Uttara* 36). However, the lower world is not only a place occupied by hell-beings, but its uppermost region known as Ratnaprabhā is also the seat of gods of both the kinds mentioned above. The two kinds are not always confined to the lower world, but are at home to a great extent in the centre world also. Of the *bhavanavāsi* or *vaimānika* gods there are ten different kinds: the Asura, Nāga, Suvaṇṇa, Vijju, Aggi, Ḍiva, Udāhi, Disā, Vāu and Thānīya (*Pannā* 84). These classes are suffixed by the term *kumāra*. They all have youthful appearances and are described mainly as male, though some appear to be female. Their size is seven cubits and they differ in colour. The Asuras are black, Nāgas and Udāhis whitish, the Suvaṇṇas, Disās and Thānikas golden, the Aggis, Divās and Vijjus orange and the Vāus dark (partly different in *TTDS* 4). These colours indicate their activities, their seats and their emblems (*Uvav* 34). They act also as the *lokapālas*. The Asuras are gods of the lower world. But they may go down into the deep beyond the Ratnaprabhā and reach both the centre world and the upper world (*Viy* 169, 180). The Nāgas are water-gods and are connected with the rain clouds (*Jambu* 238), while the Udāhis seem to command the sea. The Suvaṇṇas correspond to the Buddhist and Hindu concept of the Suparṇa-Garuḍa. Their fight with the Nāgas causes earthquake (*Ṭhān* 161). The Disās are elephant-spirits, often conceived as females. They had a role in the consecreation ceremony of the Tīrthaṃkaras. The Divās are unspecified gods or demons having some connection with the lions. The Vāus occupy submarine caves and cause the movement of the wind bodies (*Viy* 212).

The Ratnaprabhā region is horizontally divided into a southern and northern half inhabited by the aforesaid beings. Each of the two halves, of which the southern one contains some more places than the northern, is governed by a prince and his counterpart. The pair of princes are Camara and Bali -Vairocana, Dharaṇa and Bhūyananda, Veṇudeva and Veṇudāli, Harikānta and Harisaha, Aggisiha and Aggimānava, Puṇṇa and Vasiṭṭha, Jalakanta and Jalappaha, Amiyagai and Amiyavahāna, Velamba and Pabhañjana, Ghoṣa and Mahāghoṣa. These are mere names and have no mythological content. But in some of these names we come across figures celebrated in the Hindu Purāṇas. Bali-Vairocana evidently refer to the great Asura chiefs Bali and Virocana. The two Aggis are the two forms of Agni, one represented in the lion-form and the other as human. Both Haris refer to some aspects of the Hindu Hari, another name of Viṣṇu. Puṇṇa is probably the Yakṣa Pūrṇabhadra and Vasiṣṭha is the celebrated traditional sage. Pabhañjana is Prabhañjana the wind-god.

The third *śataka* of the *Viy* refer to the four *lokapālas*—Soma, Yama, Varuṇa and Vaiśravaṇa—the god Śūlpāni or Śiva, described as *vasaha-vāhana*, i.e. *vṛṣabhavāhana*, seated on an ox, Indra, Skanda, etc., playing the role of the attendant of the Jina. A few malignant spirits such as Indragraha, Skandagraha, Kumāragraha, Yakṣagraha and Bhūtagraha are mentioned. These *grahas* were supposed to inflict bodily harm both to children and adults. In the sixteenth *śataka* of the same text we find Indra paying homage to Lord Mahāvīra. The fifth *adhyayana* of the *Nāyā* refers to Surapriya *yakṣāyatana* in Dvārakā while the eighth *adhyayana* refers to a Nāga temple near Saketa. In the very begnining of the *Uyav* there is a beautiful description of the celebrated Purṇabhadra Yakṣa shrine of the city of Campā, which was a favourite resort of Mahāvīra. In the *Aṅgavijjā,* Vaiśravaṇa is pictured as the god of the merchants and Śiva as the lord of cows, buffaloes and sheep. Kārttikeya is associated with the cock and peacock and Viśākha with sheep, ram, bow and sword. They are all companion deities or angels. In the list of the female deities occur some foreign goddesses like Apalā, who is the Greek Pallas Athene, Anāditā who is same as the Iranian Anahitā, Airani who is equated with the Roman goddess Irene, and Sālimālinī who is none other than the Moon-Goddess Selene. In the fifth *śataka* of the *Viy* we come across Hariṇegamesī who was responsible, according to the *Kalpasūtra,* for transferring the embryo of Mahāvīra from the womb of Devanandā to that of Triśalā. An inscription from Mathura (*EI*, 2.200) refers to Bhagavat Nemesa who is sculpted as a goat-headed deity. He is none other than Hariṇegamesī of the Jain canonical texts. The transference of Mahāvīra's embryo is represented in four statuettes now in the Mathura museum. Two of these figures are goat-headed males and two are females, each holding an infant in a dish.

The earliest extant literary Śvetāmbara work appears to be the *Paumacariya* of Vimala, the Jain *Rāmāyaṇa* written according to the testimony of the poet himself, 530 years after the demise of Mahāvīra. Vimala had a thorough acquaintance with the Sanskrit *Rāmāyaṇa* of Vālmīki, but he thought that Vālmīki was a liar who had not given the correct version of the legend. The first canto of his poem contains the table of contents. In the second Vimala has raised certain important questions. How is it that insignificant monkeys could kill the powerful and aristocratic Rākṣasas who were versed in different sciences and had complete faith in the Jinas? How is that the demons with Rāvaṇa at their head, who were certainly of noble descent, are said to have eaten meat? Is it not ridiculous that Rāvaṇa's brother Kumbhakarṇa slept for half a year, and on awakening, devoured elephants and again slumbered for half a year ? Is it not funny that Rāvaṇa on vanquishing Indra in battle brought him in chains to the city of Laṅkā? Who can conquer Indra who is capable of uprooting the whole world and has Airāvata as his vehicle and the terrible *vajra* as his weapon ? This is why Vimala wanted to give the correct version of the Rāma story. In this Prakrit poem Padma (Pauma) is the name of Rāma, though the latter name occurs frequently. The narrative begins with the third canto and a description of the universe and the history of Ṛṣabha. The story of the race of monkeys is told in the sixth canto. According to the poet the monkeys are in reality a race of Vidyādharas, which is so called because their city has monkeys by way of a symbol on the arches of the gates, banners and the like. The seventh canto treats of Indra, of the guardians of the universe, of Soma, Varuṇa, Kubera and Yama, of the Asuras and Yakṣas and of the birth of Rāvaṇa, his sister Candramukhā, and his brothers Bhānukarṇa and Vibhīṣana. Rāvaṇa and his brothers acquired enormous magic powers by virtue of asceticism. The Rākṣasas are not man-eating demons but adherents of the race of the Vidyādharas. Rāvaṇa's mother hanged around his neck a wondrous string of pearls in which his face was reflected nine times, which is why his epithet was *daśamukha*, 'the man with ten faces' (7.95-6) . The succeeding cantos deal with the heroic activities of Rāvaṇa who was a great devotee of the Jinas, and restored ruined Jain shrines and established the Jain faith.

The Jain attitude towards the traditional demons is revealed in Vimala's treatment of the Rākṣasas. According to him the Rākṣasas of Laṅkā were not meat-eaters. He likes to call them Vidyādharas, though in many cases he forgets and calls them Rākṣasas. Rāvaṇa and his followers are described as staunch Jains. The *Paumacariya* purports to narrate the story of Padma or Rāma, but the actual hero is Rāvaṇa. He tells about Rāma's exile, Sītā's kidnapping by Rāvaṇa, death of Jaṭāyu, Rāma's meeting with Sugrīva, Hanumat's departure for Laṅkā, his meeting with Sītā, the battle of Laṅkā and the rescue and ultimate banishment of Sītā. But Rāvaṇa is Vimala's favourite. His killer Laksamaṇa is described as a lusty and sentimental hero. He has changed the legends of the Uttarakāṇḍa which describes Rāvaṇa's discomfiture. In an Uttarakāṇḍa legend Rāvaṇa is shown of having suffered a humiliating defeat at the hands of Vālin. But Vimala describes Vālin as a Jain ascetic who pressed the mount Kailāsa with the finger of his feet when Rāvaṇa had lifted the mount. The twelfth and thirteenth cantos tell of a fight between Rāvaṇa and Indra. The latter, being defeated, was brought to Laṅkā, but was released. The reason for his humiliation was that in a previous incarnation he had molested a Jain monk. Through Rāvaṇa's influence Hanuman was converted to Jainism and married thousand wives. Vimala's work probably served as a model for all the later adaptations of the Rāma legend among the Jains. In AD 678 Ravisena wrote the *Padmapurāṇa*. This work is a slightly extended recension of the *Paumacariya* in Sanskrit. Here, too, Padma is the name given to Rāma, the character of Rāvaṇa is glorified, and the monkeys are described as Vidyādharas. *Parvan* seven of Hemacandra's *Triṣaṣṭiśalākāpuruṣacaritra* is also known as the *Jaina-Rāmāyaṇa*, which starts with the stories of the Rākṣasas and monkeys and depicts Rāvaṇa as a great and mighty ascetic. Devavijayagaṇi's *Rāmacaritra*, a late-medieval Jain work in prose, has also the same approach. These Rāma legends clearly show that the Jain attitude towards the Rākṣasas was basically different. While in the Brahmanical tradition the Rākṣasas were treated as demons hostile to gods and humans beings, the Jains had an entirely different view.

Details about the Rākṣasas, Vidyādharas, Piśācas, Asuras, Yakṣas, and Nāgas are found in Jain Prakrit narrative literature. The *Vasudevahiṇḍi* written by Saṅghadāsagaṇi Vācaka is probably the eariest imitation of Guṇāḍhyas *Bṛhatkathā*. It says that the gods move a finger's breadth above the ground, the Rākṣasas have a huge body and the Piśācas are scared of watery land. The Rākṣasas, Yakṣas and Piśācas have no power during the day. They are dazed with the brightness of the sun, and therefore delight in the night. They never attack chaste men, heroes, or men awake (*VH* 135.20.21). In the *KVLM* (66.4; 67.15) it is said that the merchants on their journey to the island of Ratnadvīpa faced dreadful storms created by the Rākṣasas. The feet of the Rākṣasas leave deeper footprints (*VH* 135.10). Occasionally Rākṣasas are identified with tribal people like the Pulindas (*KVLM* 132.1-3) and described as experts in Śabarī-spells. The Rākṣasas along with the Bhūtas, Piśācas, Yakṣas, Kinnaras, Kimpuruṣas, Mahoragas, and Gandharvas are often described as *vyantara-devatās* (*Uttara* 3). These eight *vyantara* gods have been assigned to various trees, e.g. the Piśācas to the *kadamba* (a tree with orange-coloured fragrant blossoms), the Yakṣas to the *vaṭa* (*banyan* tree), the Bhūta to *tulasī* (holy basil), the Rākṣasas to the *kandaka* (reed), Kinnaras to the *aśoka* tree, Kiṃpuruṣa to the *campaka* (*michelia campaka*, with its yellow fragrant flower), Mahoragas to the *nāga* (the *nāgakeśara* tree with a folded kind of flower), and Gandharvas to *tinduka* (*Diospyros embryopteris*). These trees have been assigned to the *bhavanavāsi* gods among whom the Asuras and Nāgas are more prominent: *aśvattha*, *saptaparṇa*, *śālmalī*, *udumbara*, *śirīṣa*, *dadhiparṇa*, *vañjula*, *palāsa*, *vapra* and *karṇikāra* (*ibid.* 10.461). We have already had occasion to refer to the Jain conception of the Asuras. It is interesting to note that in the lists of goddesses, as found in the *Aṅgavijjā*, occur Asurakanyā and Asurāgramahiṣī. The cave of the Asuras is also mentioned in which connection the hand of an Asura maid is fervently sought (*KVLM* 192.26). The Nāgas were invoked along with the Yakṣas and Bhūtas when a ship in the sea was in danger (*Nāyā* 17.201), and for granting progeny and fulfilling other wordly desires (ibid. 2.49f). They are represented as guarding fields and dwelling in the ant-hills. Mathura has been mentioned in the Jain texts as a centre of Nāga worship and here a good number of Nāga sculptures have been recovered. Some more information on the Nāgas will be provided later.

In Jain demonology the Bhūtas have an interesting role. Exorcists are supposed to be possessed by them (*Jambu* 120). They are invoked to avert terrible cyclones (*Nāyā* 17.201) and are regarded as one class of *vyantara* gods (*Uttara* 3). They have the power of granting offspring to deserving candidates if properly propitiated (*Nāyā* 2.49-50). In most cases they are mentioned along with theYakṣas, Rākṣasas, and Piśācas. The festivals of the Bhūtas were celebrated on the full-moon day of the month of Caitra. It is interesting that the Bhūtas were considered marketable commodities: during the reign of king Pradyota there were shops (*kuttiyāvana*) in Ujjayinī and Rājagrha where Bhūtas were sold (*Bṛhatkalpabhāṣya*, com. 3). *Kuttiyāvana* or *kautukīkaśāla* conveys the meaning of a shop where curious articles are available. A merchant from Bhṛgukaccha is said to have purchased a Bhūta from Ujjayinī and made him excavate a pond known as the Isitaḍāga. The name Isitaḍāga is referred to in the Hathigumpha inscription of Khāravela. Hiuen Tsang while visiting Magadha in the early part of the seventh century AD had heard the legend that the emperor Aśoka commanded genii and spiritis to raise Stūpas throughout the country. The *Mañjuśrī mūlakalpa* describes how the Yakṣas in Aśoka's service erected thousands of monoliths and Stūpas within half a night. The Bhūtas are described as dancing with spear, javelin, club and axe. They wear the skin of deer. Their yellow hair is dishevelled. They are covered with a mantle of black serpents. Around their neck coils the boa-constrictor. They have protuberant bellies and large faces, and ear-rings of iguana, mouse, mongoose, and lizard (*VH* 386.4-7). Ghost-houses (*bhūtagṛha*) were situated on the corner of a road (ibid. 144.8). A forest known as the *bhūtaramaṇa* has been referred to as a place of sports for the Bhūtas (ibid. 84.15). *Bhūtabali* or offerings made to the Bhūtas was a common practice. The *Nāyā* (1.23) refers to Bhūtayātrā, a special festival dedicated to the Bhūtas which the *Rāyapaseniya* describes as Bhūyamaha. References to temples dedicated to the Bhūtas are found. In one story we find that Dhamila used to meet his lover Vimalasena at a Bhūta temple (*VH* 54.15). The Jain term for demonology is Bhūtatantra.

The Pretas in Jain tradition are disembodied spirits. But they are also conceived as deities. The *Aṅgavijjā* refers to extensive Preta worship prevalent among the common people. In the Hindu tradition some of the Pretas in course of time become Pitṛs. The latter term is Pitara among the Jains. The Piśācas are classed with the Rākṣasas and Yakṣas in the *VH* (135.20-1) and *KVLM* (132.14-15). They are also included in the list of *vyantara-devatās* (*Uttara* 3). The *kadamba* trees are their favourite haunts. The Vānaras or monkeys are generally good fellows, but spells were often executed by assuming the form of a Vānara (*KVIM* 131.32ff.). Magic spells were known as *vidyās* and were sometimes connected with monkeys. In Jain demonology the Vidyādharas have a special place. We have seen above that in Vimala's *Paumacariya* Hanumān belongs to the race of Vidyādharas (lit. masters of magic art). In some texts we find Vidyādharas making the narration pleasant like a fairy tale. Kidnapping of another man's wife or a maiden was common among the Vidyādharas. According to the Jain tradition during the time of the dissolution of the world the Vidyādharas and heavenly gods will descend to the earth and pick the pairs of human beings and carry them to some caves where they could live on fish, tortoise and dead bodies (*Jambu* 2.18.40). It is said that Somadatta's snake-bite was cured by the touch of a Vidyādhara (*VH* 47.5-6). The hair and the clothes of a long-lived Vidyādhara had permanent fragrance. His hair was glossy with its roots unbroken (*VH* 138.10-11). They were also associated with low-class people. In order to attain magical power, two Vidyādharas are said to have resolved to marry a girl of low extraction. Each of them found a deformed girl (*Pari* 2.645-55). In order to gain efficiency in a spell a Vidyādhara went to a bamboo-grove, where, having fastened up the bamboo tree and hung himself upside down, he started inhaling smoke (*Uttara* com. 15.189). Vidyādhara Aṅgāraka having lost his magic spell is seen inhaling smoke of *Mersal farrea* (*VH* 179.16-18). It is said that Śabaraśila, the lord of the Vidyādharas, was exceedingly powerful and a treasurehouse of the Śabara spells. Later he renounced the world. His son installed Ṛṣabha's image in a cave which became the place of attainment (*siddha-kṣetra*) of the Vidyādharas (*KVLM* 133.8-18). We have the story of Mānasavega, the Vidyādhara lord who, enamoured of the beauty of Madanamañjukā, wife of Naravāhanadatta, kidnapped and detained her, though he did not molest her. It is due to the fact that any Vidyādhara who offends Jain monks or is guilty of violating a Jain temple or a couple, or one who seizes another man's wife against her wishes, shall be deprived of his magical spell (*VH* 227.14-15). Even Rāvaṇa, who was a powerful Vidyādhara monarch, did not violate the virtue of Sītā for fear of the consequences. We also read about the fight between two Vidyādharas when the stronger one destroyed the spell of the weaker (*VH* 250. 8-9).

Before dealing with the Nāgas and the Yakṣas we present here the Jain version of the legend of the demon Bali. The nucleus of the story is found in the *RV,* in connection with the description of Viṣṇu. The most prominent anthropomorphic trait, the main characteristic of the nature of Viṣṇu in the *RV* is his three steps which give him the exclusive epithets *uru-gāya* (wide-going) and *uru-krama* (wide-stepping). Two of his steps are visible, but the third or highest is invisible, far beyond the flight of the birds, and is like an eye fixed in heaven, shining brightly down. Since he is described as setting in motion his ninety seeds (*days*) with their four names (seasons), Viṣṇu is a personification of the activity of the sun, whose passage through the earth, air and heaven is referred to as his three steps. This conception of the three steps of Viṣṇu later gave rise to the Puranic conception of his *vāmana* incarnation in which he subjugated the demon Bali. According to the Puranic legend, (also found in the epics) Bali was a powerful demon. Since he was also an embodiment of virtue, his mental faculties together with his physical prowess and commanding nature frightened the gods. They approached Viṣṇu and requested him to destory Bali so that they might not be dislodged from the heaven. While Bali was performing a grand sacrifice, Viṣṇu descended on the earth assuming the form of a dwarf (*vāmana*) and disguised as a mendicant he went to the place of Bali's sacrifice and begged of him as much earth as he could cover in his three steps. Śukrācārya, the preceptor of the Asuras, understood the intention of the dwarf Viṣṇu and he asked Bali not to grant the prayer of the dwarf because the time for making gifts was already over. But Bali was too proud to refuse those who begged anything of him. And so without paying any heed to Śukra's word he maintained his commitment. When his request was granted, Viṣṇu assumed a mighty form and covered the entire earth with his first step, all the heavens with his second one, and sought a place to set his third step. Then the valiant Bali himself came forward and said: 'Please place your third step on my head.' Thereupon Viṣṇu placed his foot directly on Bali's head and pushed him down to the underworld.

Modified versions of this legend occur in Jain works. Budhasvāmin, while describing the marriage of Gandharvadatta (*Bṛhtkathā-ślokasaṅgraha* 17.112-14), has noted the Bali legend as follows: In ancient times Viṣṇu, the holder of the disc, took the form of a dwarf in order to humble Bali, and overpowered the heaven with three steps. The earliest form of the story is found in *VH* (128.18; 132.3) in which it is said that Namuci, the minister of king Mahāpadma of Hastināpura, was hostile to Jain monks and started giving them trouble. Thereupon the sage Viṣṇu was called to rescue the monks. He asked the minister to grant him space for three steps so that the Jain monks could live peacefully. The minister reluctantly agreed. Viṣṇu flared up his body. He placed his right foot on the peak of mount Mandara and the whole earth began to tremble. This is an adaptation of the Puranic Bali legend. Jinasena in his *Harivaṃśapurāṇa* (20.1-65) mentions Bali as one of the four ministers of the king. The sage Viṣṇukumāra asked Bali to permit him three steps on the earth. He took one step of the mount Meru, the other on mount Mānasottara, and as there was no space left for the third, he moved it around in the heaven. According to Guṇabhadra (*Uttarapurāṇa* 70.274-300), Viṣṇukumāra assumed the form of a dwarf Brāhmaṇa and asked Bali for three steps on the earth. Nemicandra (com. on *Uttarapurāṇa* 18.249) and Hemacandra (*Triṣaṣṭai* 6.8) went still further and addressed Viṣṇu by the name *trivirakama* in his dwarf incarnation.

The legends of king Sagara's sacrifice, destruction of his sixty-thousand sons, the bringing of the river Gaṅgā by Bhagīratha, etc., as narrated in the Hindu epics and Purāṇas are brought in relation to the Nāgas in the Jain tradition in which it is said that king Bhagīratha, the grandson of Bharata, was the founder the of the Nāgabali. When the dwellings of the Nāgas were disturbed, Jvalanaprabha, the king of the Nāgas, was annoyed and by his poisonous eyes burnt the sons of king Sagara to ashes. Then in order to pacify the king of the Nāgas, Bhagīratha visited the Aṣṭapada mountain and presented him a respectful offering consisting of garlands, perfumes and incense. From that time onwards people started offering *bali* to the Nāgas (*Uttara*, com. 18.234ff).

Dharaṇendra was another powerful king of the Nāgas. Pleased with the services of the Vidyādharas, rendered to lord Ṛṣabha, he bestowed upon them numerous magic arts. He is depicted as a moral authority on acts of omission and commission of the Vidyādharas. A miraculous image of Dharaṇendra was installed in the law-court of the Vidyādharas. His image was also installed in the cities of the Vidyādharas and the assembly halls. Allā, Akkā, Saterā, Sayāmaṇī, Inda and Ghanavijjuya are said to be the chief queens of Dharaṇendra who is highly respected among the Jains. It is said that he will be reborn as a future Tīrthaṃkara in the descending age (*VH* 303.6, 305, 26). In Merutuṅga's *Prabandhacintāmaṇi* (311). Dharaṇendra, the king of the Pātāla, cures Jain Ācārya Abhayasuri by licking his body with his tongue. Afterwards he shows the Ācārya the *stambhanaka,* the holy place of Pārśva. In the *Kathākośa* (184), Dharaṇendra rescued king Cetaka when he fell into a well holding an image of Jina. Dharaṇendra is also known as the Yakṣa of Pārśva. His image whether Śvetāmbara or Digambara, has the common features of snake-hoods, snake attributes and a tortoise as vehicle. The Śvetāmbara texts make him appear with four hands holding an ichneumon, snake, *citrus* and a snake again. The Digambara texts give to his hands the snake, noose, and *varada* pose. In connection with the origin of Dharaṇendra, there exists in Jain literature a mythological story as to how he was saved by Jina Pārśvanātha from being burnt in the sacred fire of a false ascetic Kaṭha (afterwards Meghamalin) and how, when attacked by Meghamalin, in his *kāyotsarga āsana,* Pārśvanātha was gratefully waited on by the same serpent, born next as Dharaṇendra or Nagendra Yakṣa of Pātāla. Apart from this mythology, the very name Dharaṇendra or Dharaṇidhara signifies his identity with Śeṣanāga, the king of the serpents. In iconographical representations we find his snake symbols and snake-hood. He holds also Vāsuki, the king of snakes, said to be a son of Kaśyapa. His vehicle the tortoise (*kaśyapa*) might suggest his superiority to that species who had been his and his master's enemy for ages.

Among the Yakṣa personalities mentioned in the Jain texts, the Ghaṇṭika Yakṣa was worshipped especially by Dombas. Consecrated tiny balls were rung around the ear of a Domba on which the Ghaṇṭika was expected to utter spells (*Nisi, Su* 13.26ff., *Bhā* 19). Likewise the Mātaṅgas (a tribe) had Āḍambara or Hirimikka or Hiridikka Yakṣa, whose shrine was constructed on the bones of the newly dead (*Āva Cu* 2.227-8). Bhandira was a popular Yakṣa of Mathura and a festival (*jāttā*) was celebrated in his honour (*Āva Cu* 281). His shrine at Mathura was presided over by Sudarśana Yakṣa (*Viy* 2.120). Bibhelaka Yakṣa used to attend on Mahāvīra during his ascetic life (*Āva Nir* 487). Among the more important Yakṣas mentioned in Jain texts we have Pūrṇabhadra, Maṇibhadra, Śvetabhadra, Haritabhadra, Sumanobhadra, Vyatipātikabhadra, Subhadra,

Sarvatobhadra, Manuṣyayakṣa, Vanādhipati, Vanāhāra Rupayakṣa, and Yaśottama. The *Uvay*(2) mentions a *caitya* shrine of Pūrṇabhadra Yakṣa where all kinds of actors, dancers, rope-walkers, wrestlers, boxers, jesters, story-tellers and lute players assembled and people offered *pūja* with flags, bells, peacock feathers, fly-whisks, sandalwood paste, flowers, sweets and lamps. The shrine was especially furnished with flowers, colours and fragrant substances. The aforesaid description pertains to the Pūrṇabhadra shrine at Campā. Pūrṇabhadra and his brother Maṇibhadra were very popular Yakṣas in those days. We are told that when the ascetic Mahāvīra arrived at Campā, he was attended to by Pūrṇabhadra and Maṇibhadra (*Āva Cu* 320, *Pannā* 2.192; *Pauma* 62.28-49). According to the Buddhist text *Mahāmāyurī*, Pūrṇabhadra and Maṇibhadra were brothers and presiding deities of Brahmavali. Maṇibhadra is said to be one of the foremost among the Yakṣas and his command was next to Kubera. He was considered as the presiding deity of an auspicious jewel, known as *bhadramaṇi*. Mithila is said to have had a shrine of Maṇibhadra Yakṣa. It is said that in the outer garden of the city of Samilla there was a shrine of Maṇibhadra. Once there was an outbreak of small-pox in the city and after it subsided through propitiation of the deity, the citizens were pleased to appoint a priest who regularly worshipped him and cleaned the assembly hall by smearing it with cow-dung (*Piṇḍa Nir* 245f).

Śvetabhadra was also considered a principal Yakṣa (*Viy* 5.32), but no details are known about his activities. The same holds good in the case of Haritabhadra, Sumanobhadra, Vyatipātikabhadra, Subhadra, Sarvatobhadra, Manuṣyayakṣa, Vanādhipati, Vanāhāra, Rūpayakṣa and Yaśottama. It appears that Purṇabhadra and Maṇibhadra were gods or demons of antiquity with large followings, who were accepted in Buddhism and Jainism and given new dimensions as devotees of the Buddhas and Jinas. The other names are mere fabrications, figments of imagination, which is why they have no place in subsequent literature. Among Yakṣas having a distinct personality, Geṇḍitinduga of Vārāṇasī, who was a devotee of sage Mātaṅga, punished the princess Bhadrā for showing disrespect to the sage (*Uttara* 12). Sailaka was a benevolent Yakṣa who rescued people from danger on assuming the form of a horse (*Nāyā* 9.127). The *Viy* (7.42ff) records that a lady named Gaṅgadattā with plenty of clothes, flowers, garlands and ornaments, and accompanied by relatives and friends visited the shrine of the Yakṣa Umbara in order to beget children. She cleaned the image with a peacok-feather brush, washed it with water, wiped it with a soft woollen cloth and clothed it nicely. Then she worshipped the Yakṣa, praying for a child. Umbara granted her prayer and the child she bore was given the name Umbaradatta. Subhadrā, another woman, promised the Yakṣa Surambara to offer him a sacrifice of one hundred buffaloes provided a son was born to her (*Āva Cu* 2.193). Mudgarapāṇi Yakṣa was a chastiser of evil and in order to save his devotee Arjunaka did not hesitate to kill his wife (*Anta* 6). A fight has been noted between Yakṣa Asitākṣa and king Sanatkumāra (*Uttara*, com. 18). An image of Yakṣa Vaiśramana is said to have been destroyed by Indra (ibid. 242). There were also malignant Yakṣas. Śūlapāṇi Yakṣa spread pestilence and killed any person who dared to dwell in his shrine. He forced people to leave their habitat and was not satisfied until people constructed his shrine on the bones of human beings (*Āva Cu* 272-4). Surapriya was another Yakṣa who spread epidemics. He was appeased only when he saw his likeness being painted. But as soon as the painting was over he killed the poor painter (ibid. 67-8). Sometimes, malevolent Yakṣas were appointed by influential persons to harm others. Thus Kaṃsa appointed the Black Yakṣas to kill Kṛṣṇa. They arrived at the cow-pen of Nanda and assuming the forms of donkeys, horses and bulls began to harass people (*VH* 369.30; 370.2). Jain texts refer to other Yakṣas such as Lepyaka, Niddhamana, Amoghadarśi, Śvetabaddha, Soriya, Dharaṇa, Liṅgalakṣa, Kāpardika and Sāṅkha.

In Jainism Yakṣas of the highest rank were the archangels of the Tīrthaṃkaras, and no Jain temple is considered safe without them. We come across Yakṣa statues with Jain images on their heads. We hear of Jinaśekhara Yakṣa, who projected a pearl-image of himself with the image of Ṛṣabha on his crest (*KVLM* 120.15-17). The image of Pārśvanātha is noticed on the head of goddess Padmāvatī. As a matter of fact, each Tīrthaṃkara has been assigned a Yakṣa on his right and a Yakṣiṇī on the left. Thus they also came to be called Śāsanadevatā or attendant spirits. As first in the order of the Yakṣas, Gomukha is attached to Ṛṣabhanātha. In Vasunandi's *Pratiṣṭhāsāroddhāra* he is described as four-armed, of golden colour, seated on an ox (*caturbhujaḥ suvarṇābho gomukhe vṛṣavāhanaḥ*), holding an axe (or noose) and a rosary (*hastena paraśum ghatte vījapūrākṣasūtrakaṃ*), showing *varada mudrā*, and wearing a *dharmacakra* on his crest (*varadānaparaḥ samyak dharmacakrañca mastake*). Mahāyakṣa is attached to Ajitanātha. Śvetambara and Digambara texts describe him as riding an elephant and having four faces and eight hands armed with weapons. Trimukha is Sambhavanātha's attendant. Texts of the Śvetambaras and Digambaras are concordant in describing this Yakṣa as possessed of three faces, six arms and riding a peacock (*trinetrastrimukaḥ syāmaḥ ṣaḍbāhurbarhi vāhanaḥ*). Yakṣeśvara is the attendant spirit of Abhinandana. He is characterized by the symbol of an elephant. According to the Śvetambara view, this Yakṣa holds in his right hand a citrus and a rosary and in his left hand a mongoose and a goad. According to the other view, he has a bow, a shield and a sword. He resembles the Buddhist Jambhala. Tumbara is attached to Sumatinātha as an attendant Yakṣa. His vehicle is Garuḍa and his colour is white (*śvetāṅgastārksyavāhanaḥ*). His attributes according to the Śvetambaras are *varada*, club and the noose (*varadaśa-ktidharau gadādharau pāśayuktau*), whereas the Digambara variants are two snakes, fruit and *varada*. Tumbara in Hindu mythology is said to be a divine musician and a Gandharva. Kusuma or Puṣpa Yakṣa is the attendant of Padmaprabha, his name having direct connection with that of his master. His symbol is the antelope. According to the Śvetāmbaras his four hands hold respectively a fruit, *abhayamudrā*, a rosary, and a mongoose (*kuraṅgavāhanaścaturbhujaḥ phalābhayayuktadak-ṣiṇapāṇidvayo nakulākṣasūtrayuktavāmapāṇiśca*). According to the Digambaras he has a lance, *varada-mudrā*, shield and *abhayamudrā* in his four hands.

Mātaṅga or Varanandi is the attendant Yakṣa of Supārśvanāthā. According to the Śvetāmbaras his vehicle is the elephant and attributes the *vilva* fruit, noose, mongoose and goad. The Digambaras hold that his vehicle is the lion and atributes the staff, spear, *svastika,* and flag. Vijaya or Śyāma Yakṣa belongs to Candraprabha. He has three eyes and holds in this hands a fruit, rosary, axe, and *varamudrā.* Ajita is the attendant Yakṣa of Suvidhinātha. His vehicle is the tortoise and he holds in his hands a *citrus*, rosary, mongoose, and spear. The Digambaras give him the attributes of a *śakti*, *varamudrā*, fruit, and rosary. Śītalanātha's Yakṣa is known as Brahmā who has four faces, three eyes, eight hands and a lotus seat. The Yakṣa of Śreyāṃsanātha is known as Īśvara who has a bull vehicle, three eyes, and four hands. The Digambaras place on his hands a trident, a staff, a rosary, and a fruit, while the Śvetāmbaras sustitute a mongoose for the trident. Vāsupūjya has as his Yakṣa, Kumāra whose vehicle is swan and complexion white. The Digambara view makes him three-headed and six-armed holding a bow, ichneumon, fruit, club, and *vara* respectively. According to the Śvetāmbaras he has four hands holding a *citrus*, arrow, mongoose, and bow. It is rather curious that this Yakṣa, who bears the analogous name to Kumāra or Kārttikeya, should have a peacock instead of a swan (*trimukhaḥ ṣaḍbhujaḥ śvetaḥ surūpo haṃsvāhanaḥ*) as his vehicle, while the next Yakṣa who is called Catrumukha, an epithet of Brahmā, has a peacock as his vehicle. The latter is the Yakṣa of Vimalanātha. The Śvetāmbaras, however, conceive him as Ṣaṇmukha or six-faced with twelve arms, each holding an object. The Yakṣa of Anantanātha is known as Pātāla who has three faces, six arms, and a dolphin as his vehicle. He bears a canopy of a three-hooded snake and one of his hands carries a plough. He is associated with Ananta, the serpent-king of the nether world. He seems to be the presiding spirit of the Nāga world and the plough suggests his connection with agriculture.

The attendant Yakṣa of Dharmanātha is Kinnara who is three-faced and six-armed. His vehicle is the tortoise though the Digambaras hold it to be a fish. The conception of this Yakṣa is borrowed from an older tradition. The Kinnaras are supposed to be human figures with horse-heads and Kubera is their leader. Under diverse conditions the Yakṣas were associated with the Nāgas, as is attested to by the case of the erstwhile Pātāla, Kinnaras, Garuḍas and Gandharvas. The names of the subsequent Yakṣa attendants of the Tīrthaṃkaras point to the same. Thus Garuḍa is the name of the Yakṣa of Śāntinātha. His vehicle is a boar, though Hemacandra (*Śāntināthacarita* 5.5) holds it to be an elephant. The objects borne by his four hands are the usual. His elephant association may be a distant allusion to the Puranic Garuḍa holding the warring elephant (*gaja*) and tortoise (*kacchapa*) in his claws. The Yakṣa of Kunthunātha is known as Gandharva, having four hands and a bird (swan according to the Śvetambaras) as his vehicle. The Gandharvas, as we have seen above, are a class of demi-gods regarded as the musicians of the gods, and are said to give good and agreeable voice to girls, though sometimes very wicked. Conceptually they are also related to the Yakṣas, both having many features in common. Yakṣendra or Khendra is the Yakṣa of Aranātha. He is described as having six mouths and twelve arms with the usual attributes. In description and name he seems to be the Jain counterpart of Kārttikeya. The vehicle of peacock is the same as Yakṣa Ṣaṇmukha referred to above. This Yakṣa also holds a thunderbolt. The Yakṣa of Mallinātha is Kubera, whose iconographic marks are his rainbow colours, elephant vehicle, eight hands, and four faces. He is the king of the Yakṣas as well and is related in one or other capacity to all the religious and mythological systems of India. Varuṇa is the Yakṣa of Munisuvrata. This is another instance of blending the conception of Varuṇa, the guardian deity of the ocean and the western quarter, with that of a Yakṣa. Eight-headed Varuṇa holds the citron club and mongoose—the symbols of Kubera and Jambhala of Buddhism. The

Yakṣa of Naminatha is known as Bṛukuti with four faces, eight hands and a bull as the vehicle. This Yakṣa, called Nandiga, has a mysterious connection with Nandi, the chief attendant of Śiva. Neminatha's Yakṣa is known as Gomedha or Gomeda who has three faces, six hands and a man as vehicle. He is probably a form of Kubera. His epithet, *naravāhana* (riding a man), is also an epithet of Kubera. He is also called *puṣpayāna* which is again indicative of his Kubera affinity inasmuch as Kubera's chariot is called Puṣpaka. The Yakṣa of Pārśvanātha is Dharaṇendra having snake-*hood* and snake attribute. We have already had occasion to deal with this character, who is the lord of the Nāgas. There exists a mythological story as to how he was saved by Pārśvanātha form being burnt in the sacred fire of the false ascetic Kaṭha and was born again as Dharaṇendra or Nagendra Yakṣa of Pātāla. The attendant Yakṣa of Mahāvīra is Mātaṅga who is described as two-handed and riding an elephant. His other symbols such as the ichneumon and citron are only too evident to bear some relationship with Kubera. The *dharmacakra* symbol on his head would indicate, as in the case of Gomukha, that this Yakṣa attached to Mahāvīra was the renovator of Jainism, the upholder of the 'wheel of law'.

Each of the Tīrthaṃkaras has also a Yakṣiṇī as his attendant. The Yakṣiṇī of Ṛṣabhanātha was known as Cakreśvarī, described as holding the symbol of the disc (*cakra*) and riding a Garuḍa. By all these, she pertains to the nature of Vaiṣṇavī, the wife of Viṣṇu, whose other name is Cakreśvara. The Yakṣiṇīs, associated with the Tīrthaṃkaras, as a rule, combine in them influences from the Brahmanic goddesses as well as the primitive Yakṣas. Ajitanātha's Yakṣiṇī is Ajitā, also known as Rohiṇī. The former name is a feminine form of her master and the latter denotes a star. The Digambara texts give her an iron seat (*lohāsana*) while the Śvetāmbara *Ācāradinakara* makes her vehicle a bull. In her hands she carries the usual Jain symbols. Duritāri is the Śvetambara and Prajñapti the Digambara name of the Yakṣiṇī of Sambhavanātha. The symbol of ram in the case of Duritāri implies her connection with the wife of Agni. The symbols of *vara* and rosary also support this supposition. The conception of Prajñapti seems clearly to be derived from that of Sarasvatī the goddess of learning. Her vehicle the bird appears to be a peacock, as her husband is represented as riding on the same bird (*barhivāhana*). The Yakṣiṇī of Abhinandana is known to the Digambaras as Vajraśṛṃkhalā and to the Śvetambaras as Kālī. Vajraśṛṃkhalā or Kālī is both a Yakṣiṇī and one of the Vidyādevīs. Her Yakṣiṇī character is symbolized by the presence of a *citrus* and a goad and her Vidyādevī character is symbolized by a swan and a rosary. The gradual influence of the Śākta goddess Kālī on Jainism is evident in the name of Mahākālī attributed to the Yakṣiṇī of Sumatinātha in the Śvetāmbara tradition. In the Digambara tradition she is known as Puruṣadattā. The Yakṣiṇī of Padmaprabha is known to the Śvetambaras as Acyutā or Śyāmā and to the Digambaras as Manovegā. The name Acyutā or Śyāmā might have originated from Acyuta, or Viṣṇu, or Śyāmā. Kāli symbolism again comes in the Digambara concept of Kālī as the Yakṣiṇī of Supārsvanātha, though the Śvetambaras call her Śāntā. Kālī's bull vehicle and trident, make her resemble the Hindu goddess on the one hand and the *citrus* makes her unmistakably a Yakṣiṇī on the other. Bhṛkuṭi or Jvālamālinī is the Yakṣiṇī of Candraprabha. The former, which is also the name of a Buddhist goddess, has a swan as her vehicle and her hands are adorrned with various weapons, Jvālamālinī has a buffalo as her vehicle which shows her symbolic connection with her husband Vijaya who, in Brahmanism is synonymous with Yama, whose vehicle is also buffalo.

Suvidhinātha's Yakṣiṇī is known as Sutārā or Mahākāli, the former being also the name of Buddhist Tārā who in the Hindu Tantras is equated with Kālī. The vehicle of the former is a bull and of the latter a tortoise. Apart from Kālī, other Hindu goddesses also formed part of the Jain Yakṣiṇī pantheon. Śītalanātha's Yakṣiṇī, Aśokā or Mānavī, also found in the pantheon of the Hindu goddesses, has both warlike and benign character. Śreyāṃśanātha's Yakṣiṇī is Gaurī according to the Digambara tradition and Mānavī or Śrivatsā according to the Śvetāmbara. The name Gaurī is evidently of Brahmanic origin. The name Mānavī presents an anomaly due to her identity with the Yakṣiṇī of Śītalanātha bearing the same name. As regards the attributes, some of them are warlike as worthy of a Yakṣiṇī and others are benign, symbolic of a Vidyādevī. The Yakṣiṇī of Vāsupūjya is known as a Caṇḍā and Pracaṇḍā, the names being evidently derived from those of the demonic goddesses of the *Devīmāhātymya*. She is also known as Gāndhāri. Other Yakṣiṇīs, such as Viditā, or Vijayā or Vairotī of Vimalanātha, Aṅkuśā or Anantamatī of Anantanāthā, Kandarpā or Pannagadevī or Mānasi of Dharmanātha, Nirvāṇī or Mahāmānasī of Śāntinātha, Balā or Acyutā or Vijayā of Kunthunātha, Vairotī or Aparājitā or Dharaṇapriyā of Mallinātha and Naradattā or Bahurūpiṇī of Munisuvrata, are abstractions, and though endowed with vehicles and attributes, have no solid foundation in Jain or non-Jain tradition, notwithstanding some of these names have Hindu parallels. To the same category belongs Siddhāyikā, the Yakṣiṇī of Mahāvīra, who represents the principle of attainment.

In the case of Dhāraṇī or Tārā, the Yakṣiṇī of Aranātha Buddhist influence is clearly discernible. Naminātha's Yakṣiṇī Gāndhārī or Cāmuṇḍā already occurs in connection with the Yakṣiṇī of Vāsupūjya, but in this case the vehicles and attributes have interchanged. Neminātha's Yakṣiṇī Ambikā (also known as Kuṣmāṇḍī or Āmrā) finds mention in the Vedic texts as the spouse of Śiva and is later known as the general name of the Devī. But the Yakṣiṇī Ambikā is a popular goddess of children, often represented with a bunch of mangoes and a child. Her Buddhist counterpart is Hārītī. Padmāvatī is the Yakṣiṇī of Pārśva. She is the snake goddess, her Hindu counterpart being Manasā. It is likely that the connection between the Jain Padmāvatī and the Hindu Manasā originated in Jain legends. Jaratkāru, an ascetic in Brahmanic tradition, stands for Kaṭha in the Jain legend who later became one with Śeṣa, the lord of the netherworld.

When and how the Yakṣas and their spouses, otherwise known as Śāsanadevatās, first appeared in the Jain pantheon is not precisely known to us. They do not represent purely Jain elements, and the form in which we find them reveals a mixture of ideas. Some of their names betray unmistakable identity with those found in Brahmanical literature. The same holds good in the case of their symbols. The Yakṣas are in Indian tradition regarded as spirits presiding over wealth and therefore it is easy to see why the Jains who represent a mercantile class especially favoured this cult and appropriated them especially among the class of their *dhundhi-devas* or highest divinities. The Yakṣiṇīs are also not purely fanciful creations. They were female attendants of the Tīrthaṃkaras, being the leaders of the women converts. As they appear in the Jain representations they are endowed with semi-divine attributes and symbolism of various kinds. Of the Yakṣiṇīs, a good number pass into an order of Jain female deities, the Vidyādevīs or goddesses of learning, who share in a great measure forms of the Brahmanical goddesses. Equally with Brahmanism the Jains made room for the Dikpālas to guard the quarters. They are all Vedic deities who were made subordinate to the Jinas.

NOTES AND REFERENCES

As has been in the case of the preceding chapters, names of the original Jain texts are given here in abbreviations. For their complete names, edition, translation date and place of publication see Abbreviations. Among the secondary sources the following works deserve mention, J. Fergusson, *Tree and Serpent Worship*, London,

1873; Maurice Bloomfield, *Pārśvanathacaritam: the Life and Stories of the Jain Saviour Parsvanatha*, Baltimore, 1919; J. Hartel, *On the Literature of Śvetāmbaras of Gujarat*, Leipzig, 1922; M. Winternitz, *History of Indian Literature*, vol. II, Calcutta, 1933, rpt. New Delhi, 1977; U.N. Barodia, *History and Literature of Jainism*, Bombay, 1909; H.R. Kapadia, *History of the Canonical Literature of the Jains*, Bombay, 1947; V.A. Smith, *Jaina Stūpa and other Antiquities of Mathura*, ASI, New Imperial Series, Allahabad, 1901, rpt. Delhi, 1969; C.J. Shah, *Jainism in Northern India*, Bombay, 1932; R. Ayyangar and B. Seshagiri, *Studies in South Indian Jainsim*, Madras, 1922; A.K. Coomaraswamy, *Yakṣas*, 2 vols., Washington, 1928, 1931, rpt. New Delhi, 1971; B.C. Bhattacharya, *Jain Iconography*, Lahore, 1939 (Sanskrit quotations used in this chapter are taken from this volume). W. Schübring, *The Doctrine of the Jains*, Delhi, 1962; J.C. Jain, *Life in Ancient India as Depicted in the Jain Canons*, Bombay, 1947; *Prākrit Sāhitya Kā Itihās*, Varanasi, 1961; *The Vasudevahiṇḍi—An Authentic Jain Version of the Bṛhatkathā*, Ahmedabad, 1977 (References from *VH* in this chapter have been adopted from this book); *Prakrit Jain Narrative Literature*, New Delhi, 1981; V.A. Sangave, *Jaina Community: A Social Survey*, Bombay, 1959; V.S Agrawala, *Ancient Indian Folk Cults*, Varanasi, 1970; N.N. Bhattacharyya, *Jain Philosophy: Historical Outline*, New Delhi, 1976, rpt. 1999; *Indian Religious Historiography*, vol. I (which contains the entire list of Jain Studies), New Delhi, 1996; A.K. Chatterjee, *A Comprehensive History of Jainism*, 2 vols., Calcutta, 1978, 1984. A few other works connected with the contents of this chapter may also be cited here. *Prabandha cintāmaṇī*, ed. Jinavijaya, Santiniketan, 1933; Eng. trans. C.H. Tawny, Calcutta, 1899, 1901; *Prabandhakośa*, ed. Jinavijaya, Santiniketan, 1935; *Jinaratnakośa*, vol. I, ed. H.D. Velankar, Pune, 1944; Buddhasvāmin, *Bṛhatkathāślokasaṃgraha*, ed. and French trans. Felex Lacote and Louis Renou, Paris, 1908-28; also ed. V.S. Agrawala, Varanasi, 1974; Kṣemendra, *Bṛhatkathāmañjarī*, Bombay, 1901; Somadeva, *Kathāsaritsāgara*, Bombay, 1889; trans. C.H. Tawny, *Ocean of Story* in 10 vols. ed. N.M. Penzer, rpt. Delhi, 1968; *Śukasaptati*, Varanasi, 1966; *Velālapañcaviṃśati*, Varanasi, 1968; *Aṅgavijjā*, ed. Muni Punyavijaya, Varanasi, 1957; Haribhadrasuri, *Samāraicchakathā*, ed. Bhagavan Das, Ahmedabad, 1938-42; Hariṣena, *Bṛhatkathākośa*, ed. A.N. Upadhye, Bombay, 1943; Hemacandra *Pariśiṣṭaparvan*, ed. H. Jacobi, Calcutta, 1932; *Triṣaṣṭiśalākāpuruṣacarita*, trans. by H.M. Johnson, vols. I-VI, Baroda, 1931-62; Guṇabhadra, *Uttarapurāṇa*, Kasi, 1968; Jinasena, *Harivaṃśapurāṇa*, Kasi, 1962; Nemicandragaṇi, *Taraṅgalolā*, ed. H.C. Bhayani, Ahmedabad, 1979; Saṅghadāsagaṇivācaka, *Vasudevahiṇḍi*, eds. Muni Caturvijaya and Muni Punyavijaya, Bhavnagar, 1930-1; C.H. Tawny, *Kathākośa*, Eng. trans., New Delhi, 1975; Udyotanasuri, *Kuvalayamālā*, ed. A.N. Upadhye, Bombay, 1959, 1970; Vimalasuri, *Paumacriya*, ed. Muni Punyavijaya, Varanasi, 1962, 1968.

CHAPTER V

Epic Demonology

In the two great epics, the *Mahābhārata* and the *Rāmāyaṇa,* we come across an elaborate demon lore in which the nebulous conceptions relating to the demons and spirits as found in the Vedic literature, or their idealized version tailored to suit the religious compulsions of the Buddhists and Jains, have been greatly modified. Epic demonology concerns various subdivisions of the Asuras, Dānavas, Daityas, Rākṣasas, Yātudhānas, Piśācas, Gandharvas, Yakṣas, Apsarases, Nāgas, Bhūtas, Pretas, demoniac animals, birds and a host of other spiritual entities in which certain characters stand out more as individuals than as members of a category. The higher demons are not exactly evil forces, yet not divine enough to be regarded as gods. Many individual Asuras maintain a very high standard of character and ability, but to the epic poets the Asuras as a class denote the average ungodly demons. They are the sons of either Diti (called Ditija, Daitya or Daiteya) or Danu (called Dānava or Dānaveya) and to them are also attached groups such as the Kāleyas (Kālakeyas, Kālakañjas) and other 'children of darkness' who uphold the great serpent demon Vṛtra in his battles with the 'children of light', and are regarded as the tribes (*gaṇas*) of the Dānavas and Daityas. Among the Asuras are often giant Rākṣasas, who in turn are sometimes confused with Piśācas or Yātudhānas. When it is found that the Asuras are equated with the Rākṣasas, and the latter with the Piśācas, no clear line of demarcation can be drawn among them, though the Piśācas are too mean and low to be confused generally with the demons of the higher types. Though specifically different, the Asuras, Dānavas, Daityas and Rākṣasas are generically alike. The interrelation of the groups is so close that marriage connections continually occur among the males and the females of these groups. They also have matrimonial relations with human beings and heavenly beings. The attitude of the epic poets to these demonic beings is rather ambivalent. Some demons are considered to be 'fallen angels' in the sense that they were originally gods or human beings or celestial entities who were cursed for their misdeeds. The ambivalence in their conceptualization is revealed by the facts that they are sometimes very friendly to the gods, but at other times hostile. Sometimes they appear to be weaker than the gods, though it is often found that they overcome the gods at ease. At times they are beautiful, at times they are hedious. They are protectors but also destructive. They are not irreligious but they are against the Vedic sacrificial cult. Like sages or spiritually advanced people, they believe in meditation, penance and austerities (*tapas*). They are favoured by Brahmā who increases their strength by granting them boons. In many cases they are protected by Śiva and Devī. They are simple-minded, rather naive and believe in the promises and assurances of the gods only to be cheated time and again.

The traditional struggle between the gods and the Asuras is found in the narrative of churning of the ocean. According to the version as given in *Rām* (1.45), the gods and the Asuras once thought about how they could be immortal and free from disease and old age. They began to churn the ocean with the Mandara hill as the churning rod and the serpent-king Vāsuki as the cord, to obtain *amṛta* or the nectar of immortality. After churning for a thousand years, the serpent Vāsuki began to vomit virulent poison which, like fire, began to scorch the world. Finding the gods and the Asuras in distress, Śiva drank the dreadful poison and saved the world. The churning was resumed and from it arose Dhanvantari, the father of medicines. Then arose the beautiful Apsarases—so called because they emerged from water—then Vāruṇī, the goddess of wine, who looked for takers. The Asuras did not take her (which accounts for their name) because they were not fond of wine and the gods accepted her. Then arose Uccaisravas, the best of the horses and *kaustabha*, the best of gems. At last *amṛta* appeared from the sea bed. This caused a great fight between the gods and the Asuras and in the havoc that ensued Viṣṇu appeared in the form of an exceedingly beautiful woman, stole the nectar for the gods, and destroyed the Asuras.

The *Mbh* (1.16-17) version is more elaborate. After the prolonged churning, the mild moon of a thousand rays emerged from the ocean. Thereafter sprung Lakṣmī dressed in white, then Soma, then the white steed, and then the celestial gem *kaustabha* which graced the breast of Viṣṇu. Then arose the divine Dhanvantari with the white vessel of nectar in his hand. The great elephant Airāvata who arose next was taken by Indra. With the churning still going on, the poison *kālakuṭa* appeared and blazed up like a fire to destroy the three worlds. And then, being solicited by Brahmā, Śiva swallowed the poison. Seeing all these wondrous things, the Asuras were filled with despair and prepared for war for the possession of Lakṣmī and *amṛta*. Thereupon Nārāyaṇa assumed the form of an enticing female and took away the *amṛta* from the hand of the Dānavas (Asuras) and gave it to the gods. A Dānava named Rāhu came to know of the trick and in the disguise of a god drank the nectar. When the *amṛta* reached Rāhu's throat, however, Nārāyaṇa instantly cut off his head. Then commenced a dreadful battle between the gods and the Asuras. Nārāyaṇa of fierce energy, accompained by Nara, began to destroy the Asuras, Dānavas and Daityas, who in their turn ascended the sky and by hurling down thousands of mountains continually harassed the gods. Eventually the great battle went in favour of the gods. The disappointed demons, in order to save themselves entered the interior of the earth or plunged into the sea.

The genealogy of the demons (Asura, Daitya, and Dānava) is given in *Mbh* (1.59. 17-36). Of the six spiritual sons of Brahmā, Marīcī was the father of Kaśyapa who married the thirteen daughters of Dakṣa (Aditi, Diti, Danu, Kālā, Danāyu, Siṃhikā, Krodhā, Pradhā, Viśvā, Vinatā, Kapilā, Muni and Kadru). From Aditi sprung the twelve Ādityas. Diti had a son called Hiraṇyakaśipu and he in turn had five sons, all famous throughout the world. The eldest of them was Prahlāda, the next was Sahrāda, the third was Anuhrāda, and after him were Śibī and Vāskala. Prahalāda had three sons. They were Vairocana, Kumbha and Nikhumbha. And unto Vairocana was born a son, Bali of great prowess. The son of Bali is known to be the great Asura Bāṇa. Blessed with good fortune, Bāṇa was a follower of Rudra. Danu had forty sons. They are Prathama, Rājā, Vipracitti, Mahāyaśāḥ, Śambara, Namuci, Pauloman, Viśruta, Asiroman, Keṣī, Durjaya, Dānavan, Ayaḥśiras, Aśvaśiras, Asvaśaṅku, Viryavan, Gaganamurdhan, Vegavat, Ketumat, Svarbhānu, Aśva, Aśvapati, Vṛṣaparvan, Ajaka, Aśvagrīva, Sukṣama, Tuhuṇḍa, Mahāvala, Ekapāda, Ekacakra, Virupākṣa, Mahodara, Nicandra, Nikumbha, Kupaṭa, Kapaṭa, Śarabha, Śalabha, Sūrya, and Candramas. Ekākṣa, Amṛtapa, Pralambha, Naraka, Vatrapi, Śatrutāpana, Śaṭha, Gaviṣṭha, Vanāyu and Dīrghajīva are ten great Asuras and their sons and grandsons are numerous. Siṃhikā gave birth to Rāhu, the persecutor of the Sun and the Moon, and to three others, Sucandra, Candrahantrī and Candrapramardana. Countless are the progeny of Krurā who were a wrathful tribe and crooked beings. Danāyu also had four Asura sons who were Vikṣara, Vala, Vīra and Vṛtra. And the sons of Kālā were Vināśana, Krodha, Krodhahantri, and Krodhaśatru. There were many others among the sons of Kālā. Śukra, the son of a *ṛṣi*, was the chief priest of the Asuras; he had four sons, Taṣṭadhara and Atri, and two others of fierce deeds. They were like the Sun himself in energy and set their hearts on acquiring the regions of Brahmā.

Quite a good number of the aforesaid demons have a Vedic background. Most important among them is Vṛtra who is described (*Mbh* 3.98-100) as the leader of a tribe (*gaṇa*) of Dānavas known as Kāleyas or Kālakeyas, who were of immeasurable energy. Invaded by them, the celestials led by Indra went to Brahmā, who advised them to request the sage Dadhīca to renounce his body so that from his bones a deadly weapon capable of killing Vṛtra could be made. At the request of the gods led by Nārāyaṇa, Dadhīca sacrificed his body, and from his bones Tvaṣṭṛ forged the fierce weapon called *vajra* and handed it over to Indra. Armed with this weapon, Indra attacked Vṛtra who was then occupying the entire earth and the heaven. In the terrible battle that ensued the gods were defeated. Viṣṇu, finding Indra depressed in the battle, then enhanced his might by giving him his own strength. Thus favoured by Viṣṇu, Indra hurled his *vajra* upon the Asura chief and killed him so that the other demons fled to the depth of the sea. In another version of the myth (*Mbh* 5.9-10) it is said that Triśirā, the son of Prajāpati Tvaṣṭṛ, who was endowed with all virtues and free from all sins, was practising severe austerities for gaining the post of Indra. Indra, being afraid of Triśirā's spiritual progress, tried to dissuade him by applying methods and temptations of all sorts. But Triśirā remained unmoved. When Indra failed to break his morale, he pierced him with the *vajra*. Triśirā was dead but lay covered by his energies, this frightened Indra to the extreme. Then with the help of a carpenter he had the three heads of Triśirā divided into parts. At this Tvaṣṭṛ, the father of Triśirā, became angry with Indra and created Vṛtra to destroy him. Vṛtra, at the command of Tvaṣṭṛ occupied heaven. In the battle that ensued Indra was defeated and left the celestial region in fear. Thereupon the gods went to Viṣṇu and requested him to find a way to kill Vṛtra. Viṣṇu said that Vṛtra could not be killed in a straight war. He would himself enter the *vajra* of Indra which was to be hurled at Vṛtra at the right moment. He also advised the gods to make a temporary settlement of peace with Vṛtra. When the gods approached Vṛtra with the peace proposal, he made them promise they would not hurt him during day or night and not use any type of weapon for the purpose of killing him. One evening Indra found Vṛtra walking on the sea-shore. He also saw in the sea a mass of froth. He thought: 'It is neither day nor night, and the froth is neither dry nor wet, nor is it a weapon. Let me hurl it at Vṛtra.' Instantly he threw at Vṛtra that mass of froth, blended with the thunderbolt. And Viṣṇu, having entered within the froth, put an end to the life of Vṛtra. The story resembles that of killing Balder with the help of mistletoe, as is found in Scandinevian mythology. In the *Rām* (1.25) Kausalyā blessed Rāma saying that he would achieve the same merit as was achieved by Indra after killing Vṛtra. But Indra achieved no merit since he had killed Vṛtra in an unethical way. Moreover, he was overpowered by the sin of *brahma hatyā* or murdering a Brāhmaṇa.

The third version (*Mbh* 12.270-3) describes Vṛtra as a devotee of Viṣṇu. Asked by Uśanaḥ or Śukra about his discomfiture in bắttle against the gods, Vṛtra said that by the grace of Lord Viṣṇu he was quite conversant with the mysteries of life and the universe and felt no special joy in success or sorrow in failure. According to him, the world is an illusion and the eternal wheel of time run by Viṣṇu creates and destroys everything. That is why one should fix one's mind to the ultimate reality, the supreme *brahman*, who is none other than Viṣṇu. Just as the Buddhists and Jains had admitted the demons of the earlier tradition into their creed and made them staunch devotees of the Buddha and Lord Mahāvīra, so also the followers of Vaiṣṇavism, in the Vaiṣṇavite didactic portions of the great epic depicted some of the celebrated demons of the past like Vṛtra as great devotees of Viṣṇu. Having learnt of Vṛtra's virtues and his firm devotion to Viṣṇu, Yuddhiṣṭhira wanted to know from Bhīṣma details of Vṛtra legends. Thereupon Bhīsma told that having seen the vast army of Vṛtra, Indra developed an abscess in his thigh in fear. The gods were terrorized having seen the might of Vṛtra. In order to save the frustrated gods, Bṛhaspati and other divine sages repaired to Śiva and urged him to destory Vṛtra and other Asuras. Vṛtra was overtaken by a violent fever produced from Śiva's energy and thus suddenly attacked by this form of illness he became pale and began to yawn. Indra took advantage of the situation and killed Vṛtra with his thunderbolt. Having slain Vṛtra, Indra incurred the sin of *brahmahatyā* which was, however, expiated by the combined efforts of the gods.

The rivalry between the gods and the Asuras had influenced the preceptors of both the clans. Those demons who were slain in the battle against the gods were all revived by their preceptor Śukra by the power of his secret knowledge (*sañjīvanī*). Bṛhaspati, the preceptor of the gods, had no such knowledge of restoring the dead to life. So the gods, consulting among themselves, sent Kaca the son of Bṛhaspati to Śukra to learn the secret knowledge by any means. Kaca was able to become a favourite student of Śukra whose daughter Devayānī fell in love with him. It was due to Devayānī's pressure that Śukra eventually imparted the secret knowledge of *sañjivanī* to Kaca, but the latter, having accomplished his mission, did not hesitate to ditch her (*Mbh* 1.71-2). Like the love story of Kaca and Devayānī, the story of the Asura brothers Sunda and Upasunda is well known. In the lineage of the Daitya Hiraṇyakaśipu was born Nikumbha, whose sons were Sunda and Upasunda. The two brothers were close to each other, as one soul in two bodies. They received from Brahmā the boon of invincibility. Thereupon the two set out to conquer the three worlds. The earth was easily conquered. Thousands of kings and Brāhmaṇas were killed. Then they invaded the heaven with a huge army. In order to get rid of their torture the celestials met Brahmā who asked Viśvakarman to create a woman of unparalleled beauty. Viśvakarman did so by collecting atoms from beautiful objects over the world hence the paragon of beauty came to be known as Tilottamā. Brahmā then sent her to the place where Sunda and Upasunda were staying. Both of them lusted for her, fought over her and were killed (*Mbh* 1.201-3). Among the Asuras, a great builder was Maya Dānava,who was previously saved by Arjuna during the burning of the Khāṇḍava forest (*Mbh* 1.219, 35-40). It was he who constructed for the Pāṇḍavas a palatial assembly hall that was wide, delightful, refreshing, made of excellent materials, furnished with golden walls and archways, adorned with gems and encircled by a peerless tank containing a flight of crystal stairs (*Mbh* 2.1; 2.3).

Among the Asuras mentioned in the genealogy of the demons in the *Mbh* (1.59.17-36), Śambara of the Vedic and Buddhist tradition occurs in the *Rām* (2.9) as the king of a city called Vaijayanta in the Daṇḍakāraṇya region. He was also known as Timidhvaja. It is said that when Śambara was fighting the gods, king Daśaratha of Ayodhyā came to fight with his troops in favour of the latter and was severely wounded. He was healed by the care of his wife Kaikeyī and promised to grant her two boons which she begged of him at the right time, the first being the banishment of Rāma and the second installation of Bharata on the throne of Ayodhyā. The *Rām* itself is demon lore, the characters being Rākṣasas and not the Asuras. Only the Uttarakāṇḍa refers to a few Asura legends which we shall discuss in the next chapter. But there is reference to Maya the brother of Namuci, who was admonished by Indra (*Rām* 4.51.14) because he violated the Apsaras Hemā. Vālmīki knows him as the great magician architect who made a magic cave, a Dānava palace, and also various weapons for the demons (*Rām* 4.43.31; 4.51.14-15; 5.7.24; 6.101.2). Hemā was his wife, and his daughter was Mandodarī who was married to Rāvaṇa. Māyavin and Dundubhi were his sons (*Rām* 4.9.4; 4.10.22; 7.12.6;

7.12.13-14). They were very distinguished Asuras. Dundubhi was bull-shaped, said to be like a cloud roaring like a drum, who had challenged the ocean, the Himālaya and Vālī.

Among the Asura legends as found in the *Mbh*, that of Ilvala and Vātāpi is important. They are described as sons of Diti, Daityas. The Asura Ilavala was a destroyer of Brāhmaṇas. With the power of illusion he would transform his brother Vātāpi into a ram. After cooking the flesh of that ram Ilvala offered it to the Brāhmaṇas as food. And after they had eaten the flesh, Ilvala would call Vātāpi to come out, and hearing that call Vātāpi used to come out tearing the entrails of the Brāhmaṇas, thus killing them. Since Ilvala was a wealthy Asura, the sage Agastya, for the purpose of maintaining his wife Lopāmudrā, went to him being desirous of wealth. The wicked Asura at once agreed to fulfil his desire, and with his usual evil intention offered his hospitality. Then he transformed his brother Vātāpi into a ram, cooked his flesh and offered it to Agastya. Agastya ate all the meat and made a loud-sounding wind-break. The dinner over, Ilvala began to summon his brother, 'Come Out, O Vātāpi'. Thereupon Agastya, bursting out into laughter, said: 'How can he come out? I have already digested that great Asura'. Ilvala was sad and got rid of Agastya after offering him the wealth he desired (*Mbh* 3.94-7). The concept of abstract Asuras created by the energy of austerity is also found in the epic. The old sage Cyavana was restored to youthfulness by the divine physicians Aśvins who held an inferior rank among the gods and were not entitled to the drinking of *soma*. The grateful Cyavana wanted to raise their status, but when Indra, the king of gods, paid no heed to his request, the sage himself consumed *soma* on their behalf. Indra in anger wanted to vanquish Cyavana with his *vajra* when the sage by his special power created the Asura Mada who with his appearance created havoc among the gods. When Indra saw Madāsura coming towards him looking like the god of death himself, he began to tremble in fear and offered an unconditionally apology to Cyavana. The Aśvins were now entitled to *soma* and Cyavana was appeased. Thereupon Cyavana distributed the Asura Mada in wine, women, gambling, and hunting (*Mbh* 3.224).

The story of Jaṭāsura is rather dull. This Asura in the guise of a Brāhmaṇa had constantly remained in the company of the Pāṇḍavas. His object was to possess himself of the bows, quivers and other implement belonging to the Pāṇḍavas. And he had been watching for an opportunity of ravishing Draupadī. One day when Bhīmasena was out hunting Jaṭāsura assuming a gigantic, monstrous and frightful form, captured the Pāṇḍavas including Draupadī, collected all their weapons, and hastened to his own resort. Meanwhile Bhīmasena made his appearance with a mace in his hand challenged the demon, and clenching his fist like a five-headed snake dealt a severe blow on his neck. Then he lifted Jaṭāsura, dashed him on the ground and broke his head (*Mbh* 3.154). The story of Arjuna's destruction of Dānavas called Nivātakavacas who dwelt in the womb of the ocean seems to be a little more interesting. Indra's car, used to subdue Śambara, Namuci, Vala, Vṛtra, Prahlāda, and Naraka, was given to Arjuna, and Mātali, the charioteer, took him to the bottom of the great ocean where he found the abode of the Dānavas. He blew his conch *devadatta* hearing which the offspring of Diti, the Nivātakavacas, made their appearance in the thousands with various weapons. Many Asuras were shattered by the chariot-wheels owing to the expert driving of Mātali, and many of them were shot by Arjuna with his arrows. The Asuras then resorted to their *māyā*, threw missiles in torrents, emblazed and finally made walls of water within which they vanished. The Asuras began to hurl weapons without showing their presence. Arjuna thereafter fired a special weapon named *viśoṣana* that he had received from Indra. By this weapon the illusion created by the Asuras was removed. Thereupon the Asuras created darkness and began to shower stones from all sides on Arjuna. Then, advised by Mātali, Arjuna used the *vajra* against the Asuras as a result of which they were exterminated. Looking at the places of the Nivātacavacas, Arjuna wondered why the gods did not live there since the city of the demons was far better than that of the gods. In reply Mātali told him that it was originally the residence of the gods but that the Asuras got its by pleasing Brahmạ (*Mbh* 3.165.20-4; 3.166-9).

On his way to Amaravati Arjuna saw a beautiful city of the Asuras which was the residence of the Kālakañjas (or Kāleyas) and Pulomajas who were the descendants of Danu. According to the version of Mātali, two female Asuras, Pulomā and Kālakā, practised severe austerities for a period of a thousand years as a reward for which their offspring received this heavenly city. Brahmā also granted them the boon that they could not be killed by any god. Arjuna being mortal decided to destory them and the city of Hiraṇyapura where they lived. Arjuna won by discharging the *pāśupata* which he received frorn Śiva. The Dānavas left the city in despair. The Kālakañjas and Pulomajas, peaceful though they were, did not offend Arjuna in any way; their destruction pleased the gods (*Mbh* 3.170).

In the epics we find that the task of fighting the Asuras gradually devolved on human beings. The Asura Dhundhu was killed by the

Ikṣvaku king Kuvalāśva at the instigation of the sage Utaṅka. The legend of Dhundhu is as follows. During the dissolution of the world when Viṣṇu was asleep on the hood of the serpent Śeṣa, from his navel sprang a lotus containing Brahmā, who was the four Vedas and had four forms and four faces. Some time later, two Asuras, Madhu and Kaiṭabha, found the resplendent Viṣṇu lying on the serpent and were filled with astonishment. Seeing them Brahmā trembled in fear, and at his trembling Viṣṇu was awakened from his slumber. Seeing Madhu and Kaiṭabha in front of him Viṣṇu welcomed them and wanted to grant them boons, but the demons said they would be happy to grant Viṣṇu a boon. Then Viṣṇu said he was willing to receive from them a boon whereby they would offer themselves to be slain. Hearing these words Madhu and Kaiṭabha said: 'We have never spoken an untruth, not even in jest. . . . We have ever been firm in truth and morality. . . . So you accomplish what you desire. . . . But we have one condition. You must slay us at a spot that is absolutely uncovered. . . . We also desire to become your sons.' Viṣṇu slew them with his sharp discus.

Dhundhu was the son of Madhu and Kaiṭabha. Possessed of great energy and prowess he underwent severe ascetic penances and received the boon from Prajāpati that no one among the gods, Dānavas, Rākṣasas, Nāgas, or Gandharvas could kill him. Remembering the death of his father, the wrathful Dhundhu began to trouble the gods. Then he lay in his subterranean cave underneath the sands in the observance of severe austerities to destroy the triple world. While the Asura lay breathing near the asylum of sage Utaṅka, king Kuvalāśva was passing with his troops, and urged by the sage and encourged by the celestial ones, resolved to slay Dhundhu. Aided by his sons, king Kuvalāśa excavated the sea of sands where Dhundhu was staying and hurled weapons on him. The Asura rose from his recumbent posture and threw flames from his mouth, which consumed the sons of the king. By his *yoga* force Kuvalāśva extinguished the flames and killed the demon with an arrow named after *brahman*. Thereafter king Kuvalāśva came to be known as Dhundhumāra (*Mbh* 3. 192-4).

The slaying of the Asura Mahiṣa is ascribed to Skanda-Kārttikeya in the *Mbh*. It is said that the gods were attacked by the Asuras and the celestial army was thrown into a state of confusion by a shower of weapons. The celestial troops then seemed as if they were about to turn their backs upon the enemy. But under Indra's leadership they again rushed against the Asuras. Then a powerful demon known as Mahiṣa, taking a huge rock in his hands, appeared as if the sun peering forth against a mass of dark clouds. The gods fled in confusion and were pursued by Mahiṣa who hurled that hillock at them. This struck terror in the hearts of the gods, and they fled. Mahiṣa advanced to the chariot of Rudra and seized its pole with his hands. He sounded his war-cry. While the gods were in that fearful predicament, the mighty Mahāsena (Skanda-Kārttikeya), burning in anger, advanced to the rescue. Clad in an armour of gold and seated on a chariot as bright as the sun, he rushed into battle. At this sight the army of the Asuras was suddenly dispirited. The mighty Mahāsena discharged a bright *śakti* for the destruction of Mahiṣa, which cut off the head of the demon. His head, massive as a hillock, barred the entrance to the country of the northern Kurus (*Mbh* 3.221). Elsewhere (*Mbh* 9.43-5), Kārttikeya's destruction of the Asura Bāṇa, son of Bali, is described. He is also credited for slaying the great Asura Tāraka (*Mbh* 13.86). The destruction of Tripura by Rudra or Śiva is narrated at two places in the *Mbh.* Tarakākṣa, Kamalākṣa, and Vidyunmālin, sons of the Asura Tāraka, received a boon from Brahmā that they were to be destroyed only when their cities would be united into one and pierced by a single shaft. Maya, the celestial artificer, constructed for them three cities, respectively of gold, silver and iron. Tārakakṣa had a heroic and mighty son named Hari who underwent austere of penances and received permission to excavate a lake to revive the dead. Emboldened by these boons the Asuras became invincible. Faced with the danger created by them, the gods, resorted to Rudra for their protection. They made for him a chariot designed by Viśvakarman which represented all the power-potentialities of the gods and the universe. Agni became the staff, Soma the head, and Viṣṇu the point of his arrow. And Śaṅkara cast on that arrow his fierce wrath. Brahmā acted as the charioteer and urged his steeds towards that spot where the triple city stood, protected by the Daityas and Dānavas. When Śiva set out towards the triple city, his bull uttered a tremendous roar hearing which many of the demons breathed their last. As Rudra thus stood holding his bow, the three cities losing their separate character became united and the joy of the gods knew no bounds. Then drawing his celestial bow Rudra sped that shaft at the triple city. At once loud wails were heard. Burning these Asuras, he threw them down into the western ocean (*Mbh* 7.113.52ff; 8.24).

It appears from these legends that the Asuras, both of the Dānava and Daitya categories, were originally pious and moral. Like the gods, they practised austerities according to the rules prescribed by the Śāstras and were granted boons by the creator himself. One should not fail to notice in this connection that they all craved immortality, which was refused to them, but they were compensated by the assurance that they could only be killed under extraordinary circumstances. Pride and arrogance contributed to their downfall. They are represented as associating with the gods and the Nāgas, and as worshipping Varuṇa. While dealing with Vedic demonology we have seen that Varuṇa himself was known as Asura in the Indo-Iranian tradition, which accounts for their special devotion to this particular god. The assembly of Varuṇa was adorned by great Asuras such as Bali, Virocana, Naraka, Prahlāda, Vipracitti, the Kālakañjas, Suhanu, Durmukha, Śaṅkha, Sumana, Sumati, Ghaṭodara, Mahāpārśva, Krāthana, Piṭhara, Viśvarūpa, Svarūpa, Virūpa, Mahaśiras, Daśagrīva, Vālī, Meghavāsaḥ, Daśāvasa, Tittiva, Viṭabhūta, Indratāpana and Saṃhrāda (*Mbh* 2.9.12-16). The Asuras Madhu and Kaiṭabha, never told a lie. The goddess of fortune Śrī (Lakṣmī) told Indra that previously she had graced the Asuras because they were worshippers, sacrificers, strong, masters of hundreds of illusions, observers of the vow of truth, devoted to the Vedas and endowed with noble qualities, but eventually had left them because time proved stronger (12.221). Prahlāda, Bali, and Namuci were highly respected Asuras in the great epic who taught Indra, the king of gods, the doctrine of *karma*, the virtues of giving up pride, the value of patience and the means of salvation (*Mbh* 12.172, 216-18, 220). In some cases the terms Daitya and Dānava are applied to the Asuras rather indifferently e.g., in the case of Vipracitti. Both groups of the Asuras are said to be strong, but often they are described as weaklings, when it is said that the Dānavas fall from their cars and are eaten by fishes and the Daityas are routed by the wind. They were driven from heaven at the end of the Kṛta age and took refuge in the caves, beside the sea, in mountains, in forests, under earth, but chiefly in ocean. They often appear as animals. They are opposed to the caste system, the seers, and Brahmānic power (*Mbh* 1.58.32, 36). A number of inconsistencies are found in their genealogies. As priest of the Asuras appear not only Śukra but also his sons. The Asuras are frequently identified with natural phenomena and get their names in part therefrom, especially cloud-phenomena, to which they are often compared. Opposition to light and goodness, love and the use of *māyā*, illusion or tricks, a roaring voice, the ability to assume any shape or disappear, are their general characteristics, in which they do not differ from the Rākṣasas, and not even from the gods.

The Rākṣasas in the epics were not very different from the Asuras and there were matrimonial alliances between them. The approach of the epic writers towards the Rākṣasas is that they were harmful spirits, nocturnal powers, demons of darkness and injurers of those opposing them. At the same time the Rākṣasas were the protectors of what they valued in their distinct culture, by no means inferior to that of gods and men. Notwithstanding their difference from theYakṣas, they duplicate in part the qualities of the latter because it is stated many times in the epics that the two species were born of the same mother who was a daughter of Dakṣa. Red eyes and dark bodies charcterize the Yakṣas who guard Kubera. The same features and functions apply also to the Rākṣasas. There are instances of appointing Rākṣasas as guards or protecting spirits, making the powers of evil converted to good use. They are very often confounded with the Daityas, Dānavas, and Piśācas. They display human qualities. Even they can assume human form. Rāvaṇa had ten heads and ten or twenty arms (Daśagrīva, Daśakandhara) but sometimes had only two arms and in other respects was handsome. Hanuman on seeing him exclaimed on his beauty. He said that if he were not lawless Rāvaṇa could be a protector of heaven. Even Rāma called him pious, and learned in the Veda (*Rām* 6.112.24). Besides Vibhīṣaṇa, the epics present Avindhya as a moral Rākṣasa who advised Rāvaṇa not to harm Sītā (*Mbh* 3.264.53.58; *Rām* 5.37.11ff). His daughter Kalā was also kind, as was the Rākṣasī Trijaṭā. Alongside fierce Rākṣasas, there are others who are friendly to gods and men (*raudrā maitrāśca*). In the Rāma legend of the *Mbh*, Rāvaṇa the king of the Rākṣasas is less royal-human than in Vālmīki's version. Prominent Rākṣasas of the *Mbh* are typical ogres, while in the *Rām* they are quite gentlemanly. Even Kumbhakarṇa of abnormal excess in form and habits was a rational and ethical being who had the courage to chide Rāvaṇa for his foolish act. (As Rāvaṇa was his king he was bound to honour the royal command.) Paulastyas and Yātudhanas are classes of the Rākṣasas. In the Bhārata war, Rākṣasas also participated, some in favour of the Pāṇḍavas, others in favour of the Kauravas. Again Meruvajra was a high-minded Rākṣasa who was a devout worshipper, well-versed in Śāstras and a liberal bestower. He is an instance of the tendency to convert a fiend into a guardian of virtue. Another illustration of the possible transference of functions in the nature of the Rākṣasas is Jarā, a female ogre living on meat and blood, who was appointed by Brahṃā to destroy the evil Dānavas. Her image may be painted on the wall of a pious man's house to keep evil away. As such she came to be known as the Gṛhadevī, goddess of the house (*Mbh* 2.16.38; 2.17).

Historically, as we have seen above, the Rākṣasas were indigenous tribes hostile to the Vedic or Brahmanical culture, though from their legends it appears that in course of time they were also influenced by the latter. In contrast the Asuras were a collateral branch of the Vedic Indians, originally Iran-based, having settlements in different parts of India. The contemptuous attitude of the followers of the Brahmanical culture towards the indigenous Rākṣasas and blood-feuds with the Asuras were combined and both classes were looked down upon as beings with pointed ears, stiff hair, sunken belly, red eyes, thick nose, copper-coloured face, long reddish tongue, and mouth stretching from ear to ear. This explains why in the epics the Rākṣasas and the Asuras are confounded. We have already referred to the fact that there were matrimonial alliances between the Asuras and the Rākṣasas. Rāvaṇa's wife was Maya's daughter, Kumbhakarṇa's wife was Vairocana's daughter and Vibhīṣana's wife was the daughter of the Gandharva Śailuṣa. Later the Rākṣasas became abstractions of all evil forces. According to the *Mbh*, all Rākṣasas are sons of Pulastya, but those called Nairṛtas are in particular sons of Nirṛti (destruction) who is the wife of Adharma and mother of Fear, Terror and Death (*Mbh* 1.60.7; 52-3). In the *Rām* (3.32.23; 6.114.53-4) the Rākṣasas are also said to be the sons of Pulastya. Though somewhat late as regards the period of composition, the seventh book of the *Rām* gives a detailed genealogical narrative about them. Pulastya was the son of Brahmā and of very noble character. His son by his wife Tṛṇavindu was Viśravā who was also righteous and well versed in the Vedas. He married Devavarṇinī, daughter of the sage Bharadvāja, who gave birth to a son named Vaiśravaṇa after his father. He practised severe austerities for many thousand years, as a result of which, by the grace of Brahmā, he became a Lokāpala (guardian of a quarter) and the lord of wealth. He was given for residence the city known as Laṅkā on the Trikuṭa mountain, constructed by Viśvakarman. This city originally belonged to the Rākṣasas, but they had left it in fear of Viṣṇu (*Rām* 7.2-3).

How did the Rākṣasas come into existence? Brahmā at first created water and some beings to protect it. Some of them said, *yakṣāma* (we shall worship it) and others said *rakṣāma* (we shall protect it). The former became the Yakṣas and the latter the Rakṣasas. From the Yakṣa-Rākṣasas were born two brothers, Heti and Praheti. Since Praheti was pious, he repaired to the forest to practise austerities. Heti married Bhayā, the sister of Yama, who gave birth to a son named Vidyutkeśa. He married Sālakaṭaṇkaṭā, daughter of the demoness Sandhyā. She gave birth to a child, deserted it on a mountain and returned to her husband. Hearing the cry of the deserted child, Śiva and Pārvatī who were travelling on the sky came to the place and had compassion for it. Pārvatī made the child equal to its mother's age and declared that henceforth the children of the Rākṣasīs, as soon as they were born, would receive their mothers' age. The son of Sālakaṭaṅkaṭā came to be known as Sukeśa. Having found him virtuous and gifted, the Gandharva Grāmaṇī gave his daughter Devavatī in marriage to him. Mālyavan, Sumālī and Mālī were the three sons of Sukeśa and Devavatī. They practised severe austerities and by the grace of Brahmā became invincible. At their command Viśvakarman, the divine architect, built the city of Laṅkā where they resided with their kinsmen. The three brothers married the three daughters of a Gandharvī (female Gandharva) named Narmadā. The wife of Mālyavāna was Sundarī who bore seven sons named Vajramuṣṭhi, Virūpākṣa, Durmukha, Suptaghna, Yajñakopa, Matta and Unmatta and a daughter name Amalā. Sumāli's wife Ketumatī bore ten sons named Prahasta, Akampana, Vikaṭa, Kālikāmukha, Dhumrākṣa, Dambha, Supārśva, Saṃhrādi, Praghasa and Bhāsakarṇa and four daugthers Rākā, Puṣpotkaṭā, Kaikasī and Kumbhīnasī. Mālī's wife Vasudā gave birth only to four sons whose names were Anila, Anala, Haya and Sampāti. The Rākṣasas became arrogant and hostile to the gods as a result of which they were defeated by Viṣṇu who drove them out of Laṅkā and sent them to the nether regions. The deserted city of Laṅkā was given to Vaiśravaṇa whose other name was Kubera (*Rām* 7.4-8).

Some time thereafter Sumālī left his residence in the netherworld and began to travel on the earth. He saw Kubera in his resplendent form on his flying Puśpaka chariot. He was sad and contemplated on the means by which the fallen fortune of the Rākṣasas could be restored. He asked his beautiful daughter Kaikasī to meet sage Viśravā and request him to marry her, so that her sons by the auspicious power of the sage could be equal to Kubera in brilliance and prosperity. Kaikasī however went to Viśravā at the wrong time, when the sage was performing the Agnihotra sacrifice. Having seen her standing calmly before him, the sage understood her purpose and agreed to marry her. Rāvaṅa was the first son of Kaikasī; the second was Kumbhakarṇa; the third was a daughter Śūrpanakhạ; and the fourth was Vibhīṣaṇa (*Rām* 7.9). In the *Mbh* (3.249.5-9) the mother of Rāvaṇa and Kumbhakarṇa was Puṣpotkaṭā; the mother of Vibhīṣaṇa was Mālinī and the mother of Śūrpanakhā and Khara was Rākā. The Rāmopākhyana section of the *Mbh* differs in places from Vālmīki's account. There it is stated that Prajāpati's son was Pulastya and the latter's son was Vaiśravaṇa. Pulastya did not like Vaiśravaṇa, a favourite of his grandfather Prajāpati. Vaiśravaṇa had received from him the post of Lokapāla, lordship of wealth, the flying Puṣpaka chariot and the city of Laṅkā. An angry Pulastya left his body; with one-half of his entity he was reborn in a Brāhmaṇa lineage and became famous as Viśravā. Vaiśravaṇa or Kubera tried to keep Viśravā in good humour and appointed three Rākṣasīs, expert in music and dance, to serve him. They were Puṣpotkaṭā, Rākā and Mālinī who gave birth to Rāvaṇa and his brothers. The story of the austerities performed by Rāvaṇa, Kumbhakaraṇa and Vibhīṣaṇa and the boons they received from Brahmā is also found in the *Mbh*. But there it is stated that when Rāvaṇa defeated Kubera and seizing all his valuables including the Puṣpaka chariot drove him out from Laṅkā, the pious Vibhīṣaṇa was on the side of Kubera. Highly pleased with Vibhīṣaṇa's act, Kubera conferred upon him the lordship of the Yakṣa army. The remaining part of the Rāmopākhyāna tallies with the *Rāmāyaṇa* story with minor differences here and there, e.g. Kumbhakarṇa was not killed by Rāma but by Lakṣmaṇa (*Mbh* 3.259-83).

The Rākṣasas of the *Mbh*, as we have said above, are not as refined as those of the *Rām*. In *Mbh* (1.5-7) we come across the legend of the origin of Cyavana in which it is said that an unnamed Rākṣasa (whose name appears to be Pulomā) was promised a human bride of his namesake but subsequently she was given in marriage to the sage Bhṛgu. The Rākṣasa abducted her while she was pregnant and on the way she gave birth to the sun-like Cyavana, at whose sight the Rākṣasa dropped dead and burnt to ashes. The slaying of the Rākṣasa Hiḍimba, the marriage of his sister Hiḍimbā to Bhīma, and the birth of their son Ghaṭotkaca is narrated in *Mbh* (1.139-43). Hiḍimba was, like a class of the Rākṣasas, a *puruṣādin*, a *narāśana*, or cannibal. He lived in a Śāla tree and had eight fangs, pointed ears, red hair, was very strong and was as much pleased with the smell of man. His sister Hiḍimbā could assume human form, fly through the air, and know both past and future. She ate people and then danced with her brother. And she is also described as virtuous and wise, which is why she married Bhīma and was accepted by the Pāṇḍavas. After their marriage Bhīma left his brothers and stayed with his wife's people until Ghaṭotkaca was born. Ghaṭotkaca was thus only half-Rākṣasa but he had the nature of his maternal kin and was accompanied into battle with the recognized classes of Rākṣasas, called Paulastyas and Yātudhānas, who rode indifferently on cars and animals and appeared in any shape they chose. Although Ghaṭotkaca fought on behalf of the Pāṇḍavas, crushed many Kaurava chiefs, killed the Rākṣasa Alāyudha who was fighting for the Kauravas, and died a hero's death, slain by the dart kept by Karṇa to kill Arjuna, Kṛṣṇa could not hide his joy at Ghaṭotkaca's death. This was for two reasons. First, the special weapon of Karṇa which was effective only for once and sure to kill anybody having used against him lost its power, and thus Arjuna was saved from being killed. Second, Ghaṭotkaca was an ally of the Pāṇḍavas, but by nature a wicked Rākṣasa who hated the Brāhmaṇas and was a destroyer of sacrifices. Kṛṣṇa went so far as to say that if Karṇa did not kill Ghaṭotkaca, he himself would have done it (*Mbh* 7.156. 25-8).

One of the chief Rākṣasas of the *Mbh* in independent tales was Baka who bore the epithet Asurarājā and dwelt in a cave near the city of Ekacakrā. He was red-haired and had pointed ears. He used to get one human being daily to eat from the city. The Pāṇḍavas happened to live for some time in this city, and witnessed the plight and suffering of those unfortunate families bound to send the Rākṣasa a member for his meal. At the command of Kunti, Bhīma hacked him to death and saved the people of the city (*Mbh* 1.143-52). Demons like Alāyudha, Alambuṣa, Kirmira and Hiḍimba were relations of Baka, some of whom sought to take revenge against the Pāṇḍavas, especially against Bhīma, in the ensuing Bhārata war. Baka's brother was Kirmira who lived in the Kāmyaka forest. This was a resort of the hermits, but they had left owing to the torture inflicted on them by Kirmira. He appeared before the Pāṇḍavas in his illusory form which was, however, dispelled by the incantation of the Pāṇḍava priest Dhaumya. The Rākṣasa in order to revenge the killing of his brother attacked the Pāṇḍavas, but Bhīma killed him in a straight fight (*Mbh* 3.12.1-75). Alāyudha was also probably a brother of Baka, who was a lord of the Rākṣasas. He joined the Kauravas in the Bhārata war, defeated even Bhīma, but was eventually killed by Ghaṭotkaca (*Mbh* 7.152-3). Jaṭāsura's son Alambuṣa, also somehow a brother of Baka, and a descendant of Ṛṣyaśṛṅga (Ārṣyśṛṅgī), who as Rākṣasendra had the best chariot of the Rākṣasa army drawn by horse-faced Piśācas, was opposed to the Pāṇḍavas. Ranked as a Mahāratha and called a descendant of the kings, he fought in the Bhārata war because of an ancient grudge (*pūrvavairaṃ anusmran*). Though apparently of human ancestry in part, he was a true Rākṣasa, descending into earth, rising into air again and having any form at will. Eventually he was killed by Ghaṭotkaca (*Mbh* 7.84.1-30).

In the *Rām* we come across Yakṣi Tāḍakā who destroyed two flourishing settlements, Malada and Karuṣa, where Indra had the expiation of his sin of killing the Brāhmaṇa Vṛtra. She was the daughter of Suketu, wife of Jambha's son Sunda and mother of Mārīca. Both mother and son were transformed into Rākṣasas owing to a curse of Agastya for their misdeeds. The sage Viśvāmitra induced Rāma to kill Tāḍakā, despite her being a woman, quoting the precedent of Indra's slaying Mantharā, the daughter of Virocana, who had planned to destroy the three worlds. The Rākṣasī used her power of creating illusion to defeat Rāma but the latter killed her with sharp missiles (*Rām.* 1.24-6). For carrying out her wicked designs Tāḍakā was assisted by her son Mārīca and another Rākṣasa called Subāhu. In fact, for killing both these demons, who used to ravage the hermitages of the sages, Viśvāmitra had selected Rāma and Lakṣmaṇa. With a huge Rākṣasa army Mārīca and Subāhu came to fight with them. The sky grew cloudy and loud with thunder, as the Rākṣasas began to pour in. The *mānava* weapon hurled by Rāma rolled back the Rākṣasas with Mārīca into the sea and then with the *āgneya* weapon Rāma killed Subāhu (*Rām* 1.30). Mārīca however, had to meet a different fate. When Rāvaṇa was determined to abduct Sītā, he came to Mārīca and sought his help, but Mārīca advised Rāvaṇa to give up the evil idea. He described Rāma's qualities in detail and warned him that if he came in conflict with Rāma the entire Rākṣasa race would be destroyed. As one desirous of death does not take any medicine, so Rāvaṇa did not agree. Mārīca said: 'I shall not be least sorry if I lose my life even now in the hands of Rāma, but I am really sorry to think that you will be soon destroyed with your army.' So saying he agreed to carry out Rāvaṇa's order. They together got upon the heavenly car and soon arrived at the Daṇḍaka forest. Thereupon, Mārīca assumed the form of an enchanting golden deer and in order to attract Sītā's notice began to move about slowly. Sītā fondly gazed on the wonderful deer; she wanted to have it. Rāma chased it, but it went far away, and unable to catch it he discharged from his bow a sharp arrow which struck the heart of Mārīca. But at the time of death, the Rākṣasa cried in the voice of Rāma, 'Alas Sītā'! Alas Lakṣmaṇa! (*Rām* 3.35-44).

Arriving at the Daṇḍaka forest Rāma and Lakṣmaṇa saw a terrible Rākṣasa, huge as a mountain-peak, with wide mouth, sunken eyes and protruding belly and clad in a blood-stained tiger-skin. He snatched away Sītā, introduced himself as Virādha, son of Yava and Śatapradā, and declared that having gratified Brahmā with penance and devotion he had received a boon: no weapon would be able to destory him. Rāma and Lakṣmaṇa attacked him, but Virādha caught hold of them and dragged them into the forest. Rāma and Lakṣmaṇa then broke his arms, showered kicks and blows on him, but finding him invulnerable to weapons, proposed to bury him alive. Then the monster recognized them as Rāma,

Lakṣmaṇa and Sītā and said that originally he was the Gandharva Tambaru but became a Rākṣasa because of a curse of Kubera for his attachment to Rambhā. Kubera, however, granted that when king Daśaratha's son Rāma would kill him in fight, he would go back to his former state (*Rām* 3.1-4).

More interesting is the story of Śūrpanakhā, the sister of Rāvaṇa. Seeing Rāma she was smitten in love and expressed her desire to marry him. In a lighter vein Rāma asked her to take Lakṣmaṇa as her husband. Refused by Lakṣmaṇa, the Rākṣasī became furious. In great anger Lakṣmaṇa chopped off her ears and nose (3.17-18). She then went to her brother Khara in Janasthāna and told him about her predicament. An angry Khara sent a Rākṣasa army to punish Rāma, but they were routed. Thereupon Khara made extensive preparations for war, with an army comprising fourteen thousand Rākṣasas. His generals were Śyenagāmi, Pṛthugrīva, Yajñaśatru, Vihaṅgama, Durjaya, Karavirākṣa, Puruṣa, Kalkamuka, Meghamālī, Mahāmāli, Varaṣya and Rudhirasan. Four generals were under Khara's assistant Duṣaṇa. They were Mahākapāla, Sthulākṣa, Pramatha and Triśira. By and by Rākṣasa hordes surrounded Rāma. Then Rāma began to ward off their blows and weapons. As dry wood is consumed by fire, so the Rākṣasas were scorched and overwhelmed by Rāma's arrows. The army of Duṣaṇa were scattered by Rāma's shafts. Duṣaṇa and his commanders were slain. The same was the fate of Khara's generals and army. Only Triśira fought with some courage but he, too, lost his life. Khara was alarmed at Triśira's death and the destruction of his troops which Rāma effected quite single-handed. He rushed towards Rāma violently and after a brief encounter also met his doom. In that great fight only one Rākṣasa, Akampana, survived to convey the news of their destruction to Rāvaṇa (*Rām* 3.19-30).

While Rāma and Lakṣmaṇa were searching for Sītā in the dense forest, a Rākṣasī named Ayomukhī tried to seduce Lakṣmaṇa, but the latter, greatly enraged, cut off her nose, ears and breast. Then they came across a formidable Rākṣasa with no head or neck. His mouth was set on his belly and there was only one eye on his brow. He was Kabandha. He caught both Rāma and Lakṣmaṇa and attempted to devour them. But they cut off his right and left arms respectively. The Kabandha then recognized them as Rāma and Lakṣmaṇa and said that his Rākṣasa form was due to a curse of Indra, because having received a boon from Brahmā for his austerities he became arrogant. He was, however, assured that he would recover his original body after being killed by Rāma and Lakṣmaṇa. After his cremation he assumed his original form, clad in white garment and decked with beautiful ornaments. He advised Rāma to meet Sugrīva, residing on the bank of the Pampā, who would be of greatest help in rescuing Sītā (*Rām* 3.69-73).

While crossing the sea Hanumān was caught by the Rākṣasī Siṃhikā who opened her mouth wide to devour him. Hanumān, finding her vital spot, at once reduced his size, entered her mouth and tore her heart into pieces with his sharp nails (*Rām* 5.1). At the gate of Laṅkā Hanumān met a protector deity of the city who was also a Rākṣasī. Notwithstanding his fervent requests she did not permit Hanumān to enter the city. Thereupon Hanumān roared in anger and struck her with his left fist. Then the Rākṣasī with a hideous grimace reeled on the ground. She said in a submissive voice that once god Svayambhū had said to her that her defeat at the hands of a monkey would be indicative of the destruction of the Rākṣasas (*Rām* 5.3).

Mention has already been made of the kind-hearted Rākṣasī Trijaṭā who scolded other Rākṣasīs disturbing Sītā. She consoled Sītā assuring her that her good days would return (*Rām* 5.27). Even Mandodarī, the chief queen of Rāvaṇa, was a virtuous lady. She warned Rāvaṇa not to bear hostility against Rāma. According to her, Sītā was superior to Arundhatī and Rohiṇī in every respect. She said that Sītā's fortitude was unparalleled, that she was more forbearing than the earth, more beautiful than beauty itself, highly devoted to her husband and that Rāvaṇa had committed a heinous sin by abducting her (*Rām* 6.112).

These stories suggest that, whether good or bad, in appearance, character and conduct, the Rākṣasas of the *Rām*, are very human. While in the court of Rāvaṇa Rākṣasas like Nikumbha, Rāṣabha, Sūryaśatru, Suptaghana, Vajrakopa, Indrajit, Prahasta, Virupākaṣa, Vajradanta, Dhumrāksa, Durmukha and many other heroes expressed their desire to fight Rāma, Vibhīṣana said that war is a last resort. It is not wise to despise an enemy without knowing his strength. He had the candour to say that the act of stealing Sītā was reprehensible. He repeatedly urged Rāvaṇa to return Sītā to Rāma and seek peace with him (*Rām* 6.9-10, 14,16). The old Rākṣasa Mālyavāna who was the uncle of Rāvaṇa's mother and once engaged in prolonged fight with the gods, advised Rāvaṇa to act in conformity with laws and customs and fourteen kinds of knowledge required of a king, and to conclude peace with Rāma by returning Sītā to him with grace and honour (*Rām* 6.35). Even what Kumbhakarṇa, the mountain-like super-Rākṣasa, said to Rāvaṇa is worth-quoting:

> O king, the time for decision was already passed the moment you abducted Jānakī, being bewitched by her beauty. There was time of our decision

before that. Wise is that monarch who does thoughtfully and never repents any deed done in indecent haste. It was highly wrong of you to carry one's wife by force. . . . It is rather your good fortune that you have not been yet destroyed by Rāma. . . . O king, what we apprehended at the time of holding consultation with Vibhīṣaṇa, has befallen you for neglecting our good counsel. As the sinner is damned to perdition, so you have to reap the consequences of your wicked deed of abducting another's wife. Formerly you did not out of pride calculate the evil consequences of this foul act. Therefore this crisis has arisen. The king who performs late what is to be done early, and does that first what is to be performed last, is devoid of any sense of polity. He who has no regard for time and opportunity becomes futile as clarified butter offered to unsanctified fire. . . . The king who cannot decide what is best or what is preferred, all his knowledge of Śāstras goes in vain. . . . Some advisers in order to ruin their master incite him to wicked deeds by their ill advice, and some join the powerful enemies of their master. . . . The king who is fickle and meddles in everything is doomed to be ruined. . . . O king, what queen Mandodarī and brother Vibhīṣaṇa have said formerly appear to me to be good and beneficial (*Rām* 6.63).

The character of Rāvaṇa is complex. Astonishing was his prowess. Not to speak of man, even the gods could not stand his might. In the introductory portion of the epic he is depicted as an embodiment of power and terror who oppressed the inhabitants of the three worlds. His wrath did not spare the gods, Maharṣis, Yakṣas, Gandharvas, Brāhmaṇas, or even the Asuras. Continually harassed by him, the gods requested Viṣṇu to appear on earth in the form of Rāma to destroy him. Viṣṇu complied and was born as Rāma. His associates, the monkeys, were created from gods, sages, Gandharvas and other divine beings (*Rām* 1.5-17). But despite his arrogance and evil propensities, Rāvaṇa had a greatness of character. When he was slain by Rāma, Vibhīṣaṇa lamented saying that he was the shelter of the virtuous, the image of righteousness and the protector of the valiant. This hero had granted more than what was asked of him. He supported his dependants and friends liberally, enjoyed everything precious or delicious and contributed to the prosperity of his friends and to the destruction of his enemies. He was well-versed in the Vedas and the Vedāṅgas, a great yogī and was the chief amongst the performers of Agnihotra sacrifice and other rites. Rāma also paid him a glowing tribute saying that he died as a brave Kṣatriya. One should not lament over the death of Rāvaṇa who put even Indra to flight in battle (*Rām* 6.110). He was cursed by so many that it is doubtful whose curse effected his downfall whether of Rambhā, or of Vedavatī, or of Umā or of Puñjikasthalā or of Nandīśvara. Rāvaṇa stopped the sun, conquered the gods, overran Bhogavati, forced the Dānava Madhu to marry his sister and many to give him his daughter as wife, stole Soma and conquered Jaṭāyu.

The character of Vibhīṣaṇa seems to have been modelled after Prahlāda. He and his wife Saramā have no demonic features. In appearance and conduct they are fully human. The figure of Kumbhakarṇa inspires popular imagination. He has enormous hunger and sleeps six months at a time. When he was awakened he quenched his thirst with two thousand jars of wine. As soon as he was born he devoured a thousand creatures and swallowed his foes. But his mental structure, as we have seen above, was that of a rational and ethical being. Apart from Indrajit, who is endowed with certain noble qualities, other sons of Rāvaṇa are formidable and bellicose. The same holds good in the case of the generals of Rāvaṇa such as Dhumrākṣa, Vajradaṃṣṭrā, Akampana, Prahasta, Narāntaka, Devāntaka, Trimurdha, Mahodara, Triśira (son of Rāvaṇa), Atikāya, Kumbha, Nikumbha and Makarākṣa.

The Yātudhānas and Piśācas are mentioned as a class, and none belonging to these classes is referred to by individual name. The words Yātu and Yātudhāna, as we have seen, occur in the earlier literature, basically in the sense of a class of black magicians or sorcerers or hostile forces and secondarily as a class of lesser demons and evil spirits. Likewise the word Piśāca originally denoted a human race subsisting on raw flesh, an indigenous tribe opposed to the Vedic ritual and culture. The latter, to show them as inferior, attributed to them repulsive practices. Later their real human existence was stamped out and they came to be regarded as demons. It should be pointed out in this connection that the epic writers have not consciously attributed the eating of uncooked flesh or other derogatory practices to the Asuras. They have done it only in some places where they could not distinguish between an Asura and a Rākṣasa. They had to attribute cannibalism and other repugnant practices and horrible physical appearance to the Rākṣasas or else it would be difficult to distinguish between the Rākṣasas and the gods. Behind such conceptualizations the function of the *varṇa* system had also a significant role. Those who were close to the Vedic or Brahmanical culture were placed in the higher ranks. The functioning of this hierarchical process is found in the arrangement of the eight valid forms of marriage which explains the Asura form of marriage as higher than the Rākṣasa form and the latter above the Piśāca form. Thus the Piśācas, though they were associated with the Rākṣasas and often identified with them, belonged to an inferior category owing to their remoteness from Brahmanical culture. Even so the *Mbh* (1.1.33) traces their origin to the cosmic egg along with the Yakṣas, Sādhyas, Guhyakas and Pitaras. The Piśācas are said to be the gods of the Dasyus. They are described in the *Rām* as the companions of the Rākṣasas in war. Dancing and drinking blood are traits connecting the Piśācas and Rākṣasas. Although the Piśācas have occasionally been identified with the Yātudhānas (*Rām* 6.67ff.), the latter were probably the same as the Rākṣasas since Rāvaṇa himself is *yātudhānasya dauhitraḥ*, which means that his mother's father Sumālī and uncles Mālyavāna and Mālī who were Rākṣasas *par excellence* were Yātudhanas as well. The Yātudhanas are said to have guarded the mountain of Kubera and appeared as demons in battle, being raised by fire *mantras*. One sort of Rākṣasas is called Mandehas. He hangs upon rocks and falls into water at sunrise, dying daily in fighting the sun. As Siṃhikā is a Rākṣasī, her son Rāhu who devours the sun and the moon should belong to this category. But the latter is an Asura or Dānava in the earlier tradition.

The Bhūtas in the epics are not clearly ghosts. They are between ghosts and anthropomorphized demons. The term *bhūta* also means material elements and the philosophical literature of the age (*c*. 400 BC-AD 400) is replete with analyses of the nature of the five *bhūtas* or elements. In the epics, the term *bhūta* is often prefixed with personal names such as Bhūtadhaman, son of Indra or Bhūtakṛt or Bhūtakarman, names of the creator. The earth is called Bhūtādhāra which is, however, suggestive of the philosophical definition of *bhūta* meaning elements by which the earth and earthly beings are made. Śiva is very frequently called Bhūtapati. Here the Bhūtas are attendants of Śiva. The aerial Bhūtas are known as *khecaras*, which applies to gods, Gandharvas, and Rākṣasas as well. Even the Siddhas are described as *bhūtāni khecarāni* (*Rām* 4.49.18-19). As they travel by night, they are called *naktaṃcaras* or *niśācaras* (*Rām* 5.5.9) but the term is also attributed to the Rākṣasas. Elsewhere in *Rām* (1.134) Bhūtas are *ākāśaga* and *naiśāni*, aerial night wanderers, going with Yakṣas and Rakṣas in troops all described as *raudrāḥ, piśitāśanāḥ*. Often they are invisible beings travelling in space. In the *Rām* (2.33) when people assembled to see the exiles, they said to one another that it was really heart-rending to see Sītā whom the Bhūtas even did not see from space walking in the street like an ordinary woman. The *Rām* often used the term Sattva or 'being' to denote the Bhūta. The people said in regard to the unjust act of banishing Rāma that Daśaratha had done this vile act because he was possessed by a Sattva or ghost. The Bhūtas are generally of three kinds—indifferent, hostile and good.

All the night-wanderings belong among the hostiles ones. In the *Mbh* (11.9ff), the deserted battle field after the war is described as a field of corpses filled with Bhūtas, Piśācas, Rākṣasas, and other flesh-eating night-wanderers. On the whole the epic Bhūtas, as mythologically restricted, designate beings of a rather vicious disposition, though a kindly Bhūta honours a hero, guards him and laments his fall (*Rām* 3.52.41; 6.91.62). Often they are recipients of offerings (*bali*), after gods and guests and before the Pitṛs in the order of distribution. But as ghosts are also malicious, the concept of Bhūta had a tendency to interchange with Preta.

The latter is, as we have seen above, an embryonic Pitṛ. The newly dead is a Preta or departed ghost, only those long dead are Pitṛ, father-divinity. In both epics Preta is the usual form, but the *Rām* (263.15; 3.51.31) uses also Pareta. After Daśaratha was dead for years, he appeared in the sight of Rāma and said he would never forgive Kaikeyī. Later he changed his mind, blessed Rāma, and finally went back to Indra's heaven (*Rām* 6.120). Usually the Pretas appear in ghostly battle scenes as demons dancing with Piśācas and Bhūtas amid carnage (*Mbh* 3.170.43ff). While dealing with the noise of the battle field, the epic poets frequently refer to the screaming of the Pretas with such expressions as *pretānāṃ krandatāṃ iva.* Those who are killed are said to have gone to the power of the Pretas (*pretavaśam, pretarājavaśam, pretagatam, pretabūtam.*) The identity of Pretas and Pitṛs may be shown by the remark of Bhīma that he would kill Kīcaka and make him see the *pretas* of his ancestors (*Mbh* 4.21.4). They do not appear as individuals but as hosts or troops. Pretarājapura is the city of Yama which is full of them. Together with the Bhūtas, the Pretas are often associated with the Piśācas and other wanderers of the night. Pretas are disembodied spirits and until and unless they are honoured by their relations with proper funeral rites, they do not get the status of the divine fathers (Pitṛs), thus belonging neither to gods nor men and remaining outcasts.

The Gandharvas denote a class of aeriel beings in the epics in conformity with the same conception enunciated in the Vedic, Buddhist and Jain tradition; but the existence of people of the same name, musicians by occupation in north India shows that they were not the creation of pure imagination. From the viewpoint of kinship they were related to the gods, demons, and human beings. At times they were friendly to these three classes of beings and at times hostile. In general they had a leaning towards goodness, but many were not very different from the Rākṣasas. Again, they were interlinked with the clan of the Yakṣas. Many of the important Gandharva personalities were Yakṣas at the same time. Kubera was the lord both of the Gandharvas and of the Yakṣas. Kubera's court was attended by such eminent Yakṣas as Maṇibhadra, Dhanada, Śvetabhadra, Guhyaka, Kaseraka, Gaṇḍakaṇḍu, Mahāvala, Pradyota, Kustumburu, Piśaca, Gajakarṇa, Viśālaka, Varāha-karṇa Tamauṣṭha, Phalakakṣa, Phalodaka., Haṃsacuḍa, Śikhāvarta, Hemanetra and others (*Mbh* 2.16.14-17). The name is derived from *gandha* or scent. In the *AV* (12.1.23; cf. 8.10.27) the Gandharvas and Apsarases are said to share the scent of the earth-mother; this idea is also found in the epics. While dealing with the origin of the Rākṣasas, we have also referred to the birth of Kubera, how he became one of the *lokapālas* and the lord of wealth. The mothers of the Gandharvas were the daughters of Dakṣa. Among them Muni gave birth to Bhīmsena, Suryavarcā, Suparṇa, Varuṇa, Gopati, Dhṛtarāṣṭra, Satyavāk, Arka, Parṇa, Prayuta, Bhīma, Citraratha, Śālisirāḥ, Parjanya, Kali and Nārada. Pradhā gave birth to eight daughters and ten sons whose names were Siddha, Pūrṇa, Barhi, Pūrṇāyu, Brahmācārī, Ratiguṇa, Suparṇa, Viśvāvasu, Bhānu and Pracandra. Kapilā was the mother of the celebrated Apsarases and such known Gandharvas as Atibāhu, Hāhā, Hūhū, Tumburu, etc. (*Mbh* 1.59.41-53). The Gandharva king Viśvāvasu was both an ascetic and a skilled musician and a *tīrtha* was established in his name. He was the father of Pramadvārā, who became the wife of Ruru, by the celestial damsel Menakā (*Mbh* 1.8.5-11). The *Gītā* authoritatively makes Citraratha foremost of the Gandharvas (*Mbh* 6.32.25). All Gandharvas have sweet voices (*valguvadinaḥ*) and are radiant like the sun (*sūryavarcasaḥ*). The association of the Gandharvas with music is so close that the term *gandharva* itself denotes music. *Yuddhagandharva* is war-music (*Rām* 1.4.10; 6.52.24); *gandharvaśāstra* and *ganharvaveda* mean the science of music. Among the important Gandharvas we have names such as Atibāhu, Anagha, Arkaparṇa, Alambuṣa, Ugarsena, Umbara, Ūrṇāyu, Ṛtvan, Karāla, Kali, Kārṣṇī, Gopa, Gopati, Golabha, Grāmaṇī, Citrāṅgada, Citraratha, Citrasena, Dumbara, Tamburu, Tṛaṇapa, Dhṛtarāṣṭra, Nandī, Nārada, Parjanya, Parvata, Pūrṇa, Pūrṇāyu, Prayuta, Babhru, Barhi, Bahugaṇa, Bṛhaka, Bṛhatvan, Brahmacārin, Bhānu, Bhīma, Bhīmasena, Bhumanyu, Yugapā, Ratiguṇa, Varuṇa, Viśvāvasu, Śaru, Śāliśiras, Śikṣa, Śuka, Śailuṣa, Satyavāk, Satvan, Siddha, Sucandra, Sutanu, Suparṇa, Sumanyu, Suvarṇa, Sūryavaracas, Hāhā and Hūhū.

There is no Gandharva lore in the *Rām* as we have in the *Mbh*. In the *Rām* their role is rather decorative. They, together with the Apsarases, Yakṣas, Kinnaras and other aerial beings, have a mirthful presence on such auspicious occasions as the Putreṣṭi sacrifice of Daśaratha, the birth of Rāma, the breaking of Śiva's bow and Rāma's wedding (1.15, 18, 67, etc.). They followed Bhagīratha in the company of gods, sages, Yakṣas, Kinnaras, Apsarases, Daityas, Dānavas and Rākṣasas while he was bringing Gaṅgā to earth (1.42). They were also present along with Yakṣas, Rakṣas, Kinnaras, Apsarases, Siddhas, Cāraṇas and Uragas in the sky to see the fight between Rāma and Paraśurāma (*Rām* 1.76). The Gandharvas are frequently identified with the Yakṣas, but the Yakṣī Tāḍakā, whom Rāma vanquished, was not a Gandharva but a Rākṣasa (*Rām* 1.25). The Gandharvī Somadā, daughter of Urmila, had a pious son named Brahmādatta having united with a powerful sage named Culi (*Rām* 1.33). When the sage Bharadvāja determined to offer royal hospitality to Bharata and his troops he commissioned the Gandharvīs as well as Ghṛtācī, Viśvācī, Miśrakeṣī, Alambuṣā, Nāgadattā, Hemā, Somā and a host of others to entertain them. The Gandharva king Nārada, Tambaru and Gopa as also Viśvāvasu with Hāhā-Hūhū sang before Bharata (2.91.16ff). Although the Gandharvas were in forests and caves (*Rām* 3.67.5ff), their natural abode was in the air (*Rām* 1.63.34), the realm of fog and rain (*Rām* 3.65.14; 5.1. 165ff), described as the cities of the Gandharvas. Cars as bright as the cities of the Gandharvas, the bright deer that tempted Sītā like the *gandharvapura-saṃnibhaḥ* (*Rām* 3.43.6), and such other expressions of the aerial phenomena appear as mirages to commoners. The Gandharva king was a model of beauty (*Rām* 2.3.27; 2.37.111) and as a class they gave their name to the free-love union called the fifth form of marriage. Their weapons were also famous (*Rām* 3.25.36, etc.). While giving directions to his troops searching for Sītā, Sugrīva referred to the settlements of the Yakṣas, Cāraṇas, Kinnaras, and Apsarases around the Kṣīroda ocean. Towards the southern ocean on the Ṛsabha hill lived the formidable Gandharva called Rohita and there were five Gandharva chiefs named Śailuṣa, Grāmaṇī, Śikṣan, Śuka and Babhru. Near the western ocean on the Pārījāta mountain lived twenty-four million fiery Gandharvas. Sugrīva advised his troops not to touch any fruits or roots there which were guarded by those vicious and dreadful Gandharvas. Beyond the sea lay the Sumeru mountain which was a favourite resort of the Gandharvas. Towards the north, adorned by the Himalaya, gods and Gandharvas dwelt in the Somāśrama. In Kailāsa stood the magnificent palace of Kubera which was of yellow colour and ornamented with gold. There Kubera sported with the Guhyakas. In the Maināka hill was the palace of Maya Dānava where roamed Kubera's elephant, Sārvabhauma. Beyond this was the country of Uttarakuru which was the land of the Siddhas, Gandharvas and Kinnaras. They were holy but were ever engaged in sporting with men. Sweet music and pleasant sound of laughter were always found there (*Rām* 4.41ff).

In the *Rām* among the associates of the Gandharvas we come across a class of beings called the Siddhas. Like the Vidyādharas (see chapter four) and Kinnaras they lived in the *antarīkṣa* or the aerial region. The Siddhas of the upper air were experts in singing, dancing and playing flute (cf. *Meghadūta, Pūrvamegha* 46). In Jain literature they are described as *vyantara-devatās* or intermediate gods. Associated with the Gandharvas was another class of beings known as Sādhyas. They were a class of celestial beings belonging to the *gaṇa-devatā*. They are mentioned even in the Vedas (10.90.16). According to Yāska (*Nir.* 12.41) their locality was in *bhuvarloka* or middle region. They are variously described as created after the gods with nature's refined objects, as children of Somasads, as sons of Vīrā or Sādhyā, and so on. They seem to have been superseded by the Siddhas.

In the *Mbh* however, individual Gandharvas and their activities are given prominence. In the Caitrarathaparvan the story of Gandharva Aṅgāraparṇa is narrated. When the exiled Pāṇḍavas arrived at the bank of the Ganges, it so happened that at that time the proud Gandharva king Aṅgāraparṇa, a friend of Kubera, was sporting with his wives in water. He considered the Pāṇḍavas to be tresspassers and asked them to leave. Arjuna refused and Aṅgāraparṇa challenged him to fight. He hurled at the Gandharva a blazing weapon which at once burnt his chariot. Arjuna then seized him by the hair of his head and brought him before his brothers. Aṅgāraparṇa's wife Kumbhīnasī begged Yudhiṣṭhira for the life of her husband and the prayer was granted. A grateful Aṅgāraparṇa then taught Arjuna *cākṣusī-vidyā*, the science of producing illusions. He also gave Arjuna a number of horses of superior quality and received from him in exchange the weapon of fire (*Mbh* 1.58). In the city of Indra, Arjuna was received by the Siddhas, Sādhyas, Cāraṇas, Gandharavas, and Apsarases. He was entertained with music by the Gandharvas Tumvura, Nārada, Hāhā, and Hūhū and dance by the celestial nymphs. The Gandharva Citrasena became a friend of Arjuna and taught him carefully the mysteries of the unrivalled dance and music practised by the Gandharvas (*Mbh* 3.44-5). When Bhīma went to fetch a divine lotus for Draupadī in the lake of Kubera he had an encounter with the guards who were Yakṣas, often described by the epic writers as Rākṣasas. They were defeated and when Kubera was informed of the discomfiture of his attendants he took no offence against the Pāṇḍavas (*Mbh* 3.151-4). The story in itself is not very significant, but a point to be noted is that here the Gandharvas are openly equated with the Yakṣas and Rākṣasas. At Dvaitavana, Duryadhana angered the Gandharvas by his haughty behaviour and was defeated and humiliated by the Gandharva king Citrasena. Karṇa was defeated, Śukunī ran away from the battlefield, Duḥśāsana was crushed and Duryodhana was made captive along with the Kaurava ladies. Gandharva chiefs like Citrasena, Vimiṃśati, Vinda, Anuvinda, etc., created havoc among the Kaurava army. The ministers of Duryodhana thereafter went to Yudhiṣṭhira and humbly sought his help. Bhīma was happy at the course of events and said mirthfully that by exterminating the Kaurava army and making the wicked Duryodhana a captive the Gandharvas had accomplished the great task which the Pāṇḍavas were destined to do. But Yudhiṣṭhira said that although Duryodhana was an enemy of the Pāṇḍavas and rightly served by the Gandharvas, the question of kinship remained. After all the Pāṇḍavas also belonged to the Kaurava family and family-prestige should be retained. So the Pāṇḍavas fought the Gandharvas and Arjuna defeated the Gandharva chief Citrasena, who was a friend. At the request of Yudhiṣṭhira Citrasena freed the Kauravas (*Mbh* 3.229-36). In the concluding portion of the Āraṇyaparvan we find that Dharma (the principle of righteouness) assuming the form of a Yakṣa wanted to test the wisdom of the brothers. Sahadeva, Nakula, Arjuna and Bhīma were sent respectively to fetch water from a tank possessed by the Yakṣa. Each of them was warned not to drink it before answering his questions. In eager haste none paid heed to his words and they perished instantly. Yudhiṣṭhira was the last to go there. A wise person as he was, he restrained himself, listened patiently to the questions relating to the mysteries of life, principles of ethics, the path of happiness and spiritual progress, gave answers to each of them, and got his brothers restored to life by satisfying the Yakṣa by his wisdom and knowledge (*Mbh* 3.295-7). When the Pāṇḍavas stayed in disguise in the kingdom of Virāṭa, Draupadī, the Pāṇḍava queen, who was serving as a female attendant in the royal household, made the fact known to others that she was guarded by five Gandharva husbands. When the wicked Kīcaka and his associates were destroyed by the Pāṇḍavas, the latter intentionally spread the rumour that it was an act of the Gandharvas (*Mbh* 4.22-3). Sthuṇākarṇa, a Yakṣa vassal of Kubera, lent his manhood to Śikhaṇḍī for which he was severely reprimanded by his overlord and cursed to remain a female for ever. Later Kubera was softened and he assured Sthuṇākarṇa that he would regain his manhood after the death of Śikhaṇḍī in war (*Mbh* 5.192.19-30; 5.193).

The Apsarases are so regarded, though they form a class by themselves. They were celestial nymphs, though born of the waters. There were many groups of the Apsarases among which the most revered was Vaidika to which belonged Menakā, Sahajanyā, Parṇinī, Puñjikasthalā, Ghṛtasthalā, Ghṛtācī, Viśvācī, Urvaśī, Anumlocā, Pramlocā and Manovatī. A good number of Apsarases were born of Dakṣa's daughter. One of them Muni gave birth to eighteen Apsarares, most prominent among them being Tilottamā, Rambhā, and Miśrakeśī. Others were born of Kapilā and Pradhā (*Mbh* 1.59.41-53). Some of their names coincide with the Gandharvas in feminine gender such as Gopālī, Citrāṅgadā, Citrasenā, etc. Though they technically belonged to the inverted pantheon and associated with the Yakṣas, Gandharvas, Rakṣas, Nāgas, and others, they did not show any evil propensity. In some cases, however, we find that an Apsaras was a harmful creature. They graced the assembly of the gods. They were sometimes employed by the Gods to deflect powerful sages. They were skilled in music and dance. There were sixty crores of them, not to speak of their countless attendants. They were adorned with gems and ornaments (*Rām* 3.35.16-17). Ordinarily they were not shy. Often they were heartless. Menakā did not hesitate to leave her newly born child in the hermitage of Sthulakeśa and run away (*Mbh* 1.8.5-8). They also maintained contact with the human world and would dance at weddings (*Rām* 1.73.35). The sound of their songs had three waves (*Rām* 5.4.10). They sang at the magic entertainment prepared by Bharadvāja for the army of Bharata (*Rām* 2.91.16ff). The love-legend of Urvaśī and Purūravas is indirectly mentioned in *Rām* (3.48.18) where Rāvaṇa tells Sītā about the repentance of Urvaśī for her wrong dealings with Purūravas. It speaks of the tank of five Apsarases who were ordered to seduce the aged Māṇḍakarṇi and succeeded so well that being rejuvenated by them he built a house and kept them all (*Rām* 3.11.12ff). Viśvamitra was seduced by Menakā (*Rām* 1.63.5) or by Ghṛtācī (*Rām* 4.35.7). Again he cursed Rambhā to become a stone for attempting to deflect him (*Rām* 1.64.12). Ghṛtācī bore Kusanābha's daughters (*Rām* 1.32.10). Hemā's lover, was admonished by Indra and thereafter she met Rāvaṇa (*Rām* 4.50.39; 4.51.10ff, etc.). Another Apsaras was Puñjikāsthalā, cursed to be born on earth as Añjanā, daughter of Kuñjara and wife of Keśarin who bore Hanumān (*Rām* 4.66.8ff). She was a Varuṇakanyakā and cursed Rāvaṇa in her former existence as an Apsaras in Varuṇa's realm (*Rām* 6.13.11; 6.60.11). In the Śakuntalopākhyāna of the *Mbh*, Śakuntalā telling the story of her birth to Duṣyanta said that the Apasaras Menakā was asked by Indra to deflect the sage Viśvāmitra whose performance of severe austerities aroused terror in his heart. Menakā at first declined fearing the sage's power and position. But later she revived her confidence and neatly accomplished the task of seducing the sage. She lived for some time with Viśvamitra as his spouse, gave birth to a girl-child on the bank of the river Mālinī, and then went back to the court of Indra. The sage Kanva saw the new-born girl guarded by *śakuna* birds and adopted her, naming her Śakuntalā (*Mbh* 1.65.16-42; 1.66.1-17). This was not, however, the first act of Menakā of this kind. She left her daughter Prāmadvārā in the same way (*Mbh* 1.8.5-8). Arjuna during the period of his exile, while having his bath in a lake, was caught by a crocodile. He pulled out that aquatic animal by force on the shore which instantly assumed the form of a beautiful maiden, well-dressed and decked with all sorts of ornaments. The maiden introduced herself as an Apsaras named Vargā and said that she and her four friends were cursed to remain crocodiles because they disturbed the meditation of a powerful Brāhmaṇa. Having seen their repentence the Brāhmaṇa, however, assured them that they would regain their original form if someone dragged them out of the waters. Thereafter Arjuna rescued four other Apsarases in the same way. Their names were Saurabheyī, Samīcī, Budbudā and Latā (*Mbh* 1.208.7-21; 1.209.1-24). Apsarases such as Miśrakeśī, Rambhā, Śucismitā, Citrasenā, Cārunetrā, Ghṛtācī, Menakā, Puñjikasthalā, Viśvācī, Sahajanyā, Pramlocā, Urvasī, Irā, Vargā, Saurabheyī, Samīcī, Budbudā, Latā and others were regular members of Kubera's assembly (*Mbh* 2.10.10-11). Urvaśī was sent by Indra to entertain Arjuna sexually. But on Arjuna's refusal she cursed him, saying that 'since you have disregarded a woman who came to your place at her own will being pierced by the shaft of Kāma, O Pārtha, you will have to pass the time among females unregarded, as a dancer, destitute of manhood and scorned as a eunuch' (*Mbh* 3.45-6 *K*).

The Kiṃpuruṣas and Kinnaras (Kiṃnaras) are not formally distinguished in the epics. The Kinnaras are said to have been descended along with the Rākṣasas and Vānaras from Pulastya and the Kiṃpuruṣas from Pulaha along with stags, lions and tigers (*Mbh* 1.60.7). There is no doubt that like the Asuras, Rākṣasas and Gandharavas, the Kinnaras and Kiṃpuruṣas were originally human beings, in all probability of the trans-Himalayan region, whose manners and customs differed from the dominant section of plains dwellers. In many respects they had similarity with the Gandharavas with whom they are sometimes identified. It is said that the Gandharavas called Kinnaras and others called Naras (*Kiṃnara nāma gandharava nara nāma tathāpare*) as well as

Maṇibhadras and other Yakṣas wait upon Kubera (*Mbh* 2.10.13ff). Śiva is described as the lord of the Naras, Kinnaras and Yakṣas (*Mbh* 14.44.14). They are described as terrible in appearance (*raudradarśiṇah*) and a race of separate spirits. The Kiṃpuruṣas accompany gods, sages, serpents, Gandharvas and Yakṣas to see the ocean drunk up (*Mbh* 3.104.21 *K*). Their lord is Druma (*Mbh* 2.10.29 *K*) and his son, Drumaputra was the fighting lord of the Kiṃpuruṣas in the northern White Mountain (*Mbh* 2.25.1). The Gandhamādana mountain has also been described as the stronghold of the 'lion of the Kiṃpuruṣas' who imparted knowledge of arms to Bhīṣmaka (*Mbh* 5.155.3ff). Like the Gandharvas, the Kiṃpuruṣas were *gītakovidāḥ*, well versed in music and wandered in the forests with friendly Yakṣas making them as charming as Nandana. They were also found near the hermitages (*Rām* 3.45.11; 3.46.28; 3.67.6) and sided with the gods at the time of danger (*Rām* 5.56.31). They go in pairs, male and female, wearing swords and fine garments (*Rām* 2.54.39; 2.93.11; 2.94.11). Their females are lovely, though fickle lovers (*Rām* 2.12.74; 3.46.22; 5.33.5ff). Women who can sing in a sweet voice were known as Kinnarodgītabhāsinī (*Mbh* 1.172.10 K). The Kiṃpuruṣas were not usually differentiated individually, unlike the Gandharvas and Apsarases. They have no personal names. Nor do we know about their individual attainments, adventures and exploits. The same holds good also in the case of the Kinnaras. The Kiṃpuruṣas, along with the Kinnaras and Vidyādharas were found on hills like Mandara, Citrakūṭa, etc., and in forests like Pampā (*Rām* 4.1.61; 5.56.31). The mount Mandara is also described as the abode of the Kinnaras, Apasarases, and gods (*kiṃnarairrapsarobhiśca devairopi ca sevitam, Mbh*. 1.16.2). There are passages which show that while the Kinnaras went with the Rākṣasas, Yakṣas, and Vānaras to make one group, the Kiṃpuruṣas formed a group with the Śarabhas (antelopes), Siṃhas (lions), Vyāghras (tigers), Ṛksas (bears), and Vṛkas (wolves). In other passages the Kinnaras are grouped with the Rākṣasas and the Kiṃpuruṣasas with milder Yakṣas.

Animals, birds, and serpents possessed by demons and the latter in the forms of the beings of the former category are of frequent occurrence in both the epics. Again there are cases in which the animals, birds and serpents assume human forms, mix with human beings and have discussions with them in regard to temporal, ethical and spiritual matters. They talk among themselves about various problems and follow codes of conduct like human beings. These zoomorphic beings may be divided into three distinct categories. To the first category belong animals, birds and reptiles, to the second mythical beings and to the third human beings with totemic affiliation. For example, Nāgas mean ordinary serpents (in some cases elephants); mythical serpents endowed with the power of speech, of changing forms and of going everywhere, even the space at will; and human groups tracing their descent form a serpent-totem. We often come across the term *manuṣyasālāvṛka* signifying *werewolf* or metaphorically 'a man with wolfish character'. The Sālāvṛkas denote wolf, hyena or jackal, but they are sometimes identified with the apes, elephants and bears and sometimes with the Śarabhas (a kind of deer whose roar frightens the animals), Bhuruṇḍas (a kind of bird which with its strong beaks used to carry corpses of the Uttarakurus and bury them in caves) and Bhūtas (ghosts). In one case they appear to be a class of fighter Brāhmaṇas (*Mbh* 12.33.29 *K*). Śarabha is sometimes a personal name. The *Rām* (6.27) knows a monkey chief of that name who was overthrown by Kumbhakarṇa. In the *Mbh* (3.134.15 *K*) it is the name of a monster and also of a Daitya or Asura (1.61.28). The Vānaras of the *Rām*, from an historical viewpoint must have been an important and powerful southern tribe with monkey-totem. When Hanumān first met Rāma and Lakṣmaṇa and talked with them, both were under the impression that Hanumān must have been well-versed in the three Vedas and a great scholar in grammar. They could not trace a single improper word in his long speech (*Rām* 4.3). Again the wise sayings of Jāmbuvāna clearly indicate that he was also the chief of a tribe whose totem was the bear. But as mythological animals, in addition to their original human qualities, they were endowed not only with supernatural power but with divine and demonic attributes as well. Birds like herons, hawks, vultures, cranes and crows used to precede the warriors in battlefield, but they affected not the warriors behind but the enemies who were advancing against them. Among the most important mythical birds whose functions are worth-remembering is Jaṭāyu in the *Rām* and Garuḍa in the *Mbh*. Rāma in the Pañcavaṭī forest met Jaṭāyu who introduced himself as a friend of Daśaratha. While describing his ancestry he said that Kaśyapa married eight daughters of Dakṣa Prajāpati. Among them Tāmrā gave birth to five daughters whose names were Krauñci, Bhāsī, Śyenī, Dhṛtarāṣṭri and Sukī. From Sukī's daughter Natā was born Vinatā. From Krodhavasā, one of eight daughters of Dakṣa married to Kaśyapa, were born, among others, Surasā and Kadru, both mothers of the serpents. From Vinatā were born Garuḍa and Aruṇa. Jaṭāyu himself was the son of Aruṇa. His mother was Śyeni and his elder brother was Sampāti (*Rām* 3.14). When Rāvaṇa abducted Sītā, Jaṭāyu tried his best to rescue her. He fought Rāvaṇa, but since he was old he was eventuallly defeated and mortally wounded (*Rām* 3.50-1). From the dying Jaṭāyu Rāma received the news of Sītā's forcible abduction by Rāvaṇa. When Jaṭāyu died Rāma and Lakṣmaṇa performed his funeral (*Rām* 3.67-8). From Aṅgada Sampāti, the elder brother of Jaṭāyu, received the news of his brother's death. He thereupon introduced himself to the monkey-troops of Aṅgada and said that after the celebrated demon Vṛtra was killed he and Jaṭāyu went to conquer Indra. When they approached the sun Jaṭāyu was unable to bear the heat and Sampāti saved his brother by spreading his wings. In consequence his wings were burnt and he fell upon the Vindhyas. He then informed that Sītā was in Laṅkā (*Rām* 4.56-8). He said that his son Supārśva used to bring his food everyday. One day Supārśva told him that in the sky he had seen Rāvaṇa carrying away Sītā in his chariot. Sampāti also told them about a prediction. When with burnt wings he was living a precarious life a great sage called Niśākara had assured him that in the distant future when troops of Rāma would come in quest of Sītā by giving them proper information he was to be physically renovated. While Sampāti was telling all this, his burnt wings came back to their original form. He then flew away saying that Sītā would be rescued (*Rām* 4.59-63).

The lord of the feathered race was, however, Garuḍa, who was also called Garutmat Suparṇa. His origin is to be traced in the Vedic concept of Garutmat. The Garuḍas (Garulas) and Suparṇas (Supannas) occur in Buddhist literature as well. The history of this 'king of birds' cannot be dissociated from that of the Nāgas or the serpents. The Rāmāyanic version of the origin of the Nāgas (*Rām* 3.14.28ff) has been given above. The same story is repeated in the *Mbh* (1.60.54ff). Regarding the birth of Garuḍa we have the following legend. Kaśyapa had two wives, Kadru and Vinatā. The former wished to have for sons a thousand snakes all of equal splendour and the latter to bring forth two sons surpassing the sons of Kadru in all respects. After a long time Kadru brought forth a thousand eggs and Vinatā two. One thousand strong Nāgas were born of Kadru's eggs, but the twins of Vinatā did not appear. Mad with jealousy Vinatā broke one of the eggs and found in it an embryo with only the upper part developed. At this the child in the egg, Aruṇa, became angry and cursed his mother saying: 'Since you have prematurely broken this egg you will serve as a slave. However, the illustrious child of the other egg will deliver you from slavery.' So saying Aruṇa went to the sun and became his charioteer. In due time Garuḍa was born from the second egg (*Mbh* 1.14) One day when Uccaisravas, the horse of Indra, was passing through the sky, Kadru asked Vinatā: 'Tell me of what colour the horse is.' Vinatā answered: 'It is certainly white. Let us lay a wager upon it.' Kadru replied: 'I think that the horse is black in its tail. Bet with me that she who loses will become the other's slave.' Kadru then ordered her thousand sons to transform themselves into black hair and speedily cover the horse's tail. Next morning Kadru and Vinatā ran to see the horse and found that its tail was black. Thus Vinatā entered into a sate of slavery (*Mbh* 1.18-20). One day while Garuḍa was sitting with his mother, Kadru asked Vinatā to take her along with her Nāga children to an island in the remote quarter of the ocean and Garuḍa had to carry them all. They travelled from one island to another and sported in those places. Having learnt from his mother the cause of her slavery, Garuḍa approached the snakes and asked them how Vinatā could be freed. The snakes agreed to free Vinatā from bondage provided that Garuḍa would bring *amṛta* for them (*Mbh* 1.21-3). Garuḍa thereupon set off to bring *amṛta* which was in the possession of the gods. The mighty gods wielded various sharp-edged weapons against him but failed to obstruct his way. Overcome by the lord of the birds, the Sādhyas with the Gandharvas fled eastwards, the Vasus with the Rudras towards the south, the Ādityas towards the west and the twin Aśvins towards the north. The Yakṣas were also defeated. Then the mighty son of Vinatā, taking up the *amṛta* from the place where it was kept, rose on his wings with great speed. He was in possession of the *amṛta* but did not drink it. Seeing Garuḍa's restraint Viṣṇu came forward and decreed that he would be immortal and free from disease without drinking *amṛta,* and that he would be Viṣṇu's carrier and sit on the flagstaff of his car. Indra established friendship with him. Garuḍa said that his purpose in taking away the *amṛta* was to make his mother free from slavery. And if that was accomplished he had no objection if Indra had it back by any means. Thereafter Garuḍa went back to the snakes and set the *amṛta* on *kuśa* grass for them. The Nāgas freed Vinatā from slavery, but when they came to taste the *amṛta* they found that it was already stolen by Indra (*Mbh* 1.24-31).

Garuḍa's carrying off the ambrosia and his receiving Viṣṇu's favour are recorded also in the *Rām* (1.23.5ff; 3.30.5; 3.35.27ff). Here he is called Tārkṣya and Vainateya (Aruṇa also has the last title. *Rām* 4.58.28). In the *Rām* he is not active except as the vehicle of Viṣṇu. He, however, frightened away the snake-arrows of Indrajit and cured Rāma and his brother (*Rām* 6.50 33ff). Vainateya is said to have told Sagara how his sons might be revived, since he was the brother of Sagara's second wife Sumati (*Rām* 1.38.14). The Garuḍas and Garutmats were birds of prey. The Vainateyas lived in the sixth upper world (*Rām* 4.58.28; 6.105.22; 6.131.51).

As has been stated above, when Kadru asked her sons to transform themselves into black hair and cover the horse's tail, not all of them agreed. So Kadru cursed them that they would be consumed by fire during the snake-sacrifice of king Janamejaya (*Mbh* 1.18). The important serpents (Nāgas, also known as Pannagas and Uragas) were Śeṣa, Vāsuki, Airāvata, Takṣaka, Karkoṭaka, Dhanañjaya, Kālīya, Maṇināga, Piñjaraka and Elāpatra (*Mbh* 1.31). Among them Śeṣa left his mother and practised hard penance, living on air and rigidly observing his vows. As a reward he was given by Brahmā the task of holding the earth (*Mbh* 1.32). Against the background of Kadru's curse Vāsuki, lord of the serpents, held a consultation with his fellow-serpents intent upon doing what they deemed best for themselves. The wise serpent Elāpatra said that he had heard Brahmā saying that only the cruel and poisonous serpents would be destroyed in Janamejaya's sacrifice, but the virtuous and harmless snakes would survive, thanks to the effort of Āstīka, the son of the sage Jaratkāru (*Mbh* 1.34-5). Vāsuki's sister was also of the same name and at his request Jaratkāru agreed to marry her. Their son Āstīka grew up in the house of Vāsūki. He studied the Vedas and their branches. Though a boy he was sober and intelligent (*Mbh* 1.41-4). Then it so happened that king Parikṣit of the Kuru race in one of his hunting expeditions reached the hermitage of a sage, hungry and fatigued, and wanted to know of a deer pierced by him. As the sage was observing a vow of silence he did not speak. The king in anger thereupon placed on his shoulder a dead snake, and left. The sage's son Śṛṅgin was not present at that time, but when he saw his father bearing a dead snake on his shoulder, he uttered a curse that he who had done it would be bitten by the terrible serpent Takṣaka (*Mbh* 1.36-7). The news reached the king who remained well guarded. On the appointed day the serpents assuming the form of learned Brāhmaṇas entered the king's court and blessed him with *kuśa* grass, water and fruits. Impelled by fate the king with his ministers felt the desire to eat the fruit. The particular fruit within which Takṣaka had entered, was taken by the king himself. Breaking it he found Takṣaka in the form of a small worm who at once assumed his serpent form, coiled around the king's neck, and uttering a tremendous roar bit him (*Mbh* 1.38-40). Parikṣit's son and successor Janamejaya, in order to avenge his father's death, determined to exterminate the race of serpents. He arranged a great snake-sacrifice under the guidance of efficient priests. They poured clarified butter into the blazing fire uttering appropriate *mantras*. And the snakes began to fall into the blazing fire. Hundreds and thousands of snakes perished on the occasion. Takṣaka sought protection of Indra, but he, too, was dragged along with his protector towards the sacrificial hall (*Mbh* 1.42-8). Thereupon Vāsuki, through his sister, requested Āstīka to save the serpents from annihilation. Āstīka went to the place of sacrifice and impressed the king with his wisdom and personality. The king wanted to bestow on him a boon. Āstīka said, 'If you want to grant me a boon, let your sacrifice come to an end and let no more snakes fall into the fire.' The boon was granted and the serpents were relieved (*Mbh* 1.49-51).

In the *Rām* (3.14.7) Śeṣa is said to be one of the Prajāpatis. He is also called Deva, moon-faced, and of a thousand heads who encircles the world and eventually curls himself over Viṣṇu, one of his titles being *dharaṇīdhara* (*Rām* 4.40.49). His other name is Ananta because he is endless. Vāsuki was also a favourite of the gods. He served as the cord during the churning of the ocean. In consequence of the churning, black vapours with flames issued from his mouth (*Mbh* 1.16). The account of Janamejaya's snake-sacrifice shows that all distinction between the snakes and Nāga clans was lost. The snakes are here called indifferently Nāgas, Bhujaṅgamas, Sarpas, or Pannagas. In *Mbh* we find that Bhīma lost his senses after eating food mixed with poison from Duryodhana. The latter then bound him with cords and threw him into the Ganges. The senseless Bhīma sank down till he reached the Nāga kingdom. The Nāgas, furnished with fangs containing virulent venom, bit him. The poison which was already mingled in the blood of Bhima was neutralized by the snake poison. Bhīma regained his senses and received a warm reception in the realm of the Nāgas (*Mbh* 1.119.22ff). In the Nalopākhyāna we have the legend of Karkoṭaka Nāga. Having deserted Damayantī under the influence of Kali who was residing in him, king Nala saw a conflagration in the forest. In the midst of that he heard a voice introducing himself as the snake Karkoṭaka. He said that under the influence of a curse he was immobile and requested Nala to rescue him from the forest fire. Nala obliged. The period of the curse was over and Karkoṭaka regained mobility. Then he asked Nala to go a few steps forward. As Nala did this, the snake bit him. He told the bewildered Nala that he had intentionally deprived him of his beauty so that people might not recognize him. The poison was not to harm him, but it would torment the evil one which was residing in Nala's body. Then he advised him to go to Ayodhyā and present himself before king Ṛtuparna as a charioteer, by the name of Vāhuka (*Mbh* 3.63.1-24).

There are instances of human beings also sometimes being transformed into serpents, especially owing to curses. The story of Dundubha whom Ruru was about to kill is an example. This poisonless serpent was formerly a sage whose name was Sahasrapat. When he was young he made a mock snake and in frolic attempted to frighten another sage named Khagama with it. The latter cursed that he bacame a snake (*Mbh* 1.10-12). But more suggestive is the story of Nahuṣa. Once when the Pāṇḍavas were staying at Dvaitavana Bhīma was caught by a great python. Bhīma could not free himself from his coil. The python introduced himself as king Nahuṣa of the days of yore and said that he was transformed into a serpent owing to a curse, the period of which could end if someone gave right answers to his questions. Naturally Bhīma was incapable of anwering his questions and he gave up his hope for life. Then Yudhiṣṭhira in search of Bhīma came there. The serpent asked him to go away, otherwise he would be his food for the next day. But Yudhiṣṭhira anwered all his questions and freed Nahuṣa from the curse. Nahuṣa said that he was a remote ancestor of the Pāṇḍavas. He was the ruler of heaven and earth. Thousands of sages used to carry his palanquin. Once in pride he had touched the sage Agastya with his foot and the sage's curse was that he would fall on earth as a serpent (*Mbh* 3.175-8). Again there are cases where the Nāgas were as good as human beings in appearance, speech and character. Arjuna's marriage with Ulupī, the daughter of a Nāga king, is an instance. One day while Arjuna was bathing in the Ganges, Ulupī had dragged him into the Nāga region and introducing herself as the daughter of Kauravya Nāga passionately requested to marry her. Needless to say a philanderer like Arjuna was not one to refuse such a tempting offer (*Mbh* 1.206.1-34). We have the legend of the Brāhmaṇa Dharmāraṇya who went to the Nāga king Padmanābha to obtain spiritual knowledge from him. This foremost of the Nāgas was not only devoted to righteousness, but had direct knowledge of the supreme soul. And this knowledge he had imparted to the Brāhmaṇa Dharmāraṇya who admitted that the deities were not superior to the Nāga chief in any respect. He told his wife that the Nāgas were by no means inferior to the gods, the Asuras and celestial sages. Beings with great energy, they were swift, had fragrance, and were capable of granting boons. They deserved to be worshipped and followed by others in their train. The Nāga chief taught the Brāhmaṇa the virtues of plain living and high thinking (*Mbh* 12.340-53).

NOTES AND REFERENCES

All the references to the *Mahābhārata* in this chapter are from the Critical Edition published by the Bhandarkar Oriental Research Institute of Poona. Only a few instances which do not occur in the Critical Edition, such as the episode of Arjuna and Urvaśī, are taken from the Kumbhakonam edition. Among the secondary sources the following works deserve consideration. V. Fausböll, *Indian Mythology*, Copenhagen, 1902; E.W. Hopkins, *The Great Epic of India: Its Character and Origin*, New York, 1901; *Epic Mythology*, Strassburg, 1915; J.N. Farquhar, *An Outline of the Religious Literature of India*, Oxford, 1920; M. Winternitz, *History of Indian Literature*, vol. I, Calcutta, 1927; C.V. Vaidya, *The Riddle of the Rāmāyaṇa*, Bombay, 1906; *Epic India*, Bombay, 1907; N.V. Thandani, *Mystery of the Mahābhārata*, 5 vols., Karachi, 1931-5; G.I. Held, *The Mahābhārata: An Ethnological Study*, London, 1935; J.C. Majumdar, *Ethics of the Mahābhārata*, Calcutta, 1953; H.C. Raychaudhuri, *Studies in Indian Antiquities*, Calcutta, 1932; A.D. Pusalkar, *Studies in the Epics and Purāṇas of India*, Bombay, 1955; S.N. Vyas, *India in the Rāmāyaṇa Age*, Delhi, 1967; S.K. Chatterji, *The Rāmāyaṇa: Its Characters, Genesis, Expansion, Exodus: A Resumé*, Calcutta, 1978; J.L. Brocklington, *Righteous Rāma: The Evolution of the Epic*, Delhi, 1984; A. Sarkar, *A Study on the Rāmāyaṇas*, Calcutta, 1987; N.N. Bhattacharyya, *Indian Religious Historiography*, vol. I, New Delhi, 1996.

CHAPTER VI

Puranic Demonology–I

The major Purāṇas began to be composed in the beginning of the Christian era. Like the epics, the composition of the Purāṇas was in a state of flux. The *Mahābhārata* was composed between 400 BC and AD 400 and the *Rāmāyana* between 200 BC and AD 200. So it appears that before the epics assumed their present form, the composition of the Purāṇas was already in the move. It is therefore natural to expect that some of the Puranic materials were incorporated in the epics and much epic material made its way into the Purāṇas. Among the major Purāṇas composed during the Gupta period, that is before AD 600, mention may be made of the *Viṣṇu*, *Matsya*, *Mārkaṇḍeya* and part of the *Vāyu*. In between the epics and the major Purāṇas fall the Uttarākāṇḍa of the *Rāmāyaṇa* and the *Harivaṃśa* of the *Mahābhārata*. The former is a later addition. It contains numerous myths and legends similar to those which occur also in the *Mbh* and the Purāṇas and have nothing to do with the Rāma legend. Even in the Uttarākāṇḍa itself there are a few sections which are regarded as *prakṣipta* or later interpolations. The *Harivaṃśa* is regarded as a supplement (*khila*) to the *Mbh*. It is not the work of a single composer. It is a jumble of texts—legends, myths and hymns—for the glorification of Viṣṇu. The connection of the *Hari* with the *Mbh* itself is purely external. The same Vaiśampāyana who is said to have recited the whole *Mbh* to Janamejaya is also regarded as the reciter of the *Hari*. The latter consists of three great sections, the first of which is entitled *Harivaṃśaparvan*. It begins in the manner of the Purāṇas with a rather confused account of creation and all sorts of mythological narratives containing the ancestry of the gods and the demons, rivalry between Viśvāmitra and Vasiṣṭha, genealogy of the solar and lunar dynasties, and so on. The second section is known as *Viṣṇuparvan* and deals almost exclusively with Kṛṣṇa. The third section is called the *Bhaviṣyaparvan*, which is a loose collection of Purāṇa texts. The text of the *Hari* consists of 16,374 verses arranged in 325 chapters.

The *Uttarākāṇḍa* (7) presents very interesting demon lore. It begins with the origin of the Rākṣasas (*Rām* 7.2-4) which has already been discussed in the preceding chapter. Rāvaṇa (Daśagrīva for his ten heads), Kumbhakarṇa and Vibhīṣaṇa performed severe austerities. Rāvaṇa sacrificed nine heads and when he was about to sever his only remaining head, Brahmā came to grant him a boon. Rāvaṇa asked for immortality, but he had to remain satisfied with the boon that he was not to be destroyed by Pakṣīs, Nāgas, Yakṣas, Daityas, Dānavas, Rākṣasas, or Devas. Kumbhakarṇa, being confused by Sarasvatī, received the boon of deep sleep for a long time (*Rām* 7.10). When Sumālī, their maternal grandfather, heard of the boons he came to Rāvaṇa with his four councillors, Mārīca, Prahasta, Virūpākṣa, and Mahodara. He told Rāvaṇa they had been banished from Laṅkā and exhorted him to take the city from Kubera. Rāvaṇa was at first reluctant, but instigated by Prahasta he sent an army towards Laṅkā and asked Kubera to vacate the city for the Rākṣasas. Thereupon Kubera left Laṅkā and retired to the holy region of the Kailāśa mountains. Rāvaṇa's wife Mandodarī was the daughter of the Dānava Maya and the nymph Hemā. Maya had two other sons, Māyāvī and Dundubhi. Meghanāda who was also known as Indrajit was born of Mandodarī. Kumbhakarṇa's wife was Vajrajvālā, grand-daughter of Vairocana and Vibhiṣaṇa's wife was Saramā, daughter of the Gandharva king Śailuṣa. Rāvaṇa's sister Śūrpanakhā was given in marriage to the demon Vidyujjihva (*Rām* 7.11-12). Having established himself at Laṅkā and encouraged by the boon of invincibility he received from Brahmā, Rāvaṇa unleashed a reign of terror in the three worlds. Kubera then sent an envoy to Rāvaṇa requesting him to stop his acts of depredations. At this Rāvaṇa was furious and launched an invasion against Kubera. In the battle both the Yakṣas and the Rākṣasas showed great valour. But Kubera was worsted and Rāvaṇa brought down the Puṣpaka chariot as a war trophy (*Rām* 7.13-15).

Victorious Rāvaṇa while returning towards Laṅkā was stopped by Nandīśvara, the attendant of Śiva, who asked him to go back, as Śiva was then sporting with Pārvatī in that hilly region. Rāvaṇa laughed at the monkey face of Nandī. At this Nandī cursed him that he was to be destroyed by apes. Rāvaṇa paid no heed and pulled down the rock which was obstructing the course of his chariot. As the rock was lifted Śiva pressed it with his toe. Rāvaṇa cried out under the pressure and felt the panic of living burial. Finding no other means to survive he began to sing the glory of Śiva and tried desperately to appease him. At this Śiva was satisfied and let him go (*Rām* 7.16). But his wicked nature did not change. Once he met an ascetic lady Vedavatī and wanted to know her identity. Vedavatī replied that her father, the saintly king Kuśadhvaja, wished to marry her to Viṣṇu, but the demon Śumbha slew her father. She was henceforth engaged in prayers to avenge her father's death. But Rāvaṇa tried to molest her. Vedavatī then cursed him saying that she would be the cause of his destruction. With these words she entered the flames and was reborn as Sītā (*Rām* 7.17) Then Rāvaṇa went to the Uśīravija country where king Marutta was performing a sacrifice. Seeing Rāvaṇa the gods disguised themselves as animals. Rāvaṇa entered in the form of an unclean dog and challenged king Marutta. The latter was ready to fight, but the priests suggested that he should complete his sacrifice. So he desisted from fighting. Rāvaṇa's minister Śuka convinced his master that he was victorious (*Rām* 7.18). Meanwhile Rāvaṇa went around the world and challenged every powerful king to battle. Duṣyanta, Suratha, Gādhi, Gaya, Purūravas and other kings acknowledged defeat. Rāvaṇa then arrived at Ayodhyā and challenged king Anaraṇya. After offering a brave resistance Anaraṇya was defeated. Before his death he foretold that Rāvaṇa would meet his death in the hands of an Ikṣvāku hero named Rāma (*Rām* 7.19).

Nārada, the divine sage, in the mean time, convinced Rāvaṇa that there was no need to torture human beings because men are subject to death. It was better to conquer Yama, the lord of death. Rāvaṇa was encouraged and Nārada himself went to the realm of death to witness Rāvaṇa's fight with Yama. Rāvaṇa's chariot was seen glittering like the sun and in that light he saw how people were suffering in hell. Rāvaṇa released all persons from torture. The minions of Death, the ghosts and goblins, at once attacked him but were worsted. Then Yama himself went to fight against Rāvaṇa which lasted for several nights. At last Yama raised his fatal sceptre and Rāvaṇa was scorched by its intense glare. Meanwhile Brahmā appeared on the spot and said that Rāvaṇa had been rendered invincible by his own boon and his words would prove false if Yama killed him. Hence Yama withdrew from battle and Rāvaṇa proclaimed that he was victorious (*Rām* 7.20-2). Thereafter Rāvaṇa entered the ocean to reach the nether region, the abode of the Urages (serpents). He entered Bhogavatī, the city of Vāsuki, and reduced the Nāgas to submission. Then Rāvaṇa proceeded to the city of jewels, the home of Daityas called Nivātakavacas who were extremely powerful. A terrible fight ensued between the two groups of demons and at Brahmā's interference the Nivātakavacas concluded peace with Rāvaṇa, who stayed at their place for some time and learnt to create various forms of illusions from them. Then Rāvaṇa came to the city of Aśmana where he fought against the Kālakeya Daityas and killed Vidyujjihva who happened to be the husband of his sister Śūrpanakhā. Then he went to the city of the god Varuṇa and defeated his son. He however, missed Varuṇa because the latter was listening to songs in the abode of Brahmā. When he returned to Laṅkā his sister Śūrpanakhā came to him with tears in her eyes and said that it was for him that she had become a widow. Rāvaṇa apologized to his sister and sent her to live under Khara's guardianship in the Daṇḍaka forest (*Rām* 7.23-4).

Rāvaṇa captured many beautiful women and landed at Laṅkā when Vibhīṣaṇa informed him that their sister Kumbhīnaśī, grand daughter of Mālyavāna, was abducted by the demon Madhu. Hearing this, Rāvaṇa was enraged and attacked Madhupura, the city of Madhu. But at Kumbhīnaśī's request he gave recognition to her marriage with Madhu and took the latter as his ally (*Rām* 7.25). One day Rāvaṇa saw the beautiful nymph Rambhā and made advances to her. At this Rambhā said that since she was his daughter-in-law, engaged to Nalakubera, son of Kubera, Rāvaṇa should not look lustfully at her. But Rāvana said that Apsarases had no husbands and even the gods treated them as wives. He threw Rambhā down on the ground and enjoyed her. After her release Rambhā came to Nalakubera, threw herself at his feet, and narrated everything to him. Then Nalakubera cursed Rāvaṇa saying, 'if henceforward he uses force upon any woman against her will his head will instantly burst into pieces' (*Rām* 7.26). Rāvaṇa next arrived at the realm of Indra. All the gods gathered to fight him, and a terrible battle commenced between the gods and the Rākṣasas. Indra fought resolutely, but in vain. Rāvaṇa's son Meghanāda availed himself of his black art and made himself invisible. Indra was exhausted and Rāvaṇa and Meghanāda repaired to Laṅkā with Indra as their prisoner. After the defeat of Indra all the gods headed by Brahmā came to Laṅkā and requested Rāvaṇa to release Indra. Rāvaṇa wanted immortality as the ransom for Indra's release. Brahmā said that there is none immortal on earth and requested him to ask for another boon. This time Rāvaṇa said: 'When I shall worship fire with due rites and shall set out for the conquest of my enemies, a chariot yoked with steeds will rise from the fire, and none will be above to slay me so long as I shall be seated on that chariot: but I shall be destroyed, if I be engaged in fight before the completion of my worship with due rites.' This boon was granted by Brahmā and Indra was then released (*Rām* 7.27-30).

But there were cases of Rāvaṇa's defeat and humiliation. Once upon a time Rāvaṇa arrived at Māhiṣmatī city. Its king Arjuna, belonging to the

Haihaya dynasty, was out sporting with women in the Narmadā. Rāvaṇa then went to fight against Arjuna. Arjuna's men asked Rāvaṇa to accept their hospitality. But Rāvaṇa mistook courtesy for weakness and began to smash Arjuna's forces. Then Arjuna came out with the mace, gave Rāvaṇa a sound beating and imprisoned him. Having heard of Rāvaṇa's discomfiture, his father, sage Pulastya, moved by fatherly affection, came to Arjuna and prayed for his release. Since Arjuna had great respect for Pulastya, he agreed to release Rāvaṇa (*Rām* 7.31-3). But Rāvaṇa learnt nothing from this. He came to Kiṣkindhyā to fight Vālī. The latter was then in meditation on the shore of the southern sea. As Rāvaṇa hastened to him, Vālī, who did not break his chanting of the Vedas, silently took Rāvaṇa in his clutch and rose up in the sky. Vālī performed his *sandhyā* rites on the banks of the four oceans without any hurry, putting Rāvaṇa under his armpit. Then he arrived at the garden of Kiṣkindhyā and released him. The latter, thus divested of his pride and arrogance made friendship with Vālī (*Rām* 7.38). In *prakṣipta* 1 of *Rām* 7 it is stated that while returning from the abode of Varuṇa, Rāvaṇa saw a house. Entering the house he found a black giant-like person guarding a room with a terrible-looking club in hand. His very appearance caused panic in Rāvaṇa's heart. His tongue became dry. His body began to tremble. That great person said softly with a smile: 'O king of the Rākṣasas. Tell me frankly what do you want? Do you want to fight with me or with the one who is inside the room?' Rāvaṇa was puzzled. The gate-keeper told him that the one who was inside the room was none other than Bali. Hearing the name of Bali, the celebrated lord of the demons, Rāvaṇa entered the room. Bali took him on his lap and asked the purpose of his visit. Rāvaṇa said that he had come to rescue Bali from his captivity. Bali said: 'My boy, the person whom you have seen guarding the gate is none other than Kāla, the personification of eternal time. Every being in the three worlds is his victim.' There was a ring in a corner of the room. Bali asked Rāvaṇa to bring that ring. But with all his strength Rāvaṇa failed to lift it. Bali said: 'That was the ear-ring of my ancestor Hiraṇyakaśipu.' Bali thus humbled his pride and said a few words to him about the greatness of Viṣṇu.

Apart from Rāvaṇa the *Utarakāṇḍa* refers to another demon known as Lavaṇāsura. Formerly there was a powerful king in the Ikṣvāku line named Māndhātā. He made preparations for the conquest of the three worlds. Indra, was frightened and approached Māndhātā and said that he should first reduce the whole earth to submission. Then Māndhātā asked Indra to tell him who was there on earth who had not yet been brought under his subjection. Indra mentioned Lavaṇa, Madhu's son, residing in

Madhuvana (Mathura). Māndhātā fought him, but was defeated and killed. Long after this event, when Rāma was the king of Ayodhyā, the sage Cyavana came to him and said that the cruel Lavaṇāsura had grown quite formidable and was a tyrant, especially over the hermits. Rāma then deputed Śatrughna to destroy Lavaṇa. The latter had a formidable lance which Rudra had presented Madhu, the son of Lola who married Kumbhīnaśī, a sister of Rāvaṇa. Their son Lavaṇa inherited that lance which kept one invincible. Rāma advised Śatrughna that Lavaṇa was to be attacked in such a time when the lance could not be with him. Śatrughna then set out for Lavaṇa with his troops. He noticed that every day at dawn Lavaṇa set out in search of food. That time he did not carry the sacred lance. So when he was out Śatrughna besieged the entrance of the Madhuvana. At midday when Lavaṇa returned with his food Śatrughna challenged him to a duel. But the Asura was more powerful and defeated him. Thereupon the desparate Śatrughna took up an irresistible shaft, which Rāma had given him knowing full well that it would be required – the shaft by which previously Madhu and Kaitabha was destroyed by Viṣṇu. Śatrughna fixed it on his bow and sent it flying towards Lavaṇa. It at once pierced Lavaṇa's heart and he fell dead on the ground (*Rām* 7.60-9). The Lavaṇa episode is also found in *Hari* 48. He challenged Rāma saying that the destruction of Rāvaṇa for an ordinary woman was not justified and that he had violated the rules of asceticism. At Rāma's command Śatrughna killed Lavaṇa.

Like the two epics the *Hari* also describes the origins of demons. From Diti, the wife of Kaśyapa, were born two sons, Hiraṇyakaśipu and Hiraṇyākṣa, and a daughter Siṃhikā who was married to the demon Vipracitti. Hiraṇyakaśipu had four sons—Hrāda, Prahrāda (Prahlāda), Anuhrāda and Saṃhrāda. Prahlāda's son was Virocana, and the latter's son was Bali. Among the sons of Bali, Bāṇa was most important. He became a favourite of Śiva. Bāṇa's son was Indradamana. Likewise Hiraṇyākṣa had five sons. From Danu, another wife of Kaśyapa were born the Dānavas among whom Śambara, Vipracitti, Śarabha and Mahāgiri were famous. Among the descendants of Vipracitti Namuci, Vātāpi, Ilvala and Rāhu deserve special mention. The Nivātakavacas were born of Saṃhrāda. From Tāmrā, another wife of Kaśyapa, were born seven daughters. Aruṇa and Garuḍa, sons of Vinatā, and the serpents born of Kadru and Surasā, were all of Tāmrā's lineage (*Hari* 3). Brahmā bestowed lordship of the Daityas and Dānavas upon Prahlāda, of the Pitṛs upon Yama, of the Yakṣas, Rakṣasas, Bhūtas, and Piśācas upon Mahādeva, of the Gandharvas upon Citraratha, of the serpents upon Takṣaka, of the

Nāgas upon Ananta, of the birds upon Garuḍa and of the Apsarases upon Anaṅga (*Hari* 4). Pṛthu, son of Veṇa, was the first to milk the earth and received crops by imagining Svāyambhūva Manu as the calf. He received ghee for sacrifice, which became his food. In the same way the serpents milking the earth received poison, the Asuras received *māyā* or illusory power, the Yakṣas received invinsibility, the Rakṣas, Piśācas, and Bhūtas received blood, the Gandharvas and Apsarases received fragrance and the mountains herbs. What they received became the means of their subsistence (*Hari* 4).

The demon lore of the *Harivaṃśa* is mainly concerned with the exploits of Kṛṣṇa or of Viṣṇu in various forms of his incarnations. Among the earlier legends the story of the destruction of the demon Dhundhu by king Kuvalāśva of the Ikṣvāku line is directly adopted, without modification or fabrication, from the *Mbh* (*Hari* 11). It should be pointed out in this connection that in both the *Mbh* and the *Hari* the person who excited king Bṛhadāśva and his son Kuvalāśva against the demon was the sage Utaṅka, who was also responsible for persuading king Janamejaya to perform the snake-sacrifice. In *Hari* 41 there is a summary treatment of Viṣṇu's destruction of various demons in his different incarnations. A serious war between the gods and the Asuras is described as Tārākāmaya. Soma abducted Tārā, the wife of Bṛhaspati. Notwithstanding requests made by the gods and the sages he did not return Tārā to her husband. Śukra, the preceptor of the Asuras, was the supporter of Soma, and as such the Asuras assembled to fight on behalf of Soma against the gods, who were supporters of Bṛhaspati. Because the conflict was centred on Tārā, the war came to be known as Tārakāmaya (*Hari* 25). Viṣṇu himself led the divine army, while the Asura army was led by such Daityas and Dānavas as Maya, Tāraka, Virocana, Hayagrīva, Rāhu and others. The Gandharvas and Yakṣas participated on either side. The Asuras employed *māyā* or illusion which covered the battlefield in the form of fire. Previously this particular fire was produced from the thigh of Ūrva who gave it to his disciple Hiraṇyakaśipu, the lord of the demons. Then the moon-god began to sprinkle dew on the fire and it was eventually extinguished. The demon Maya was fighting with the help of his fetters of illusions. Viṣṇu resisted the attack by creating counter illusion. Then Asura Kālanemi took the lead and defeated the Lokapālas. He hurled a shaft at Suparṇa (Garuḍa) which wounded him. Thereupon Viṣṇu expanded his body and cut off the head of Kālanemi with his blazing disc and shattered the Asura army (*Hari* 43-8).

The *Viṣṇuparvan* of the *Hari* deals with Kṛṣṇa's career in which his fight with numerous demons is described. It is said that the demons who fought and died in the Tārakāmaya battle were reborn on earth, e.g. Kālanemi as Kaṃsa, Hayagrīva as Keśin, Lamba as Pralamba, Khara as Dhenuka, Maya as Cānuka and Tāraka as Muṣṭika. But they were earthly demons and compared to their earlier forms essentially rustic. And the legends themselves are dull and monotonous, as the characters contained in them. The manner in which the demons are killed is also crude. Lack of imagination characterizes all the legends. Kṛṣṇa as an infant killed the demoness Putanā, who came to him in the form of a vulture, simply by sucking her breast (*Hari* 62). While still a boy he subjugated the Kālīya Nāga who was residing with his family in the Yamunā and poisoning its water. Kṛṣṇa subjugated Kālīya by standing on its hood and forced him to leave the river and settle in the ocean (*Hari* 68). On the bank of Yamunā near the Govardhana hill lived the demon Dhenuka whose form was an ass. While Balarāma and Kṛṣṇa were plucking palm fruits, this ass-demon rushed towards Balarāma and raised his foreleg to strike him. Balarāma killed him (*Hari* 69). The demon Pralamba mixed with Kṛṣṇa and Balarāma as a shepherd and at an opportune moment assuming a huge fearful form carried away Balarāma. The latter was at first bewildered, but when Kṛṣṇa by his words reminded him of his prowess, Balarāma inflicted a crushing blow upon Pralamba's head, sufficient to kill him (*Hari* 70). One day while Kṛṣṇa was tending the cows in the field the demon Ariṣṭa attacked him in the form of a violent bull. Kṛṣṇa caught him by the horns and began to twist his head in consequence of which his neck broke and he fell down dead (*Hari* 77). Kaṃsa employed Keśi, the horse-faced demon, to kill Kṛṣṇa, but the latter pushed his hand into his mouth and put him to death by suffocation (*Hari* 80). Kaṃsa and his warriors were killed by Kṛṣṇa (*Hari* 84-6), but they did not possess any special demonic attribute, except that they were very powerful. Kaṃsa is however said to have been fathered by a demon called Drumila.

The story of the Asura Naraka has many aspects and it has been reproduced in the Purāṇas from different viewpoints. The Puranic accounts of Narakāsura are anomalous. Naraka's ancestry is also problematic. He is said to be a son of Viṣṇu borne by Pṛthivī or the earth. He was pious. Though he was a womanizer like Kṛṣṇa or Indra, unlike most other demons, was well behaved to others. However, in the *Harivaṃśa* account we find that Naraka was a demon who abducted the daughter of Viśvakarman having assumed the form of an elephant. He was the ruler of Prāgjyotiṣapura or Kāmarūpa in the Brahmaputra valley and with the help of the Dānavas and Rākṣasas amassed immense wealth and collected lovely maidens from the Gandharvas, gods, and human beings for the sake of his own pleasure. For them he built a city on the Maṇiparvata. He had four commanders named Hayagrīva, Nisunda, Pañcanada and Muru (*Hari* 120). Naraka even had stolen the ear-rings of Aditi. Owing to Indra's insistence Viṣṇu agreed to destroy Naraka. Accompanied by a divine army commanded by Indra, Viṣṇu came to the territory of Naraka. He had a terrible encounter with Muru. Other generals of Naraka such as Nisunda, Pañcanada, and Hayagrīva rushed to assist Muru. But they too were defeated and killed. Entering Prāgjyotiṣa, Viṣṇu blew his conch. Having heard that tremendous sound Naraka came out in a decorated chariot with thousands of heroic attendants. After his valiant struggle he was defeated, and Viṣṇu beheaded him with his disc. After his death, the earth, assuming the form of a woman and handing two *kuṇḍalas* (rings) over to him, said: 'O Lord, you have given to me this Naraka and have taken him back to you once again. You may do whatever you like, but now receive these *kuṇḍalas* and maintain the subjects of my son' (*Hari* 121).

The legend of the destruction of Ṣaṭpura is an extension of that of the description of Tripura. It is a Śaivite legend in which Vaiṣṇavite elements and the Kṛṣṇa narrative have been grafted. The *Mbh* legend of Tripura has been narrated earlier. The three demons —their names vary in different Purāṇas—symbolically represent the coordination of the entire Asura clan residing in three cities or forts (*tripura*). The legend had it that the demons were destined to be exterminated when under special circumstances the three *puras* or forts would be joined to each other and pierced by a single shaft. This piercing was done by Śiva who thus destroyed Tripura, symbolizing the Asura power in totality manifested in its existence at three places. This symbolism is, however, dropped in the *Harivaṃśa* account in which the three chiefs were ordinary aerial demons who were destroyed by Śiva, but with Viṣṇu's assistance. The account itself is piecemeal. It begins with a description of Asuras of three castles and their movements in atmosphere. Then it says that the demons under the leadership of Sūryanābha and Candranābha obstructed the ways of the gods. This led to a conflict between the gods and the Asuras. The gods led by Śiva were initially defeated. However, the battle was resumed. Śivá's chariot did sink in the ground. Śiva was depressed. Then Viṣṇu in the form of a bull raised the chariot and Śiva revived his original form. With three arrows he shattered the three *puras* of the Asuras. The entire account is incoherent and inconsistent (Hari 323). In the episode of the destruction of Ṣaṭpura it is said that Śiva spared many Dānavas who were virtuous. They practised severe austerities and hence Brahmā wanted to grant them a boon. They wanted the power to defeat Śiva who had exterminated their clan. This boon was not granted. Instead, they received invincibility against other gods and six cities/forts (*ṣaṭpura*) under the earth, where they could live in peace and prosperity. In the Ṣaṭpura a Brāhmaṇa named Brahmadatta was performing the Aśvamedha sacrifice. The Daityas living there demanded a share of *soma* offered in the sacrifice, the daughters of Brahmadatta and valuable articles stored there. When Brahmadatta refused the demon Nikumbha and his associates forcibly abducted his daughters. Then Brahmadatta remembered Kṛṣṇa, Balarāma and Gada. Kṛṣṇa sent his son Pradyumna to rescue the daughters of Brahmadatta and he himself advanced with a large Yādava army. Meanwhile the sage Nārada tactfully misguided Nikumbha, advising him to bring in his favour the assembled kings by distributing among them wealth and the fifty daughters of Brahmadatta. The kings agreed to side with the Daityas in the battle. Among these kings were Duryodhana, Śiśupāla, Drupada, Rukmī, Śalya, Śakuni and the allies of the Kauravas. Kṛṣṇa, Baladeva, Sātyaki, Pradyumna, Śāmba, Aniruddha and other Yādava chiefs desperately fought against the Asura Nikumbha and his allies. When the battle took a severe turn Nandin, the attendant of Śiva, gave Pradyumna a special weapon of Śiva by which he put all the hostile kings in fetters. But Nikumbha remained invincible because he was favoured by the boon of immortality. The five Pāṇḍava brothers who were also fighting the Asuras could do nothing. Kṛṣṇa explained to them that the demon Nikumbha had three forms. One was his ascetic form which had been engaged in serving Aditi. The second form was destroyed by Kṛṣṇa during the time of the abduction of Bhānumati. His third form was Ṣaṭpura. While fighting with Kṛṣṇa, Nikumbha entered a cave. Kṛṣṇa chased him there. Then a voice was heard from the sky which advised Kṛṣṇa to cut his head off with the disc. Kṛṣṇa having saluted Śiva did so (*Hari* 141-3). While in the Tripura legend Śiva became victorious with the help of Viṣṇu, in the Ṣaṭpura legend the reverse had happened.

Diti, mother of the demons, seeing that her sons had perished in the hands of the gods, begged of Kaśyapa a son quite capable of vanquishing all gods. Kaśyapa assured her that she would have such a son. He would defeat every god, with the exception of Śiva who was eternally invincible. That son was Andhaka who became a terror to the gods and the three worlds. Bṛhaspati on behalf of the gods requested the divine sage Nārada to find a means of killing Andhaka. He went to the Mandara garden where Śiva was staying and brought a garland of flowers unparalled in beauty and fragrance. Seeing that garland Andhaka said that the colour and fragrance of the flowers were enchanting and asked where these could be had. Nārada said that these were from Śiva's garden where no one had the right to enter without permission. The sage also hinted that it was beyond Andhaka's capacity to have flowers from Śiva's realm. This injured the pride of Andhaka who with his followers went to ravage Śiva's garden. Initially Śiva was indifferent, but when Andhaka had transgressed the limit of propriety, Śiva killed him with a stroke of his trident (*Hari* 144-5).

The Andhakāsura legend of the subsequent Purāṇas is, however, different from this version. The slaying of the demon Nikumbha in his second form has been treated separately in the *Harivaṃśa*. He abducted Bhānumatī of the Yādava lineage and Kṛṣṇa, along with his son Pradyumna and the third Pāṇḍava Arjuna, chased the demon. The latter could not cross the Gokarṇa mountain which was the abode of Śiva and taking advantage of the situation Pradyumna rescued Bhānumatī. Arjuna with his arrows limited the space of Nikumbha's movement. But the Asura fought with his power of illusion (*māyā*) and stole Arjuna. Pradyumna also possessed some magical powers with which he could locate the invisible Nikumbha in space. Thereupon Kṛṣṇa cut off his head with his divine disc. Arjuna was also found out. The girl Bhānumatī was then given in marriage to the youngest Pāṇḍava, Sahadeva (*Hari* 148).

There are a few legends in which the traditional method of describing the fights between the gods and the demons was abandoned and attempts were made to make them more interesting. The legend of the Asura Vajranābha may be cited here as an illustration. This demon, pleasing Brahmā, received two boons. The first was that he could not be killed by any god and the second was that no one, not even the wind, would be able to enter his realm without his permission. But there was a loop-hole. This boon did not preclude the probability of his being killed by human or semidivine agencies. Accordingly, emboldened by the boons and following tradition, the demon wanted to conquer the three worlds. When he went to the heaven and demanded the submission of the gods, a frightened Indra requested him to wait till a sacrifice of his father Kaśyapa, who was to negotiate with him in the matter of war and peace, was over. Meanwhile he went to Kṛṣṇa at the city of Dvārakā for consultation. There Vasudeva held an Aśvamedha sacrifice in which an artiste named Bhadra pleased the audience with his wonderful dance. The assembled sages asked him for boons. Requested by Indra and Kṛṣṇa, the goddess Sarasvatī possessed Bhadra under whose influence the latter prayed that he may go to any place unhindered, and be indestructibile. The prayer was granted and he began to travel the three worlds, exhibiting his artistry performance to all kinds of beings. The demon Vajranābha had a beautiful and virtuous daughter named Prabhāvatī. Indra asked the divine swans to go to the city of Vajrapura and to tell Prabhāvatī about the beauty, qualities and valour of Pradyumna, the son of Kṛṣṇa, so that she falls in love with him. As Vajranābha liked the divine swans they had no difficulty entering the city. Their chief Śucīmukhī, an expert in conversation, was able to influence Prabhāvatī's mind in favour of Pradyumna. Śucimukhī also had a friendly talk with Vajranābha, in the course of which the latter came to know of the dramatic talent of Bhadra and wanted to see his performances. In the dramatic party of Bhadra, the Yādava heroes joined as actors in disguise. Meanwhile the swan Śucimukhī informed Prabhāvatī that Pradyumna had arrived at Vajrapura as an actor. Thereafter Pradyumna and Prabhāvatī used to meet secretly. Vajranābha had another brother named Sunābha who had two daughters, Candrāvatī and Guṇavatī. They were introduced to Kṛṣṇa's cousin Gada and his other son Śāmba. In the course of things the three Asura girls became pregnant. They delivered their sons in secret and by the grace of Indra the sons, grew to be valiant. When Vajranābha came to know of all this he was furious and ordered the arrest of the Yādava princes who had seduced the maidens of his family and destroyed their virtue. The three Yādava princes, Pradyumna, Gada and Śāmba began to fight with the Asuras and they were assisted by Jayanta, the son of Indra. Kṛṣṇa and Indra came there being carried by Garuḍa and in the terrible fight that ensued Vajranābha was killed by Pradyumna. His kingdom was divided into four parts, three of which were given to the sons of Prabhāvatī, Candrāvatī and Guṇavatī respectively, and the fourth to Jayanta's son Vijaya (*Hari* 149-55).

The story of the Vedic Asura Śambara has also assumed a new colour in the *Harivaṃśa*. Madana or Kāmadeva, who was burnt and reduced to ashes in the wrath of Śiva, was reborn as Pradyumna. When he was a child of seven days he was stolen by Asura Śambara. On seeing the child Śambara's wife Māyāvatī understood that in her previous existence she was the wife of this child who was none other than Kāmadeva. So instead of bringing the child up with motherly care she handed it over to an efficient nurse. When Pradyumna grew up and became a youth, Māyāvatī tried to attract him sexually. Since Pradyumna knew her to be his mother he took offence at this. Māyāvatī then disclosed his real identity. When Pradyumna learnt that he was the son of Kṛṣṇa and Rukminī and that he was stolen by Śambara he challenged the demon. An angry Śambara asked his other sons to kill Pradyumna, but they were all slain. His generals Durdhara, Ketumāli, Śatruhantā and Pramardana had also the same fate. Thereupon Śambara himself came out and used his illusory powers against Pradyumna. The latter then remembered the goddess Pārvatī with devotion and hit the demon with his *vaiṣṇava* arrow. Śambara was killled instantly. Pradyumna then returned to Dvārakā with Māyāvatī, whom Kṛṣṇa and Rukminī had accepted as their daughter-in-law (*Hari* 162-6). This story has some dramatic elements, but is not so rich as that of Vajranābha.

More interesting is the story of Bāṇa who was the son of the celebrated Asura Bali. Pleased with his severe austerities Śiva and Pārvatī accepted him as their son. The demon then became invincible and became a war-monger. One day he went to Śiva and told him that since there was no one to fight, he was depressed. Śiva smilingly asked him not to worry. When his flag with its peacock symbol would fall he was to be led to a war automatically. A happy Bāṇa conveyed this news to his minister Kuṣmāṇḍa, but the latter, wise as he was, smelt disaster. At that time the flag fell and Bāṇa was happy about the impending war, but his minister was sad. Bāṇa's daughter Uṣā wanted to fall in love with someone. The goddess Pārvatī, having understood her intention, said that she was destined to marry a person who would appear in a dream and have sexual union with her in that condition. This eventually happened, and a distressed Uṣā sought the advice of Ramā, her friend who was the daughter of the minister Kuṣmāṇḍa. Ramā referred what had happened to their friend Citralekhā who had magical powers and identified the man concerned. He was Aniruddha, son of Pradyumna and grandson of Kṛṣṇa, the arch enemy of Bāṇa. Citralekhā promised to bring Aniruddha to Uṣā and went to Dvārakā. She told Aniruddha about Uṣā's love for him, and brought him to Śonitapura (now a district of Assam), the capital of Bāṇa. The two lovers met each other and conducted their love-affair secretly. But the news leaked and an angry Bāṇa rushed with his soldiers to punish Aniruddha. The latter also prepared to fight the demons and at that period of crisis Citralekhā remembered Nārada who arrived instantly to help her as he had once promised. A terrible battle ensued. Bāṇa failed to defeat Aniruddha in straight combat. His minister Kuṣmāṇḍa then requested Bāṇa to resort to magic. This plan was successful and Aniruddha was fettered, entwined by serpents. The wise minister Kuṣmāṇḍa then advised Bāṇa to enquire who this mighty young man was. He said that this gallant boy destroyed many Asuras which proved his great skill in warfare. He must have had a secret *gāndharva* marriage with Uṣā. It was therefore better to protect him and not kill him, at least for the sake of family prestige. Meanwhile Nārada informed Kṛṣṇa of what had happened and Kṛṣṇa went on Garuḍa to the city of Bāṇa followed by a vast army led by Balarāma, Pradyumna and others. On the way he defeated an Asura named Jvara who troubled him by entering his body as fever. Then he had encounter with Bāṇa. The latter was cornered with his army which Śiva could not tolerate because Bāṇa was his protégé. He sent his army, the Pramathas having faces of various animals, and he himself came on the field. The war turned into one between Kṛṣṇa and Śiva. This created great pressure on the Earth who went to Brahmā so that she was relieved. Brahmā went to Śiva and requested him not to fight against Kṛṣṇa because both were aspects of the same divinity. At this Śiva left the battlefield, infusing his own strength into Kṛṣṇa's body. Guha or Kārttikeya was still fighting with Kṛṣṇa but the goddess Koṭavī removed him from the battlefield. Bāṇa then determined to fight alone. In that terrible fight Bāṇa faced disaster, but at the interference of Śiva, Bāṇa was saved. Thereupon Śiva granted him the boon of immortality and Bāṇa went to stay with him. Aniruddha was rescued and given in marriage to Uṣā. In the absence of Bāṇa, Kṛṣṇa handed the kingdom of Śonitapura over to Kuṣmāṇḍa and returned to Dvārakā with Aniruddha and Uṣā (*Hari* 174-89).

The third part of the *Harivaṃśa,* known as the Bhaviṣyaparvan, deals mostly with the older legends of Viṣṇu and his earlier incarnations. The story of the slaying of Madhu and Kaiṭabha by Viṣṇu as given in *Hari* 202 is the same as that found in the *Mbh*. There was another Madhu Daitya, who was neither the Madhu of the Madhu-Kaiṭabha legend nor the one who was a relation of Rāvaṇa, whom Viṣṇu in his Hayagrīva form had killed in the course of a struggle between the gods and the demons over the performance of a sacrifice (*Hari* 204-5). The demonș being repeatedly defeated resorted to religious austerities along with the gods and Brāhmaṇas to achieve a different kind of purpose (*Hari* 218). That was to extract the drug of immortality and other good objects by churning the ocean. This is, however, treated very briefly in the *Hari* 219 in a few verses. The legend of the Hiraṇyākṣa is described for the first time in the *Harivaṃśa* in a conventional way. It is said that Viṣṇu after creating the world placed Indra at the command of the gods and Hiraṇyākṣa and

Hiraṇyakaśipu at the command of the Daityas. While Hiraṇyākṣa was ruling over the Asura world he was informed that the gods were planning to destroy him. He invaded heaven, and challenged Indra to fight. As the gods were under threat Viṣṇu in his boar form appeared to save them. A terrible fight ensued between Hiraṇyākṣa and Viṣṇu. The disc of Viṣṇu cut off the head of the demon (*Hari* 226-8). More important is the story of Hiraṇyakaśipu which has various versions in different Purāṇas. Hiraṇyakaśipu was the son of Diti and as such the ancestor of all demons. He pleased Brahmā by his devotion and obtained immunity from death in the hands of the gods, Asuras, Gandharvas, Yakṣas, Rākṣasas, Piśācas, men and serpents. Emboldened by this boon he conquered the three worlds. Unable to bear his torture, the gods requested Viṣṇu to save them. Viṣṇu assured them that he would destroy the demon and reinstate them in heaven. There upon he assumed the terrible man-lion (*nṛsiṃha*) form and went to his court. There he saw Hiraṇyakaśipu and the demon-chiefs enjoying the dance of the celestial nymphs. When Viṣṇu entered the hall in his man-lion form, Hiraṇyakaśipu was surprised. Prahlāda (Prahrāda) then said to his father Hiraṇyakaśipu that he had never seen such a wonderful and awe-inspiring being in which the entire universe was reflected. He feared that this man-lion would bring peril to the demons. Hiraṇyakaśipu ordered his attendants to arrest the man-lion. They tried their best and showered all forms of divine, human, and magical weapons on him, but these were of no avail. On Hiraṇyakaśipu's side, apart from the destruction of his huge army, evil omens were looming large. Śukrācārya, the preceptor of Hiraṇyakaśipu, warned that a grave situation had arisen which he should handle with patience and care. But Hiraṇyakaśipu paid no heed. Viṣṇu in his man-lion form jumped on him and tore him to pieces with his claws (*Hari* 230-7).

A summary treatment of the story of the dwarf (*vāmana*) incarnation of Viṣṇu and his subjugation of the demon Bali is given in *Hari* 220. A detailed account is also found. It is said that among the five sons of Hiraṇyakaśipu, Prahlāda was the eldest. His son was Virocana and the latter's son was Bali. After Hiraṇyakaśipu was killed, the Daityas made Bali, who was religious, truthful, restrained, valiant, grateful and wise, their king. They wanted Bali to conquer the three worlds, defeat Indra, and restore the prestige which they enjoyed in Hiraṇyakaśipu's rule. All the demons of various races assembled under his banner. Vala and Namuci of the Vedic fame, Maya and other celebrated demons, Pulomā and Hayagrīva, even Prahlāda (Prahrāda) looking Brahmā among the gods, also joined him. Each of them were given charge of a well-equipped army. Prahlāda's son Virocana, father of Bali, Anuhrāda, son of Hiraṇyakaśipu, Kujambha, brother of Virocana, and the great Vṛtra came to Bali's assistance. The gods also made elaborate preparation for war. In the battle that ensued each of the demons fought against his counterpart among the gods. Thus Namuci fought Dhara, Maya took on Tvaṣṭṛ, Pulomā fought against Vāyu, Hayagrīva against Puṣan, Śambara against Bhaga, Virocana against Viśvakṣena, Asilomā against Hari, Vṛtra against the Aśvins, Rāhu against Aja Ekapāda, Vala against Mṛgavyādha, Prahlāda against Kākṣa, his brother Anuhrāda against Kubera and Vipracitti against Varuṇa. Bali found his rival in Indra. After the great fight the demons were victorious. The goddess Lakṣmī herself came to Bali and congratulated him saying that he had accomplished the impossible and surpassed even his illustrious great-grand father Hiraṇyakaśipu (*Hari* 238-55).

In order to celebrate his victory Bali was performing a sacrifice. There Viṣṇu appeared in a dwarf form, as if a boy. He praised the sacrifice, described it as the best of its kind he had ever seen, but explained that it was the knowledge of the self for which one should strive. Bali was pleased with the appearance and wisdom of the boy. He welcomed the boy and said: '. . . Whoever you may be, receive my salutation, and say how should I please you.' The dwarf said: 'If you are satisfied with me, if you have faith in righteousness, in that case my only prayer is that, for the sake of my preceptor and for maintaining fire, please grant me three steps of land.' Śukra, the preceptor of Bali warned of danger. 'O lord of the Asuras, don't make gift of land to him. You do not know him. He is Viṣṇu in disguise.' But Bali took a golden waterpot and said to the dwarf, 'please sit facing the east'. The dwarf said: 'I am seated'. Bali: 'Beg'. Dwarf: 'Bestow'. Bali: 'What do you want?' Dwarf: 'Land'. Bali: 'How much?' Dwarf: 'Only three steps'. Bali: 'Granted'. At this Śukra said: 'I know him very much'. Bali: 'Who is he?' Śukra: 'He is Viṣṇu'. Bali: 'Matter of joy'. Śukra: 'You have been deceived'. Bali: 'Not at all'. Śukra: 'Why?' Bali: 'When Viṣṇu, the lord of the world, is himself present at the place of my sacrifice, whatever he asks for I shall grant him. Who is a better recipient than Viṣṇu?' (*Hari* 261-2).

The *Viṣṇupurāṇa* is undoubtedly one of the oldest Purāṇas. It approaches closely to the old definition of Purāṇa containing the five characteristics (*pañcalakṣaṇa*). Its character is more that of a unified composition than a mere compilation, which is not the case with most of the other Purāṇas. The power of faith in Viṣṇu finds here the most magnificent expression in the legend of the boy Prahlāda (Prahrāda), whom his father the proud demon-king Hiraṇyakaśipu, in vain tried to dissuade from Viṣṇu worship. Although Prahlāda is treated with respect in the *Mbh* which refers to his various sermons and discourses in regard to *dharma* and other higher aspects of life, in the *Hari* he is an ordinary demon who fought against the gods. In the *Viṣṇu* we find that because of Prahlāda's devotion to Viṣṇu no weapon could kill him, neither snakes, nor wild elephants, neither fire, nor poison, nor magic-spells could harm him. Hurled from a balcony of the palace, he fell gently on the bosom of the earth. He was thrown fettered into the ocean, and mountains were piled upon him, but he was not destroyed. Questioned by his father whence his marvellous powers came, Prahlāda replied: 'Whatever power I possess, father, is neither the result of magic, nor is it inseparable from my nature: it is no more than that which is possessed by all in whose hearts Acyuta (Viṣṇu) dwells . . . I wish no evil to any, and do and speak no offence; for I behold Keśava (Viṣṇu) in all beings as in my own soul.' The *Viṣṇu* refers to the killing of Hiraṇyakaśipu by Viṣṇu in his man-lion form, but gives no detail (*Viṣṇu* 1.16-20). Other demon lores pertain to the exploits of Kṛṣṇa and many legends are directly adapted from the *Harivaṃśa*, such as the killing of Putanā (*Viṣṇu* 5.5), the subjugation of Kālīya Nāga (5.7), the slaying of the Asura Dhenuka (5.8), that of Asura Pralamba (5.9), that of Vṛṣabha (5.14), that of Keśi (5.16) and that of Kaṃsa (5.20). Besides we have the legends of the slaying of Śambara by Pradyumna and his marriage to Māyāvatī (5.27), the slaying of Narakāsura by Kṛṣṇa (5.29), and the love story of Uṣā and Aniruddha (5.32) and in that connection Kṛṣṇa's fight with the Asura Bāṇa (5.33). The stories have already been narrated, and no divergence from the Harivaṃśa accounts is found. In the *Viṣṇupurāṇa* the stories are given in brief.

The genealogy of the demons, as given in *Viṣṇu* (1.21), is based upon those found in *Mbh* (1.59.1ff) and *Hari* (3-4), but is neither comprehensive nor adequately classified. The imperfection of the *Viṣṇupurāṇa* account has been redressed and systematized in the *Matsyapurāṇa* which says that from Diti were born Hiraṇyakaśipu and Hiraṇyākṣa. Prahalāda, Anuhlāda, Saṃhlāda, and Hlāda were sons of Hiraṇyakaśipu while Uluka, Śakuni, Bhūsantāpana, and Mahānābha were sons of Hiraṇyākṣa. Āyusmān, Śibi, Vāṣkala and Virocana were sons of Prahlāda. Virocana's son was Bali. Among the hundred sons of Bali, Bāṇa was the eldest and the best. From Danu, another wife of Kaśyapa, were born hundred demons, among whom Vipracittti was pre-eminent. Others deserving mention were Dvimūrddhā, Śakuni, Śaṅkuśirodhara, Ayomukha, Śambara, Kapiśa, Vāmana, Mārīcī, Meghavān Garbhaśirā, Vidrāvana, Ketu,

Ketuvīrya, Śatahrada, Indrajit, Saptajit, Vajranābha, Ekacakra, Mahābāhu, Vajrākṣa, Tāraka, Asilomā, Pulomā, Vindu, Bāṇa Svarbhānu, and Vṛsaparvā. The daughter of Svarbhānu was Prabhā and that of Pulomā was Sacī. Upadānavī, Mandodarī and Kuhū were daughters of Maya while Śarmiṣṭhā, Sundarī and Candrā were daughters of Vṛṣaparavā. Vaiśvānara had two daughters, Pulomā and Kālakā, who were married to the demon Mārīca. Their descendants came to be known as Pauloma and Kālakeya. Siṃhikā, wife of Vipracitti, gave birth to thirteen demons, who were Vyaṃśa, Kalpa, Nala, Vātāpi, Ilvala, Namuci, Svasṛpa, Ajana, Naraka, Kālanābha, Sāramana and Kālavīra. They belonged to the sister's lineage of Hiraṇya-kaśipu. Tāmrā, wife of Kaśyapa, bore six daughters who were Śuci, Śyenī, Bhāsī, Sugrīvī, Gṛdhrikā and Sukī. They were the progenitors of the various kinds of birds and animals. Vinatā was the granddaughter of Tāmrā, who bore two sons, Garuḍa and Aruṇa, and a daughter Saudāminī. Aruṇa had two sons, Sampāti and Jaṭāyu; the former's son was Vabhru. Jaṭāyu had five sons named Karṇikāra, Śatagāmī, Sārasa, Rajjuvala and Bherunda. Surasā and Kadru, both granddaughters of Tāmrā, gave birth to serpents, important among them being Śeṣa, Vāsuki, Karkoṭa, Śaṇkha, Airāvata, Kambala, Dhananjaya, Mahānīla, Padma, Aśvatāra, Takṣaka, and Elāpatra. From Krodhavasā, another wife of Kaśyapa, were born the Rākṣasas, from Muni the Apsarases, and from Ariṣṭa the Gandharvas and Kinnaras (*Matsya* 6.7.47).

The Maruts were storm-gods *par excellence* in the *RV* who belonged to the *gaṇa* category. They were the sons of Rudra and Pṛṣṇi, also of Vāyu, and are sometimes described in the *RV* as self-born. They were all brothers of equal age, having the same birth-place and abode. In the epic-Puranic tradition they are described as sons of Diti, but they are not classed with the demons. In *Rām* (1.46-7) it is stated that after the demons were killed, Diti, much aggrieved at the destruction of her sons, requested Kaśyapa to give her a son who would be able to destroy Indra. The request was granted and she was advised to live a pure life during the period of austerities. Indra smelt danger at this and with the motive of self preservation, began to wait upon her and nurse her in various ways. A pleased Diti was softened, and assured Indra that his brother, to be born, would be friendly to him. One day, quite unknowingly, she made a violation of the rules relating to sleeping. Taking advantage of this fault, Indra entered the womb of Diti and shattered the embryo into pieces. The pieces began to cry aloud and Indra asked them not to cry (*mā ruda*). Hearing the sound Diti awakened and asked Indra to come out. Seven fragments of Diti's foetus became seven guardians of the seven realms of wind. Since Indra called them *mā ruda* they came to be known as Maruta. The same legend is found in *Hari 3*. In the account of the *Rām* Diti's fault was that during sleep she placed her feet where her head should have been. In the *Hari* account her fault was that she did not wash her feet before going to sleep. *Mā ruda* of the *Rām* has been replaced by *mā rudiḥ* in the *Hari*. In the latter text each of the seven parts of the embryo was again subdivided into seven thus making a total number of forty-nine. The *Hari* account recurs in *Viṣṇu* (1.21.29-40). It also says that Diti's fault was that she did not wash her feet before going to sleep, that the embryo was subdivided seven-fold times and that the name Marut was due to *mā rodiḥ* as uttered by Indra. *Matsya* has only a single line (1.16.47), *tata ekonapañcāśamarutaḥ Kaśyapādditiḥ*, 'thereupon Diti produced forty-nine Maruts in connnection with Kaśyapa'. But elsewhere in the same Purāṇa (146.16-37) it is said that once Diti was sleeping during the daytime and her hair touched her feet. This was her fault, taking advantage of which Indra entered her womb and subdivided her embryo into forty-nine parts. Then he begged pardon of Diti assuring her that he would give this forty-nine beings a high place in the heavens.

The story of Kaca and Devāyāni as narrated in *Matsya* (25.26) is taken from the *Mbh*. It is a love story, not demon lore. There is no need to repeat the story. The *Matsya* (170.1-30) account of the slaying of the demon Madhu and Kaiṭabha is the same as that found in the *Hari*. The *Matsya* refers to twelve struggles between the gods and the Asuras under the following captions: Narasiṃha, Vāmana, Varāha, Amṛtamanthana, Tārakāmaya, Āḍivaka, Traipura, Andhaka, Vṛtraghātaka, Dhātra, Hālahala, and Kolāhala (47.41-5). It first gives a summary account of these struggles (47.46-80) but later these are elaborated in various chapters. The story of the destruction of Hiraṇyakaśipu by the Narasiṃha incarnation of Viṣṇu is adapted in the *Matsya* directly from the *Harivaṃśa* and not from the *Viṣṇupurāṇa*. Here it is stated how the demon received the boon that he could not be destroyed by gods, Asuras, Yakṣas, Pannagas, Rākṣasas, Piśācas or human beings, how he became lord of the three worlds, how at the request of the gods Viṣṇu assumed the form of man-lion (*narasiṃha*) and entered the wonderfully decorated court of Hiraṇyakaśipu in which he was attended by the sweet music of the Gandharvas and dancing performances of such Apsarases as Viśvācī, Sahajanyā, Pramlocā, Divyā, Saurabheyī, Samīcī, Puñjikasthalā, Miśrakeśī, Rambhā, Citralekhā, Sucismitā, Cārukeśī, Ghṛtācī, Menakā and Urvasī and worshipped by hundreds of demons such as Bali, Virocana, Naraka,

Prahlāda, Vipracitti and others, how Prahlāda warned that this man-lion would bring disaster, how at the command of Hiraṇyakaśipu the demons hurled various weapons at the man-lion only to get themselves destroyed, how Hiraṇyakaśipu fought him, how evil portents began to appear, the world with all its objects began to tremble, and how the man-lion killed Hiraṇyakaśipu with his sharp claws (*Matsya* 161-3). Interestingly enough the Prahlāda episode as described in *Viṣṇu* (1.16-20) is absent, except his anticipation of the imminent danger of the Asuras at the presence of the man-lion.

Prahlāda however comes in the picture in the legend of Bali and Vāmana. It was suddenly discovered that the power and spirit of the Asuras was declining. The Asura king Bali wanted to know from his grandfather Prahlāda the cause of this sudden change, and Prahlāda after meditation ascribed this degradation of the Asuras to Hari's (Viṣṇu's) conception in the womb of Aditi. He said that Hari was the supreme soul, the lord of all, and the Asuras could be saved only if they resorted to him. Bali, who was lord of the god-like powerful demons such as Vipracitti, Śibi, Śaṅku, etc., did not pay heed to Prahlāda's words, as a result of which the latter uttered the curse that he would be subdued by Hari. Prahlāda, however, consoled the repentent Bali that he would not be destroyed, and that when he had understood the greatness of Hari the latter would protect him. The remaining part of the story has been narrated above. Having received from Bali the grant of 'three steps of land', Hari in his dwarf form asked him to reside in the nether world known as Sutala; after staying there for a *kalpa*, Bali was to become Indra in the Sāvarṇi Manvantara (*Matsya* 244-6). The *Matsya* account of Bali shows divergence from other accounts, in one of which Viṣṇu would occupy heaven and earth with two steps and with his third would push Bali into the nether region. The *Matsya* version of the churning of the ocean is also somewhat different from others. Here it is stated that since the Asuras slain in battle were restored to life by their preceptor Śukra, the gods planned to acquire *amṛta* by churning the oceans. Since it was not possible for them to do so themselves, they wanted to involve the Asuras in the task. They approached the Asura king Bali who agreed to help them with his Asura forces. When the churning commenced, Bali caught hold of the head of Śeṣa Nāga serving as the cord with his left hand and his body with the right, while Nārāyaṇa maintained the mount Mandara serving as the churning pole fixed in its right position. The *Matsya* follows the *Mbh* account regarding subsequent happenings only with the difference that in the battle between the gods and demons Nara and

Nārāyaṇa took the lead, the former destroying the demons with his sharp arrows and the latter with his disc (*Matsya* 249-51). Elsewhere in the same Purāṇa (47-8) it is stated that in the battle that took place after the churning of the ocean Indra defeated Prahlāda.

The Tripura legend is more systematized in the *Matsya Purāṇa.* The demon Maya, defeated by the gods, practised severe austerities with his two assistants, Vidyunmālī and Tāraka. They wanted an impregnable fort so that the gods could not harm them. But Brahmā said that is was impossible to give anyone absolute protection. After some bargaining they received the boon that the fort could be destroyed with a single arrow only by Śiva, and would otherwise remain impregnable. Then Maya constructed a triple city (*tripura*) made of iron on the earth, of silver in the atmosphere and of gold in the sky. This impregnable triple-city, unparalleled in beauty and splendour, became the resort of demons who stayed there happily with family and friends, devoted to religion, truth and righteousness. But with the passing of time jealousy, hatred, and greed began to emerge among the demons. Maya, the king, had an evil dream which foretold the destruction of Tripura. He told the demons about the dream and advised them to give up lust, anger, jealousy, and greed, follow the course of virtue and worship Maheśvara or Śiva. But the demons did not pay any attention to Maya's warnings. They became adamant and aggressive, ravaged repeatedly the realm of the gods and gave up their peaceful way of life. The gods resorted to Śiva Maheśvara who then resolved to destroy Tripura. A chariot representing the worlds was constructed for Śiva. It was pulled by divine horses and driven by the gods themselves. Mounted on that chariot Śiva went to Tripura, followed by his attendants the Pramathas. The battle began and the triple-city was invaded. The demon Tarakāṣa was killed. Maya assured the demons that Tripura was safe so long as the sun and the moon did not meet the Puṣyā star, when the triple-city was supposed to be combined for a moment. Tripura would be destroyed only if at that particular moment Śiva shot a single arrow. To Maya's utter despair Śiva did shoot his arrow at the right moment and Tripura was destroyed (*Matsya* 129-40).

Then comes the legend of Tarakāsura, son of Vajrāṅga. When Diti's desire to have a son capable of subduing the gods was foiled by Indra entering her womb, she again appealed to Kaśyapa for an invincible son. This time she gave birth to Vajrāṅga, so named because his body was immune to the attack of Indra's thunderbolt (*vajra*). Diti asked him to conquer Indra, which he did. When Indra was brought to Diti as a captive, Brahmā requested Vajrāṅga to release him, because Indra was sufficiently humiliated by his defeat and captivity. Vajrāṅga obliged saying that he had only obeyed his mother's command and had no personal enmity against Indra. Thereafter Vajrāṅga repaired to the forest to practise austerities. When Brahmā came to grant him a boon he wanted to live a virtuous life. But when he went to his hermitage he saw his wife Varāṇgī weeping. She informed him that during his absence Indra had disturbed her in various ugly ways. An angry Vajrāṅga complained to Brahmā, who appeased him saying that they would have a very powerful son named Tāraka. In due time Tāraka was born, and the happy Asuras made him their king (*Matsya* 146.38-77; 147). Tāraka said to his fellow demons that the gods would not allow them to live in peace and they were to be exterminated. But before the confrontation he required more power and repaired to the forest to practise severe austerities. When Brahmā came to grant him a boon he asked for immortality. But he was granted the boon that, apart from a seven-year old boy, no god or demon could kill him. Thereupon Tāraka invaded the heavens. His generals were Grasana, Jambha, Kujambha, Mahiṣa and Śumbha. Indra, Yama and other gods came to fight. The Gandharvas under Kubera came to their assistance. The demon chief Kālanemi was defeated, Grasana was killed, Mathana was crushed and Mahiṣa was humbled. But Jambha and Nimi revived the fallen fortune of the demons by defeating Viṣṇu. Thereupon Tāraka began to show his valour, and notwithstanding severe resistance, the gods were defeated, humiliated and crushed (*Matsya* 148-153).

The remaining part of the Tarakāsura saga has many episodes. When Tāraka became lord of the three worlds, Brahmā told the defeated gods that the slayer of Tāraka was yet to be born. The son born of Śiva and Umā was destined to kill Tāraka. Then Brahmā called the goddess of Night (Rātri) and told her that Dakṣa's daughter Satī (the wife of Śiva) for some reason gave up her life. She would be reborn as the daughter of Himavat and wedded to Śiva. But the fruit of their union would be of no avail unless they practised austerities before. Brahmā requested Rātri to enter the womb of Himavat's wife Menakā and give the child a black complexion. In due time Menakā gave birth to Umā. When she grew up the divine sage Nārada visited her parents and informed them that Umā was born to accomplish a divine purpose, to be the wife of Śiva. Then Nārada went to Indra and asked him to find ways and means to induce Śiva to marry. Indra sent Madana, the god of love, to excite Śiva's sexual passion. But owing to Śiva's wrath a blazing fire covered Madana and reduced him to ashes. When Umā came to know about this she wanted to purify herself and resorted to asceticism to get Śiva as her husband. Her desire was fulfilled and she was married to Śiva which was celebrated by the gods, Gandharvas, Apsarases, and sages. After marriage both Śiva and Umā had become somewhat humanized. One day Śiva jokingly referred to the black complexion of Umā. She was enraged, quarreled with Śiva, and went to practise austerities so that she could change her complexion. But before her departure she appointed her attendant Vīraka to guard Śiva's abode carefully so that no woman entered there to dally with Śiva. Now it so happened that there was a demon called Āḍi, brother of Baka and son of Andhaka, who could transform his body to anything at will. Because his father was killed by Śiva, Āḍi bore a grudge against him. Taking advantage of Umā's absence he entered Śiva's place as a snake and assumed the form of Umā to harm Śiva. But his behaviour raised suspicion in Śiva's mind and when the god understood that it was a demon in Umā's guise, he killed the demon (*Matsya* 154-6).

Her austerities over, Umā returned. The gods were eager to have among themselves the son of Śiva and Umā who would save them from Tarakāsura's tortures. They sent Agni to collect information of their nuptial life. Agni as a Śuka bird peeped through the window and saw Śiva and Umā in sexual union. Śiva noticed Agni and said angrily to him that since he had interrupted them he must consume his semen. Agni had to do so and through the gods the sperm was conserved in a lake on lotus leaves. Umā went to the lake where the Kṛttikās after bathing had pulled out all the lotus leaves. They agreed to let her drink the water contained in the lotus leaves that would make her pregnant provided that the son thus born was to be given to them and introduced by their name. After some argument Umā agreed, and having drunk the water produced a beautiful six-faced child from her right side. Another child issued from her left side. Then on an appointed day the gods united the two, who came to be known as Kumāra, Skanda, Viśākha, Ṣaḍānana, or Kārttikeya. He was worshipped by the gods as the ultimate destroyer of Tāraka. Kumāra then assured the gods that Tāraka must be destroyed. The gods then sent a messenger to Tāraka's court conveying their intention to destroy him. Tāraka thought that Indra by this time must have acquired some extra power. After a few days he saw that the army of the gods was advancing towards the Asura capital. He heard the beating of drums and praises of a young hero. Then it came to his mind that he was to be destroyed in the hands of a lad of seven. With a huge army Tāraka went to defend himself but after a severe fight he was killed. The gods regained position and worshipped Kumāra as their saviour (*Matsya* 158-60).

Another great fight among the gods and the demons is known as Tārakāmaya. The *Matsya* account of this battle does not substantially differ from the *Hari* account. In the *Kṛta* age after Vṛtra had been slain, this great battle ensued in which the Dānavas, Yakṣas, Uragas and Rākṣasas fought against the gods. The latter, who being defeated time and again, resorted to Viṣṇu for protection. Thereupon Viṣṇu promised that he would exterminate the demons. Having learnt of Viṣṇu's intention, the demons made extensive preparations for war. Among the Dānava chiefs there were Virocana, Hayagrīva, Varāha, Khara, Tvaṣṭā, Śveta, son of Vipracitti, Ariṣṭa, son of Bali, Kiśora, Pralamba, etc. The gods were led by Indra, Yama, Sūrya, and other deities. Thereupon the war began. While Indra repeatedly hurled his *vajra* against his adversaries, the Dānavas resortred to *māyā*. The illusion created by the demon Maya brought Ūrva-fire on to the battlefield, which began to burn the gods. As regards the origin of the fire the following is stated. The sage Ūrva was an exceptional person who did not believe in the concept of maintaining lineage. Being repeatedly pressed by other sages he created fire from his own thigh. This special fire, which was the son of Ūrva, was kept under the sea. Hiraṇyakaśipu, the lord of the demons and an ardent devotee of Ūrva, received from him the responsibility of tending this fire. That is why it became a regular feature of the illusion of the demons. While the fight was going on the demon Kālanemi took the lead and began to create havoc among the gods. Demons like Maya, Tāra, Varāha, Hayagrīva, Śveta, Ariṣṭa, Kiśora and Svarbhānu followed Kālanemi. The gods began to retreat. Indra and Varuṇa became inactive. Pleased with the discomfiture of Indra and Varuṇa, Kālanemi rushed towards Viṣṇu. After a prolonged fight Viṣṇu severed the head of Kālanemi with his disc. The account of the Tārakāmaya war abruptly ends in the *Matsya* (171-8) with the killing of Kālanemi.

Most of the legends about the conflict between the gods and the demons as found in the *Hari*, *Viṣṇu* and *Matsya* are basically Vaisnavite; Viṣṇu appears to be the saviour of the gods. But as we have seen, some have Śaivite affiliation. Yet even in such cases the authors of these Vaiṣṇavite Purāṇas wanted to establish the superiority of Viṣṇu over Śiva.

We shall conclude this chapter with reference to the Andhaka episode, as found in the *Matsya*, in which Śiva is the hero. This legend has elaborate representation in sculptures. The Asura Andhaka, like many others of his class, received invincibility. Once he saw Śiva playing with Pārvatī and made an attempt to abduct her. There was a forest in the Avantya country where a terrible battle was fought between Śiva and Andhaka. Śiva hurled the *pāśupata* shaft at him and the demon fell. But from his blood thousands of Andhakas came into existence and attacked Śiva. At this, an enraged Śiva created numerous Mātṛkās who began to drink the blood that gushed out from their bodies. Śiva was partly successful in getting the blood of the Andhakas consumed by the Mātṛkās, but he could not resist the emergence of the other Andhakas. Thereupon Viṣṇu created a goddess called Śuṣkarevatī who drank all the blood and stopped the further emergence of the Andhakas. Then Andhaka realised that his power to multiply himself from his own blood had lost its efficacy. He fell at the feet of Śiva and fervently appealed to him to save him, and induct him as one of his attendants. Śiva bestowed upon him what he had desired. This legend in the later Purāṇas has been fabricated to abnormal level, and the Śakti element contained in it may be regarded the precursor of many subsequent Devī legends (*Matsya* 179.1-41).

CHAPTER VII

Puranic Demonology–II

In the preceding chapter we have dealt with the demon lore in the earlier Vaiṣṇavite Purāṇas. In the *Harivaṃśa* as well as in the *Viṣṇu* and *Matsya Purāṇas* it is Viṣṇu who, either in his original form or in his incarnatory forms, is the destroyer of demons and saviour of the gods. But Śiva is not altogether ignored. While in some cases Śiva is the opponent of Viṣṇu or subordinate to him, in special cases, such as the destruction of Tripura, he is the supreme war-lord whose chariot was driven by Brahmā and in whose shaft Viṣṇu had himself entered. Likewise, among the earlier Purāṇas, the Śaivite *Vāyu* and the Devi-oriented *Mārkaṇḍeya* are not at all indifferent to the exploits of Viṣṇu. In fact, the demon lore of the *Vāyu* begins with Viṣṇu's slaying of Madhu and Kaiṭabha. Yet the *Vāyu* version of the legend differs significantly from the account given in the aforesaid Vaiṣṇavite Purāṇas and the *Mbh.* Here it is stated that after the destruction of Dakṣa's sacrifice Śiva was about to devour Viṣṇu and Brahmā. They appeased him with prayers extolling his greatness as the supreme being. A highly pleased Śiva then asked them to receive boons. Since he combined in himself both the aspects of Puruṣa and Prakṛti, he granted the Prakṛti aspect with all its static and kinetic forces to Viṣṇu. After receiving this boon a happy Viṣṇu repaired to the deep to sleep on the serpent Ananta for a *kalpa.* Brahmā, desirous of procreating subjects, wanted Śiva to become his son, and Śiva readily agreed. Then Brahmā went happily to sit and mediate on his lotus seat. At that time the demon brothers Madhu and Kaiṭabha arrived and began to toss the stem of the lotus on which Brahmā was seated. They broke the petals of the lotus and whispered to Brahmā that he would be their food. Saying this they vanished. Thinking they were ghosts (*bhūtas*), a terrified Brahmā went to the bottom of the sea, raised Viṣṇu from his sleep, and requested to save him (*bhūtebya me bhayaṃ deva trāyasvottiṣṭha śaṃ kuru*). Viṣṇu laughed and from the mouth of the serpent Ananta came the twin Viṣṇu-Jiṣṇu. Madhu Kaiṭabha saw Viṣṇu-Jiṣṇu and assuming their forms began to fight them, appointing

Brahmā as judge. A bewildered Brahmā, unable to distinguish the pairs, began to meditate and from his forehead emerged a goddess, the *mohinī* illusion of Viṣṇu, variously known as Mahāvyāhṛti, Sāvitrī, or Ekānaṃśā. At her appearance Madhu and Kaiṭabha lost their fighting spirit. They requested Viṣṇu to grant them two boons: that they would die in an open place, and that Viṣṇu would be their son. The boons were granted and at Viṣṇu's command his namesake killed Madhu and Jiṣṇu killed Kaiṭabha *(Vāyu* 25.1-52) .

Regarding the origin of demons, the *Vāyu* says that the gods, Asuras, Manu, Prajāpati, Ṛṣis, Pitṛs, Dvijas, Piśācas, Yakṣas, Uragas, Rākṣasas, and all other beings are evolutes of Prakṛti (*Vāyu* 3.13-16). Here the influence of the Sāṅkhya philosophy is discernible. In another place it is said that when Kaśyapa was performing a sacrifice four seats were placed for four priests. His wife Diti was helping him. At that time she was pregnant and at the sacrifical altar she delivered a son. The son at once took the seat of the chief priest and began to recite the Vedas. The assembled sages wondered at the knowledge of the child and gave him the name Hiraṇyākaśipu. Kaśyapa's second son by Diti was Hiraṇyākṣa. Diti also bore a daughter named Siṃhikā who was married to the demon Vipracitti. Hiraṇyakaśipu practised severe austerities and became the lord of the three worlds. He was so influential that his footsteps were saluted by the gods and sages. The *Vāyu* refers to the fact that in hoary antiquity he was killed by Narasiṃha, but gives no detail. Hiraṇyakaśipu had four sons—Prahlāda, Anuhlāda, Saṃhlāda, and Hlāda. Prahlāda's sons were Virocana, Gaveṣṭi, Kālanemi, Jambha, Vāṣkala and Śambhu. Virocana's son was Bali. The latter had a hundred sons among whom Bāṇa was the eldest and greatest. Others were Kumbhanābha, Gardhabhākṣa, and Kuśi. Bali also had two daughters, Śakuni and Putanā. Bāṇa's son by his wife Lohiti was Candramanas. Hiraṇyākṣa had five sons whose names were Utkura, Śakuni, Kalānābha, Mahānābha and Bhūtasantāpana. Their descendants were known as Kāleyas who were destroyed in the Tārakāmaya war (*Vāyu* 67.52-70, 82-5). Hlāda's sons were Nisunda and Hrāda. Nisunda had two sons Sunda and Upasunda. Sunda's wife was the Yakṣī Tāḍakā who gave birth to three sons—Brahmaghna, Muka, and Mārīca. Tāḍakā and Mārīca were killed by Rāma and Muka by Arjuna. Anuhlāda's sons were Vāyu and Sinīvālī. Their descendants were known as the Hālāhalas (*Vāyu* 67.71-5). Among the other sons of Prahlāda, Gaveṣṭi was the father of Śumbha, Niśumbha, and Viśvakṣena. Jambha had four sons—Jambhāsya, Śāladundubhi, Dakṣa and Khaṇḍa. The sons of Vāṣkala were Virodha, Manu, Vṛksāyuḥ, and Kuśalimukha. Kālanemi's sons were Brahmājit Kṣatrajit, Devāntaka and Narāntaka. The sons of Śambhu were Dhanka, Asilomā, Nāvala, Gomukha, Gavākṣa and Gomān (*Vāyu* 67.76-9). The story of Diti's prayer for a son capable of destroying the gods, Indra's entrance into her womb and cutting her embryo into pieces and the birth of the Maruts (named after Indra's utterance *mā rodī*) are also recorded. The only difference is the placement of the Maruts respectively in the regions of the earth, sun, moon, stars, planets, Great Bear and the pole star (*Vāyu* 67.86-113).

Among the sons of Danu, another wife of Kaśyapa, Vipracitti was the foremost. The *Vāyu* gives a detailed list of powerful Dānavas, prominent among them being Marīci, Suketu, Subāhu, Tāraka, Vaiśvānara, Pulomā, Svarbhānu, Vṛṣaparvā, Māhagiri, Asilomā, Sukeśa, Mahodara, Hayagrīva, Virūpākṣa, Śambara and Śarabha. Sūrya and Candramas were originally the gods of the Asuras, but later they defected and joined the gods. Svarbhānu was originally born of Diti, and Anubhānu was the son of Danu. The sons of Diti were known as Daityas and those of Danu as Dānavas. Both groups belonged to the Asura category and maintained matrimonial alliances between themselves. Among the sons of Danu with human character, and born of Daitya-Dānava union, were Ekākṣa, Ṛṣabha, Ariṣṭa, Pralamba, Kesī and Meru. The sons of Vipracitti were known as Saiṃhika. They were fourteen in number, prominent among them being Rāhu, Vātāpi, Kālanābha and Naraka. The daughter of Svarbhānu was Prabhā, of Pulomā Sacī, of Maya Upadānavī and of Vṛṣaparvā Sarmiṣṭhā. Nahuṣa was the son of Prabhā, Jayanta of Saci (married to Indra), Puru of Sarmiṣṭhā, and Duṣyanta of Upadānavī. Vaiśvānara had two daughters, Pulomā and Kālikā, both married to Mārīca. They had numerous offspring, among whom fourteen powerful Dānavas were settled at Hiraṇyapura. The Paulomeya and Kālakeya Dānavas were powerful. The sons of the demons Maya were Dundubhi, Vṛṣa, Mahiṣa, Vālika and Vajrasama. Moreover, he had a daughter named Mandodarī who was married to Rāvaṇa. Among the four sons of Danāyu, Aruru was the father of the demon Dhundhu who was slain by king Kuvalāśva; Valijanma was the father of Kumbhila and Cakravarma; Virākṣa was the father of Kālaka and Vara; and Viṣa was the father of Śrāddhahā, Yajñahā, Brahmāhā and Paśuhā. When Vṛtra was fighting against Indra many demons came into existence from the former's breath. From Pravāhī were born a good number of Dānavas whose attributes and functions were different from others of the general Dānava stock. They were known as Devagandharvas (*Vāyu* 68.1-29).

Sixteen Gandharvas, also known as Devagandharvas, belonged to the Mauneya class. They were Citrasena, Ugrasena, Urṇāyu, Anagha, Dhṛtarāṣṭra, Pulomā, Sūryavarcā, Yugapat, Tṛṇapat, Kālī, Diti, Citraratha, Bhramiśira, Parjanya, Kali and Nārada. Thirty-four beautiful Apsarases were under their control, among them are Miśrakeśī, Alambuṣā, Mārīcī, Tilottamā, Surasā and Hemā. They were known as Laukikī Apsarases. Suyaśā, Gāndharvī, Vidyāvatī, Carūmukhī, Sumukhī, and Varānanā were important female Gandharvas. Among them Suyaśā who was the wife of Pracetas gave birth to five Yakṣas known as Kambala, Harikeśa, Kapila, Kāñcana and Meghamālin. Suyaśā had also four daughters from whom the divine Viśāla had begotten four Yakṣa tribes known as Lauheya, Bharateya, Kṛśāṅgeya and Viśāleya. From Vikrānta the Vāleya class of Gandharvas came into existence, important individuals of this class being Citrāṅgada, Viśvakarmā, Mahābhāga, Citraketu, and Somadatta. The daughters of Vikrānta were married to Viśravā and they bore three important clans of the Vidyādharas known as Śaiveya, Vaikrānta and Saumanasa. From the same Vikrānta originated the clans of the horse-faced and human-faced Kinnaras. From Karālaka terrestrial and aerial Bhūtas were born. The chiefs of the terrestrial Bhūtas were Sutāra, Kālabhavana, Nirdeśaka and Videśaka. From Variṣṭhā were born eight celebrated Gandharvas named Haṃsa, Anya, Hāhā, Hūhū, Viṣaṇa, Vāsiruci, Tumburu and Viśvāvasu. The divine Apsarases belonging to the *pañcacuḍā* group were Menakā, Sahajanyā, Varṇinī, Puñjikasthalā, Ghṛtasthalā, Ghṛtācī, Viśvacī, Pūrvacī, Pramlocā and Anumlocantī. Menakā was the daughter of Menā and Urvaśī was born of Nārāyaṇa's thigh. The Apsarases belonged to fourteen tribes. Among these tribes the Śobhayantas originated from Brahmā, the Āhutas from Manu, the Vegavantas from Ariṣṭā, the Agnisambhavas from Urjja, the Āyuṣmatis from sun, the Kurus from Soma, the Śubhas from Yajña, the Vanhis from the Ṛk and Sāmans, the Amṛtās from water, the Sudās from Vāyu, the Bhumijas from Bhavā, the Jātas from Ruk and the Bhairavās from Mṛtyu. The Śobhayantis belonged to the exclusive domain of Kāmadeva. Tilottamā, Prabhāvatī, Vedavatī and Hemā were associated with Brahmā in regard to their origins (*Vāyu* 69.1-63).

The Nāgas, Yakṣas, Piśācas and Rākṣasas were related. Kadru, a descendant of Kaśyapa, was the mother of the Nāgas. Among them Śeṣa, Vāsuki and Takṣaka were the foremost. Khaśā, one of the many wives of Kaśyapa, gave birth to many children, the seniormost of them being Vilohita and the juniormost Vikala. Immediately after their birth they became adults. Being hungry the cruel Vilohita wanted to eat his mother but Vikala resisted, saying that since she was their mother she should be protected (*rakṣamāṃ mātaram*). Thereupon Kaśyapa came and said to Khaśā, 'The sons receive the nature of their mother. Aditi is by temperament righteous and religious, Diti is religious and powerful, Ariṣṭā is a master musician, Danu possesses illusory power, Vinatā is speedy, Surabhi is pious and austere, Kadru is hot-tempered and Danāyusa is merciful to her enemies. Their children have also the same qualities. You are guided by impatience and anger. So will be your sons.' He then said to Vilohita who uttered the word *yakṣa* when he was about to eat his mother (*yakṣa ityeṣa dhāturvai khādana kṛṣaṇe ca saḥ*, the meaning of the root of the word *yakṣa* is eating and ploughing) that his descendants would be known as the Yakṣas. At the same time he said to Vikala who uttered the word *rakṣa* when he was going to save his mother (*rakṣa ityeṣa dhāturvaḥ pālane sa vibhāvyate*, the meaning of the root of the word *rakṣa* is protecting) that his clan would be known as the Rakṣas or Rākṣasas. They were to work at night and sleep in the daytime. At night their power was to be doubled. One night when the Rakṣa Vikala was out searching for food he was caught by two Piśācas, named Aja and Khanda. Each of them had a daughter, Brahmadhanā and Jantudhanā, and they were both given in marriage to the Rakṣasa. Their descendants Hetṛ, Prahetṛ, Ugra, Pauruṣeya, Vadha, Sphurjja, Vidyuta, Vāta, Āpa, Vyāghra and Sarpa were the Rākṣasas of the Yātudhana category. Hetṛ's son was Laṅku, whose sons were Mālyavāna and Sumālī. Among others belonging to the Yātudhāna category mention may be made of Pulomā, Vighna Somena, Rumana and Nikumbha. Another class of Rākṣasas were known as Brahmadhāna or Brahmarākṣasa (*Vāyu* 69.68-135).

The Yakṣa Vilohita was attracted to the Apsaras Kratusthalī, but he knew that he was so ugly and repulsive the Apsaras would turn him down. So he assumed the shape of her lover, the Vasuruci Gandharva, and had sexual intercourse with her. As a result a child was born to them. As soon as he was born he became youthful with a giant-like body. His name was Nābhi. The Yakṣa brought him to his own place, a *nyagrodha* tree inhabited by the Guhyakas. Yakṣa Rajatanābha who married Anuhrāda's daughter Bhadrā, was the grandfather of the Guhyakas. Maṇivara and Maṇibhadra Yakṣas were born of Bhadrā. Both of them were equal to Indra. Maṇibhadra begot twenty-four sons by his wife Puṇyajani. Maṇivara and Devajani also had many sons, the most important among them being Pūrṇabhadra. Among other sons of Khaśā there were some well known Rākṣaṣas like Vidyujjibha, Bhīma, Mātaṅga, Triśirā, and Akampana. She had also seven daughters from whom various *gaṇas* or tribes were produced: the Ālambeyas, Kārṣṇeyas, Nairṛtas and others. The Rākṣasas were worshippers of Śiva. From the Rākṣasa Kumbha came into existence the Kāpileyas. There were several classes of Rākṣasas such as Naila-Rākṣasas born of Keśini's daughter Nīlā, Bhūmi-Rākṣasas born of Vikacā, and so on. They had eight clans, Bhadraka, Nikara, etc., whose function was to destroy sacrifices. The clan comprising Putanā, etc., caused harm to men, especially to children. Skandagraha and Apākatrāsaka clans were terrestrial enemies of human beings. The Puṇyajana and Devajana clans were Yakṣa-Rākṣasas under the broader category of Guhyakas. At the apex of the demon hierarchy were the Asuras who were equal to the gods in every respect. Next came the Gandharvas who were three steps inferior. The Guhyakas, Rākṣasas and Yakṣas were three steps inferior to the Gandharvas. The Piśācas were again three steps lower than the Rākṣasas (*Vāyu* 69.136-203). The violent Rākṣasas were descendants of the daughters of Krodhā who were wives of Pulaha. From these daughters of Krodhā were also born various classes of animals. Thus, Mṛgī was the mother of all kinds of antelopes; Mṛgamandrā of all kinds of bovine animals; Haribhadrā of the lions, tigers, monkeys, Kinnaras, Kiṃpurusas; Irāvatī of elephants and especially of Airāvata and other mythical elephants; Bhūti of the ghosts or Bhūtas of various horrible appearances; Kapiśā of the Piśācas; Daṃṣṭrā of carnivorous animals and certain kinds of serpents; Tiryā, Śvetā and Svarā of various kinds of aquatic animals and worms and Surasā of the serpents (*Vāyu* 69, 204-321).

The Bhūtas and Piśācas are described in the *Vāyu.* Born of Bhūti, the Bhūtas were attendants of Śiva. Individually they had varied appearances—plump, lean, tall, short, long-eared, etc. They lived on mountains, lakes, rivers, or sea-coasts. Several of their kind had black, blue, yellow, red, white, or a smoke-like complexion. Some wore a sacred thread made of serpents. Their eyes did not look alike, many of them having epicanthic folds. Some of them were many-eyed as well. Some were headless. They are variously described as headless, many-headed, single-headed, uneven-headed, fierce, hairy, without hair, blind, complex, dwarf, one eared, big-eared, earless, clawed, sharp-toothed, toothless, double-tongued, one-armed, many-armed, one-footed, many-footed, footless, great being, ascetic, most-powerful, having knowledge of *brahman*, capable of assuming any form and going to any place, dangerous, cruel, auspicious, inauspicious, corpse-eater, big-faced, bearing clubs, bows and arrows, swords and tridents, having flaming eyes, wearing garlands and travelling at night. They have neither wives nor children. The Piśācas were born of Kapiśā. They were also known as Piśitāsana owing to their pale-yellowish colour. They had sixteen tribes, each of which was designated after masculine-feminine pairs such as, Chagala-Chagalī, Sucī-Sucimukhī, Kumbhapātra-Kumbhī, Vajradaṃṣṭra-Dundubhi, Upacāra-Apacāra, Ulukhala-Ulukhali, Anarka-Anarkā, Kukhaṇḍa-Kukhaṇḍikā, Pāṇipātra-Pāṇipātrī, Pāṃsu-Pāṃsumati, Nituṇḍa-Nituṇḍi, Nipuṇa-Nipuṇā, Chalada-Uccesaṇā and Praskanda-Praskandikā. The Kuṣmāṇḍas were a branch of the Piśācas who were also divided into eighteen clans: Ajāmukha, Vakamukha, Puriṇa, Skandina, Vipāda, Aṅgurikā, Kumbhapātra, Prakuṇḍaka, Upacāra, Ulukhalikā, Alarkā, Kumaṇḍikā, Pāṇipātra, Paituṇḍa, Urṇāśā, Nipuṇā, Sucimukha and Uccheṣanāda. The Piśācas of the Kuṣmāṇḍa category are described as hairy, round-eyed, carved body and face on the hip. The Vakra-Piśācas were curved in figure and movement . The Nitundaka Piśācas were of dwarf form and could go anywhere. The Alarkamarka-Piśācas lived on trees . The Pāṃśu-Piśācas were dry and lived on cremation grounds. The Kumbhapātra Piśācas were animal-faced and moved about in groups. The Nipuṇaka-Piśācas had lips extended upto their ears and by them men were possessed. The Puraṇa-Piśācas were small in form and devoured new born children. The Piśitāda-Piśācas used to drink blood on the battlefield. The Skandika-Piśācas were nude, without abode and long haired. The Piśācas lived in haunted houses, dilapidated buildings, impure houses, towers, roads, rivers, *caitya* trees and other places. They were the favourites of craftsmen and those who violated the *varṇāśrama*. They were gods of dying persons, thieves and traitors. They were to be propitiated with honey, meat, rice, curds, sesamum, wine, incense, turmeric,. or black cloth. Śiva was their lord (*Vāyu* 69.242-89).

The story of Gayāsura, narrated in the *Vāyu Purāṇa*, is as follows. Among the Dānavas, the Asura Gaya was most powerful. His height was 125 *yojanas* and width 60 *yojanas*. He resorted to a mountain called Kolāhala and practised severe austerities for several thousand years. The gods, alarmed, went to Brahmā, Viṣṇu and Maheśvara so that some arrangement could be made to put him under control. The gods under the leadership of Brahmā, Viṣṇu and Maheśvara went to Gayāsura, asked him about the purpose of his austerities and wanted to bestow a boon upon him. Gayāsura wanted to become the purest of all beings, and this boon was granted. This again made the gods afraid because Gayāsura fooled them not by asking for the boon of crushing the gods by force, but for supremacy over the gods and all beings. Thereupon the gods went to Brahmā again and having a consultation with him they all came to

Gayāsura. Gayāsura was highly pleased to have Brahmā as his guest and agreed to do any work that would please him. Brahmā said that he had visited all the holy places of the world but did not find any place which was wholly pure and where a divine sacrifice could be performed. He requested Gayāsura to offer his body to accomplish this purpose. Gayāsura agreed and fell down on the south-eastern corner of mount Kolāhala. On that body Brahmā performed his sacrifice. But Gaya's body began to tremble. A gigantic stone slab from the abode of Yama was put on his head, but the movement continued. All the gods including Brahmā stood on his body, but this was of no avail. Then Viṣṇu came and put his weight on him. At this Gayā said that the gods had deceived him. If Viṣṇu requested him to stop his movement he would do it happily and there was no need to torture him. The repentant gods then wanted to grant him a boon. Gaya wanted his body to become the permanent abode of Brahmā, Viṣṇu, and Śiva and the region covered by his body to become celebrated after his name for ever. Thus the *tīrtha* (holy place) of Gayā was founded (*Vāyu* 116.1-78).

It is in the *Mārkaṇḍeya Purāṇa* that we come across for the first time the emergence of the Devī, the embodiment of the primordial energy conceived as the all pervading Female Principle of creation, in the form of the demon slayer. Apart from the *Devīmāhātmya* section, other parts of this Purāṇa have little to do with demonology except the story of Ṛtadhvaja and the usual account of creation which is found in all Purāṇas. King Śatrujit's son Ṛtadhvaja saved the Brāhmaṇa Gālava with the help of a wondrous horse named Kuvalaya. The demon Pātālaketu, assuming various forms, was destroying the hermitage of Gālava and creating obstacles to his meditation and rituals. Ṛtadhvaja pursued the Daitya Pātālaketu down to the nether region and killed him. He rescued and married the Gandharva princess Madālasā whom the demon Pātālaketu had stolen and imprisoned (*Mārkaṇḍeya* 20-2). This is not exactly demon lore, but an ordinary love story. The remaining part of the story is that the slain demon's brother Tālaketu had caused Madālasā to die on a false report of Ṛtadhvaja's death. But she was restored to life by the grace of Śiva and bore several children to Ṛtadhvaja, among whom Alarka later became celebrated (*Mārkaṇḍeya* 23-6). One chapter describes how Brahmā created the Asuras, gods, Pitṛs, mankind, Rākṣasas, Yakṣas, Nāgas, Piśācas and Gandharvas. In order to create four classes of beings Brahmā resorted to the waters. Then at first out of his buttock were produced the Asuras. He cast away that body which was composed of the particles of darkness and which eventually became night. From his mouth were produced the gods. He cast way that body also which became the day. In the same way emerged the Pitṛs which became the intervening twilight between day and night and mankind which came with the dawn between night and day. Hence the gods are powerful by day, the Asuras by night, mankind at dawn, and the Pitṛs by evening twilight. After creating these four, Prajāpatī-Brahmā created the ever hungry bearded monsters by assuming another body. Some of the monsters who said 'let us preserve the body' were called the Rākṣasas. And those who said that 'let us devour it' were called Yakṣas. When the creator Brahmā saw them, the hair of his head withered and from it were born serpents. Seeing these he fashioned beings possessed with anger, the flesh-eating Piśācas, tawny-hued and fierce. Then Brahmā meditated on the earth, and the Gandharvas were born as his offspring (*Mārkaṇḍeya* 48.1-24).

The *Devīmāhātmya* section of the *Mārkaṇḍeya* is the most important demon lore, which is recited all over India even today. King Suratha being defeated and driven from his kingdom repaired to a forest. There he met a Vaiśya who had been driven from his home by his relatives. Both met a sage and asked him about the selfish feelings that still possessed them. The sage ascribed those feelings to the goddess Mahāmāya and narrated how Brahmā had invoked the goddess at the end of a former *kalpa* in order to seek deliverence from the demons Madhu and Kaiṭabha and how the sleeping Viṣṇu, awakened by her, slew the demons (*Mārkaṇḍeya* 81.1-77). The exploits of the Devī begin in the next chapter. In the days of yore there was a fight for a full hundred years between the gods and the Asuras. The army of the gods was vanquished by the Asuras whose leader became the Asura Mahiṣa. The defeated gods with Brahmā at their head went to Śiva and Viṣṇu and told them about the tortures Mahiṣa had inflicted upon them. Viṣṇu and Śiva and also Brahmā became angry. Then issued a great energy from the anger of these three divine beings, which became more intense when the other gods added their own energies to it. From this combined energy was formed the goddess Caṇḍika. Śiva gave her his trident, Viṣṇu his discus, Varuṇa his conch, Agni his spear, Maruta his bow and quiver, Indra his thunderbolt and the bell of Airāvata, Yama his rod, Prajāpati his necklace of beads, the Sun his rays, Kāla his sword, Viśvakarman his weapons and ornaments, the Ocean a girdle of unfading flowers, Himavat a lion, Kubera a cup of wine and Śeṣa a serpent necklace adorned with gems (*Mārkaṇḍeya* 82.1-34). Honoured by the gods, the goddess gave a war cry hearing which Mahiṣa rushed out surrounded by all the Asuras. Then began the battle. Among the generals of Mahiṣa, Cikṣura, Cāmara,

Udagra, Mahāhanu, Asilomā, Vāṣkala, Ugradarśana, and Vidāla were destroyed by Caṇḍikā. The goddess hurled her weapons at the Asuras killing them in thousands. The lion on which the goddess was mounted, stalked among the Asuras like fire through the forests. Thus Ambikā (Caṇḍikā) brought the great Asura army to utter destruction. Then the Asura Mahiṣa in his own buffalo-shape rushed to attack the goddess. He repeatedly changed form, roared, and hurled mountains at Caṇḍikā. Then the goddess drank some wine and leaped upwards, sat herself on that great Asura, kicked him on the neck, and struck him with her spear. Finally she struck off his head with her great sword. The gods and the great heavenly sages poured forth praise to the goddess. The Gandharvas began to sing and the Apsarases began to dance (*Mārkaṇḍeya* 82.35-68; 83.1-41).

The second exploit of the Devī is her destruction of the demons Śumbha and Niśumbha. The Asuras Śumbha and Niṣumbha conquered the gods and drove them from heaven. The gods then went to the Himavat and invoked Caṇḍikā in a hymn, appealing to her to help them. While the gods were engaged in offering hymns, Pārvatī, came there to bathe in the Ganges. She asked the gods whom were they invoking. At once Caṇḍikā came out from the body of Pārvatī and said that the gods were invoking her for slaying the demons Śumbha and Niśumbha. Because Ambikā (Caṇḍikā) issued from the muscles (*kośa*) of Pārvatī, she came to be known as Kauśikī. Thereupon Caṇḍa and Muṇḍa, attendants of Śumbha and Niśumbha, saw the sublime and captivating beauty of Ambikā (Caṇḍikā). They went to Śumbha and, describing her beauty, urged that this gem among women be taken by the Asura chief. Śumbha sent a messenger to the goddess to invite her to marry him. The goddess explained that by a vow she could marry no one who did not conquer her in fight. The Asura monarch then became very angry and ordered his general Dhumralocana to fetch the goddess by force. Thereupon Dhumralocana went with his army and seeing the goddess stationed on the snowy mountain ordered her to come forward to the presence of Śumbha and Niśumbha. But Ambikā with a mere roar reduced him to ashes. Then two other heroic Asuras, Caṇḍa and Muṇḍa, were sent out. Seeing them Ambikā frowned and from her forehead emerged the goddess Kālī of the terrible countenance. She fell upon the great Asuras impetuously, crushed them, devoured some and battered others. She beheaded both Caṇḍa and Muṇḍa and presented the heads to Ambikā. A pleased Ambikā gave Kālī as a reward the name Cāmuṇḍā (*Mārkaṇḍeya* 85-7).

After Caṇḍa and Muṇḍa were slain, Śumbha sent out all his armies against Caṇḍikā. The gods also did not remain inactive. To help her their energies took bodily shape. On the other hand Śumbha was helped by such Asura tribes as the Kambūs, Dhaumras, Kālakas, Darhṛtas, Mauryas, and Kālakeyas. At the same time in order to assist Caṇḍikā the seven Mātṛkās, the personified energies of seven great gods, appeared in the battlefield and massacred the Asura army. Then the great Asura Raktavīja came on the scene. His characteristic was that whenever a drop of his blood fell, that moment was produced an Asura of his stature. But every drop of his blood was consumed by Cāmuṇḍā alone and Raktavīja was eventually killed. Niśumbha then attacked Caṇḍikā and was worsted. Śumbha came to his help but the goddess foiled him and slew Niśumbha. The Asura army was exterminated by the Mātṛkās, especially by Kālī and Śivadūtī. The lion devoured those Asuras whose neck he had crushed. Seeing his brother Niśumbha slain and his army slaughtered, Śumbha in wrath challenged her to fight directly. Meanwhile all the Mātṛkās became absorbed into the breast of the goddess. Thereupon commenced the battle between the goddess and Śumbha. The gods and the Asuras who were alive were mere spectators. After a prolonged fight with all sorts of weapons, Caṇḍikā lifted Śumbha, whirled him around, and dashed him to the earth. He fell lifeless on the ground. The gods then offered a hymn of praise to the goddess. She granted them the boon that she would always become incarnate and deliver the world whenever it is oppressed by demons. She said that in the twenty-eighth age of the Vaivasvata Manvantara she would slay demons by becoming the offspring of Yaśodā and dwelling on the Vindhya mountains; that becoming incarnate as Raktadantikā she would slay the demons of the Vipracitti lineage; that after a period of a hundred years of drought she would he reborn as Śatākṣī, that she would support the whole world by the life-sustaining vegetables growing out of her body during the period of a heavy rain and become famous as Śākambharī and slay the great Asura named Durgama; that taking a terrible form as Bhīmādevī on mount Himavat she would destroy the Rākṣasas, that she would slay the terrible demon Aruṇākṣa as the goddess Bhrāmarī, and that she would always save the world from the harm caused by the demons (*Mārkaṇḍeya* 88-92).

In the *Śiva Purāṇa*, closely linked with *Vāyu Purāṇa,* the earlier demon legends pertaining to Śiva have been elaborated and modified. The demon lore of the *Śiva Purāṇa* begins with the story of the destruction of the Asura Taraka which has been mentioned above. But as happens in the case of all Purāṇas, here also we have many divergences. The story of Tāraka's austerities is given here quite in accordance with what the other Purāṇas say in this regard. The only exception is that here Tāraka is represented as one who had the previous knowledge of what would happen. After he became lord of the universe, the gods, divested of their power and position, went to Brahmā and narrated their grievances (1.9.1-51). Then we have the *Kumāra-sambhava* story, inevitably with special Puranic accretions. Only the son born of Śiva's semen was destined to kill Tāraka. The preconditions were naturally created by the gods, and Umā at the command of his father attended Śiva who was practising austerities on a Himalayan peak by closing all his sense organs. At the request of Indra, Kāma or Kandarpa, the god of love and sexuality, went with his wife Rati and at his command the season of spring spread itself all over the region. Pārvatī or Umā was present there. Her presence was sufficient, and seeing her Kandarpa who was getting ready to strike Śiva with his arrow of passion forgot to fix it on his bow. Śiva opened his eyes and finding Pārvatī before him was about to embrace her. An embarassed Pārvatī left the place (*Śiva* 1.16.1-75). An angry Śiva then looked around and found Kandarpa. From his third eye a flash of fire hit Kandarpa and burnt him to ashes. His wife Rati began to lament. The gods then came to Śiva and requested him to restore Kandarpa to life since he acted according to the desire of the gods with the ulterior purpose of destroying the Asura Tāraka. Hearing this Śiva said that for the time being Kandarpa was to remain bodiless (*anaṅga*). He would then be reborn as Pradyumna, son of Kṛṣṇa, by his wife Rukminī. Pradyumna was also to be known as Kāmadeva. After his birth he was to be stolen by the Asura Sambara and kept in a city middle of the sea. Śiva advised Rati to go and reside in the city till Pradyumna was released by slaying the Asura (*Śiva* 1.11.1-30).

Pārvatī understood that physical beauty was not sufficient to charm Śiva and thereupon she went to practise austerities. In order to test her devotion Śiva came in the form of and old person and said that Śiva had neither beauty, nor wealth nor good qualities; and that it was more desirable she chose a god like Indra as her partner. Pārvatī rebuked him and was about to leave the place. Then Śiva assumed his real form and said that he was pleased with her (*Śiva* 1.11.31-8; 1.112-14). To tease Mena, the mother of Pārvatī, Śiva appeared in the marriage procession attended by all the gods and the Rsis, with his attendants, the Bhūtas, Pretas, and Piśācas blowing horrible horns, beating ill-shaped drums, and making fearful noise. Seeing all this Mena fainted. She began to scold Pārvatī and said that it was better on her part to commit suicide than to marry this devil-incarnate. Later, however, Śiva changed his form and pleased his would-be mother-in law (*Śiva* 1.15-18), and Śiva and Pārvatīl lived happily. The gods were eager to see the son of Śiva and Pārvatī who was to redeem them from the torture of Tārakāsura. Agni, assuming the form of a bird peeped into their chamber. Śiva, having understood the desire of the gods, gave him his semen on a leaf. The power of the semen became unbearable to Agni and he threw it on the Gangā, the latter was also unable to bear it and threw it among the reeds. There a beautiful child was born. Six princesses came to bathe on the Gangā. Seeing the child each of them claimed it to be her own and the child pleased them all, and suckled by developing six faces. The gods came to receive the child. He came to be known as Pārvatinandana (son of Pārvatī), Agnibhū (born of Agni), Skanda, Gaṅgāputra (son of Gaṅga), Śarajanma (born among the reeds) and Ṣaṇmātura (having six mothers). The gods made him their commander and took him to Soṇitapura, the capital of Tāraka. For ten days there was a terrible fight between the gods and the demons. Tāraka was slain by Skanda. The gods regaining their power and position propitiated Śiva (*Śiva* 1.19.1-25).

The legend of Tripura has also been fabricated in the *Śiva Purāṇa*. After the destruction of Tāraka, three of his sons, Vidyunmālī, Tārakākṣa and Kamalākṣa, began to practise severe austerities for regaining their previous position. When Brahmā came to grant them what they desired they wanted to build three impregnable cities of gold, silver and iron, and to live there undisturbed; they could be destroyed only if the three cities became united and someone pierced them by a single shaft. These clauses are known to us but the *Śiva* adds another condition. So long as the Asuras maintained their devotion to Śiva they could not be destroyed. The three cities were constructed by the great architect Maya Dānava, and the Asuras lived there a happy and pious life worshipping lord Śiva (*Śiva* 1.19.47-82). In the remaining part of the story, the Śiva account contains some additional elements. The gods knew full well that the demons had not deviated from *dharma* and hence Śiva would not destroy them. So they went to Viṣṇu who invoked the Bhūtas and asked them to destroy the three cities. They failed because the Asuras were devoted to Śiva. Thereupon Viṣṇu in order to diverge the Asuras from the path of true devotion to Śiva created an enchanting personality who with his four attendants in the guise of shaven-headed monks (*muṇḍis*) taught them anti-Vedic high-sounding philosophical doctrines regarding the problem of existence, life and universe (i.e. Buddhism, Jainism, etc.), very attractive by themselves. Even Nārada went to the cities of the demons and convinced them to embrace the new faith. The Asuras of

Tripura thus left the true faith and lost their original devotion to Śiva. Thereafter the destruction of Tripura was accomplished (*Śiva* 1.20-4). In another place recurs the story of the destruction of Tripura. Here the event happened after the death of Hiraṇyakaśipu, and the demons who performed austerities were Maya, Vidyutprabha, and Tārakākṣa. The events are the same with the exception that in this case the Asuras gradually became devoid of virtue. Maya tried his best to bring them back to the path of virtue but could not prevent the inevitable. It is also said that as a last resort, Maya tried to conclude a peace with the gods, but the wily Nārada persuaded him to fight and welcome destruction which happened eventually (*Śiva* 4. 52-4). A third version of the burning of the three cities is also found in the *Śiva*. Here the three principal demons were Tārakākṣa, Vidyunmālī and Kamalākṣa. The three forts or cities were built for them by Viśvakarman at the command of Brahmā. The boon they received was that if the three *puras* were combined at the moment of *abhijit* when the moon entered the Puṣya constellation and the clouds showered rain and Śiva pierced *tripura* with a single impossible shaft, then alone would they be destroyed. This version contains a detailed account of the burning of the combined *puras* and their innocent inhabitants (*Śiva* 7.3.1-124).

There are two legends in the Śiva pertaining to the slaying of the Asura Andhaka. The one which we have already referred to on the basis of other Purāṇas, has nothing to do with the legends narrated here. The characters bear the name Andhaka but seem to be different personalities. The first legend is simple but the second is a confused narrative from which nothing really comes out. According to the first legend, Andhaka was the son of the demon Hiraṇyākṣa. He received the boon that so long as his body would remain identical with the world he was not to be destroyed (*śarīra me brahmāṇḍaṃ vartate yadā*). Whatever its significance, the fact is that by virtue of this boon Andhaka became extremely powerful and conquered the three worlds. In order to save themselves the gods repaired to the mount Mandara. The demon also excavated a cave nearby and built a city, and from this stronghold led an invasion against the gods. There was a prolonged war. Then Śiva came to protect the gods with trident in his hand, chased Andhaka. The demon was wise. He surrendered immediately and began to propitiate Śiva. Pleased with his propitiation Śiva wanted to grant him a boon. Andhaka asked for Śiva's grace both in this world and in the next. After granting him the boon, Śiva threw Andhaka away into the cave. And for the sake of public welfare he himself entered the cave and stayed there. The cave became a sacred place in which the god was worshipped as Andhakeśvara (*Śiva* 1.43).

The second legend is marked by confusion, inconsistency and contradictions. The Puranic narrator himself has made a mess and unsuccessfully blended episodes of different ages. The legend, as reconstructed from confusing materials, runs as follows . Once Pārvatī covered the three eyes of Śiva with her sweating palms. That served the purpose of a womb out of which came a deformed being, as dark as cloud, making peculiar sounds. Seeing him, Śiva said that he would be of enormous strength. Because he was born in darkness he was named Andhaka and was adopted by Śiva and Pārvatī (*Śiva* 7.4.1-14). At that time the Asura king Hiraṇyanetra was praying to Śiva for a valiant son. Since Hiraṇyanetra said that his brother had five sons including Prahlāda, he appears to be Hiraṇyākṣa, the brother of Hiraṇyakaśipu. Śiva said that owing to some secret cause he had no chance of having a son. He advised the Asura king to adopt Andhaka as his son. The demon was very happy to receive Andhaka. Emboldened by the grace of Śiva Hirṇyanetra conquered the gods and terrorized the earth. Thereupon Viṣṇu, invoked by the prayer of the gods and sages, assumed the form of a boar and slew Hiraṇyanetra. Andhaka was declared lord of the netherworld inhabited by the demons (*Śiva* 7.4.15-31). Andhaka thereafter propitiated Brahmā and told him that he was afraid of death. He obtained the boon that he could not be destroyed in heaven or earth, during day or night, by weapon, noose, or material object. Then he set out to conquer the three worlds. The defeated gods went to Viṣṇu and sought his protection (*Śiva* 7.4.32-8).

Here the narrator of the *Śiva Purāṇa* has given a confusing account. Viṣṇu had assumed the man-lion form, entered the city of the Asuras, and killed their king by tearing him into pieces with his sharp claws. This Asura lord was not Andhaka against whom the gods sought protection, but Hiraṇyakaśipu, though the Puranic narrator does not mention his name (*Śiva* 7.4.39-53). Then the narrative goes on to say that when Andhaka was sporting with his cousins they said that he could not be king of the demons because he did not belong to their race. King Hiraṇyanetra had acted foolishly by adopting a quarrelsome, blind, and deformed being like him. At this Andhaka repaired to forest and began to practise austerities. When Brahmā came to grant him boon he asked for removal of his blindness, invincibility and immunity. He also wanted to get rid of his demonic existence. He suggested his own downfall only when evil desire would arise in his mind to have the best of all women of all the ages who was as if a mother-figure and inaccessible to all. A surprised Brahmā granted him all the boons. When the demons learnt that Andhaka had been favoured by Brahmā they made him their king. Thereupon Andhaka conquered the three worlds, forced the gods to pay him tribute, and passed his days happily in company of women (*Śiva* 7.4.54-82). But during his long career of kingship he did not perform a single pious act. He paid no respect to the Vedas, Brāhmaṇas, or preceptors. Once during his stay in the Mandara mountain his ministers Duryodhana, Vighasa, and Hastin informed him of a lady of unparalleled beauty living with her husband. They did not understand that the lady was Pārvatī and her husband was Śiva (*Śiva* 7.4.83.91). Andhaka wanted the lady and bade his ministers persuade her husband to hand her over to him. In course of conversation with her husband the ministers smelt danger. They came back and advised Andhaka to give up the idea. But Andhaka paid no heed to their words and rushed with his army to capture her by force. They could not enter the cave being resisted by Nandī at the gate. The place was filled with corpses of the demons and Śiva's Pramathas known as Bheruṇḍas danced around them (*Śiva* 7.4.92-126).

Śiva then appointed Vīraka to guard Pārvatī and repaired to the forest to perform the *mahāpāśupata* ritual to obtain extra power. In the mean time Andhaka reappeared with his generals and renewed the war against Nandī. The energies (*śaktis*) of the gods in female forms entered the cave of Pārvatī and began to fight against the demons. Vaiṣṇavī was armed with conch, disc, mace and lotus, Saṅkarṣaṇī with bow and plough, Brāhmī with rod and Aindrī with *vajra*. *Śaktis* of other gods held the weapons of their male counterparts. Pārvatī appointed Vīraka as the commander of the divine army. Nandī began to fight against a powerful demon known as Tadgila. Śiva returned after completing his rituals and took the lead. While the war was going on, one of Andhaka's generals Vighasa swallowed all the gods including Brahmā, Indra, Viṣṇu, Arka, Śaśāṅka, Yama, Varuṇa, Vāyu and Kubera. This information was provided to Śiva by Vīraka (*Śiva* 7.4.127-83). Śiva thereupon hurled a vomit-producing special arrow at Vighasa in consequence of which the gods came out. The battle went against the gods because the slain demons were all restored to life by their preceptor Śukra. It turned in favour of the gods when the *gaṇas* of Śiva captured Śukra. Śiva just devoured him. Because Andhaka received the boon that he would not be killed by any god, despite the reverses of his army, he fought terrible. What was worse, from each drop of blood which fell from Andhaka's body, there came into existence one demon of his stature. Thus one Andhaka became many. Thereupon Śiva created two serpents from his two sides pouring venom and flames by which the extra Andhakas were killed and burnt. From his ear was produced a goddess who drank all the blood. Only Andhaka remained, but he had no blood in his body. Even so he did not give up fighting. At last Śiva pierced him with his *sula* and in that condition he was left out divested of all power. But he did not die (*Śiva* 7.4.183-208). Later his mind was changed and he worshipped Śiva and Pārvatī with devotion and expressed regret for what he had done. Moved by his fervent appeal Śiva and Pārvatī accepted him as their son (*Śiva* 7.56.14-50).

A similar legend, that of the destruction of Ruru, is found in the *Śiva Purāṇa* in which the increasing influence of the Śakti cult is discernible. This shows the transformation of the benign goddess Pārvatī into a terrible war goddess of the Caṇḍikā category. A demon named Ruru practised severe austerities for a long time to obtain Pārvatī as his wife. Brahmā advised him to give up this idea since Pārvatī was the mother goddess worshipped by the three worlds. Even Śiva had obtained her not very easily. Without paying heed, Ruru continued his austerities and as a result the world became heated. Śiva told Pārvatī that the demon in order to obtain her was doing this and he was unable resist the power arising of his exertion. Only Pārvatī herself could spoil the effect of his austerities by misguiding him cleverly. Thereupon Pārvatī, here designated Gaurī, went to the Vindhyas and found a lion fighting with an elephant. She killed the lion, covered herself with its blood-stained skin, went to the demon and told him that it was for her that he was practising austerities and that since she had now come to him his purpose was served. The demon could not recognize her and bade her go away. He also hit her with his mace. The goddess thereupon made a counter-attack and created from her body a band of female army. Then assuming a terrible form, she tore the demon to pieces, ate his flesh and drank his blood. The gods, sages, Siddhas, Asuras, Kinnaras, and human beings then propitiated the goddess. Even Brahmā worshipped her because she saved the three worlds. Thereafter the goddess left her terrible form and assumed her original form which was as beautiful as the autumnal moon (*Śiva* 7.6).

The Hiraṇyakaśipu legend has been given a new turn in the *Śiva Purāṇa.* Jaya and Vijaya, two gatekeepers of Viṣṇu, were cursed by some sages as a result of which they were to be born on the earth. They were told that if they were born as devotees of Viṣṇu they would have to undergo seven births. But if they wanted to have Viṣṇu as their enemy they were to be generated only for three times. In their first birth they became Hiraṇyakaśipu and Hiraṇyākṣa, in the second Rāvaṇa and Kumbhakarṇa and in the third Śiśupala and Dantavakra. Hiraṇyakṣa carried the earth into the bottom of the sea. Then Viṣṇu, assuming the form of a boar, fought against Hiraṇyākṣa, killed him, rescued the earth from water, and gave it to Brahmā. Hiraṇyakaśipu performed severe austerities and became master of the three worlds. But his son Prahlāda was a devotee of Viṣṇu, which was not tolerated by Hiraṇyakaśipu. This father-son episode in the *Śiva* is a direct adaptation of the *Viṣṇupurāṇa* account. How Hiraṇyakaśipu was killed by Viṣṇu in his man-lion form has been described earlier. But the *Śiva* adds a new episode which became very popular in later times. Praḥlāda told his father that Hari or Viṣṇu was everywhere in all animate and inanimate objects. Hiraṇyakaśipu laughed at the words of Prahlāda and pointing at a pillar asked sarcasticallly whether Viṣṇu was in it. Prahlāda affirmed and an angry Hiraṇyakaśipu at once struck the pillar with a huge sword. It burst open and there emerged the man-lion, the slayer of Hiraṇyakaśipu (*Śiva* 1.59-61).

There are three more demon stories in the *Śiva Purāṇa,* of which the piercing of the boar-demon Muka at the same time from both sides by Śiva and Arjuna respectively recalls the *Kirātarjunīya* (1.65). The slaying of the demon Āḍi as found in the *Śiva* (7.10) is same as the one found in *Matsya* 156. The *Matsya* account is that during the absence of Pārvatī this demon assumed her form and went to Śiva to cause his ruin. But Śiva was cautious. In the *Śiva* version, Śiva was bewitched by her beauty and began to have sexual intercourse with her. When Śiva's penis penetrated the vulva of the demon, Āḍi made the organ as a stiff as *vajra* and as sharp as a razor so that it was cut off. This brought Śiva to his senses and he killed the demon. The story of the slaying of the demons Śumbha and Niśumbha as found in the *Śiva* is a restatement of what is given in the *Mārkaṇḍeya,* to which the transformation of the black muscle of Pārvatī is added. Śiva jokingly referred to the black complexion of Pārvatī and called her Kālī. An angry Pārvatī thereupon left Śiva and resorted to austerities to become Gaurī. Brahmā then came to her and told that for accomplishing this purpose her wish was sufficient and there was no need to practise austerities. But when she had taken up this course, another purpose could be served: the destruction of the demons Śumbha and Niśumbha who had conquered the three worlds and were creating havoc among the inhabitants. Pārvatī then became Gaurī, with a golden complexion, and from the black muscles (*kośa*) which she had left emerged the black goddess Kauśikī or Caṇḍikā who was destined to slay the demons (*Śiva* 5.21).

The demon lore of the *Varāha Purāṇa* which is Vaiṣṇavite in character begins with a simple narration of the Andhakāsura legend. While in the *Matsya* we find that Andhaka tried to abduct Gaurī or Pārvatī and in the *Śiva* his attraction to the goddess has been exaggerated, and he ordered Śiva to hand her over to him, the *Varāha* refers to no such incident. But it maintains the earlier tradition that from each drop of the blood of Andhaka that fell on the ground, another Andhaka sprang up and fought against the gods. In order to cope with this strange situation the Mātṛkās were produced from the energy of the gods. From Śiva's mouth issued Yogīsvarī. Subsequently emerged Vaiṣṇavī, Brāhmaṇi, Kaumārī, Aindrī, Vārāhī, Maheśvarī and Yamī. These eight Mātṛkās drank all the blood of Andhaka, and his multiplication ceased (*Varāha* 27.1-43). There is another reference to Andhaka in the *Varāha* which narrates that in order to get rid of the tyranny of Andhaka, Brahmā, Viṣṇu, and Maheśvara held a conference. Once when Śiva was sporting with Umā in the company of his Pramathas of various appearances, Brahmā and Viṣṇu came to him, and when the eyes of the three gods met a splendid maiden was born. She came to be known as Trikalā. Then she divided her body into three. A white was known as Brāhmī, a red as Vaiṣṇavī, and a Black as Raudrī. Such legends are suggestive of the growing importance of the cult of Śakti side by side with the cults of Viṣṇu and Śiva (*Varāha* 90.11-44).

The myth of the ancient demon Vṛtra has a transformation beyond recognition in the *Varāha Purāṇa*. A king called Sindhudvīpa performed austerities to beget a son capable of conquering Indra. This was because in one of his previous births as the son of Viśvakarman, he was killed by Indra who used sea-foam. This reminds us of the *Mbh* legend narrated above according to which Indra killed Vṛtra with the same material. While the king was practising austerities, the river Vetravatī, assuming the form of an exquisite lady, came to him. She introduced herself as the wife of Varuṇa and solicited him for having union with her. The king satisfied her desire and she gave birth to a son who came to be known as Vetrāsura. He became the lord of Prāgjyotiṣa, brought under control the seven continents of the earth, ascended the Sumeru mountain, and defeated Indra and other gods. The gods thereupon went to Brahmā and the latter was moved by their call, *paritrāhi* (save us). He thought that creation was coming to an end and dipped into the ocean. It was against this background that an eight-armed goddess, seated on a lion, clad in white garment and holding various weapons appeared and fought and killed Vetrāsura. She was propitiated by Śiva himself who addressed her by various names. She was none other than Durgā. So did Brahmā who had been hiding under water. He located her abode in the Himalayas and requested her to save the gods in future when they would be oppresssed by the demon Mahiṣa (*Varāha* 28.1-45).

The slaying of Mahiṣa is described in the *Varāha* with an erotic touch. The goddess Viṣṇumāyā or Vaiṣṇavi adopting the vow of remaining a maiden all her life, lived alone on mount Mandara. But one day her mind became restless in consequence of which thousands of most beautiful maidens were produced from her body. They all lived happily under her guardianship. Once the divine sage Nārada met her in the Mandara mountain and exchanged pleasant words with her. Then saluting the goddess he went to the realm of the demons, ruled by the Asura Mahiṣa. In course of conversation Nārada said to mahiṣa, 'O lord of the Asuras, I am telling you about a jewel among women. Listen carefully. O lord of the Daityas, by virtue of the boons you have received, you are the master of the three worlds. Recently from the abode of Brahmā, I went to the Mandara mountain. There I saw a city inhabited by thousands of beautiful maidens. The chief among them is an ascetic observing the vow of celibacy. I frequently travel in the realms of the gods, Gandharvas and Daityas, but such a paragon of beauty I have seen nowhere. The gods, the Gandharvas, the Siddhas, the Ṛṣis, the Cāraṇas, and the Daitya-leaders—all are engaged in the worship of that maiden. Having seen that supramundane goddess I have come to you. There is no need for you to conquer the gods or Gandharvas. Just conquer her and that will suffice because she has no second in the three worlds' (*Varāha* 92.1-33).

The *Varāha* version of the Mahiṣa legend is different from that in the *Devīmahātmya* of the *Mārkaṇḍeya*. The narrative continues. After hearing from Nārada, Mahiṣa had a consultation with his minister as to how the goddess was to be obtained. The minister Praghasa said that since she was an ascetic she should not be disturbed. Praghasa''s view was accepted in principle, but Vighasa; another minister, said that from the viewpoint of ethics the king, the symbol of sovereignty, should have the right to possess the best. He advised that the maiden should be approached directly, or negotiation for her marriage should be made with her relatives. Accordingly, Vidyutprabha went to the goddess as messenger. It was also decided that for seeking the hand of this most coveted lady, the candidate himself ought to possess some extra glamour. An ordinary king of demons would not be a suitable match for her. At least Mahiṣa should become Indra, the lord of the gods. So heaven was to be conquered and Indra to be subjugated (*Varāha* 93.1-32). Accordingly, the demons invaded heaven. The Ādityas, Vasus, Rudras and Sādhyas were defeated. Indra himself was defeated by Mahiṣa and ran away (*Varāha* 94.1-16).

Meanwhile, Vidyutprabha, the messenger of Mahiṣa, went to the Mandara mountain and saw the goddess in the company of thousands of maidens. He saluted her and presented details about Mahiṣāsura. He said that at the time of original creation a sage named Saṃvatsara was produced. From him was born Supārśva, and from the latter Sindhudvīpa. His daughter was Māhiṣmatī, named after a place on the Narmadā. She was the elder sister of Vipracitta. One day while travelling with her friends she came to a beautiful hermitage belonging to a sage known as Ambara. She was so pleased with the view that she wanted to stay. She wanted to frighten the sage away. She assumed the form of a sharp-horned buffalo and rushed towards him. The sage, with his special power, learnt about her intention and cursed her that she would become a she-buffalo. The repentance of Māhiṣmatī softened the mind of the sage who said that she would receive her original form after giving birth to a child. On the bank of the Narmadā Sindhudvīpa was engaged in meditation. A deity, a maiden named Indumati was then bathing in the river. Seeing her the semen of the sage was discharged. It was kept in a jar full of water. Māhiṣmatī in her buffalo-form drank the semen-mixed water from the jar, and became pregnant. She gave birth to Mahiṣa, lord of the three worlds. Saying all these Vidyukprabha requested the goddess to take Mahiṣa as her husband (*Varāha* 95.1-20). The proposal was after all gentlemanly, but the goddess was offended. At the instigation of Nārada there was a fight between the demons and the maidens living with the goddess. The demons were routed. The goddess—meanwhile became the supreme being, the eternally existing Female Principle—assuming the form of twenty-handed Śakti, destroyed Mahiṣa (*Varāha* 95.20-65).

The increasing importance of the concept of Śakti is manifested in the Ruru legend of the *Varāha Purāṇa.* In the *Śiva* (7.6) account, as started previously, we see how the demon Ruru made a desperate attempt to make Gaurī or Pārvatī his spouse, and how the goddess foiled his ambition. In the *Varāha* account we come across a different version. This demon of the underworld as the leader of a host defeated Indra. The gods went to Raudrī, the Śakti of Rudra, and requested her to protect them. The goddess was excited and from her mouth thousands of fearful goddesses came into existence and destroyed the Asura army. Ruru himself was slain by the goddess Raudrī, who thereafter came to be known as Kālarātri and Cāmuṇḍā (*Varāha* 96.1-33). The *Varāha* (99.1) introduces a new demon named Caitrasura who was killed by the eight-armed goddess Gāyatrī, born of Brahmā, but does not refer to any legend associated with the said demon. Even though the *Varāha Purāṇa* purports to be of the Vaiṣṇavite sect, special insistence is made on the female-force or Śakti of the gods Viṣṇu and Śiva.

The *Vāmana Purāṇa* contains two sets of demon lore, one connected with the demons belonging to the Hiraṇyakaśipu lineage and the other with those slain by the Devī. The lineage of Hiraṇyakaśipu as described in *Vāmana* (23.1-21) does not refer to Hiraṇyākṣa and his clan, but includes Maya and Śambara. This lineage is described as eternally virtuous, and the goddess Lakṣmī is said to have blessed Bali with the overlordship of the three worlds. As regards the lineage of Hiraṇyākṣa (Hiraṇyanetra of the *Śiva*), Andhaka legend is described many times in the *Vāmana* and the legends are of a different character with extra fabrications. Here Andhaka is said to have been installed as the king of the Asuras by Prahlāda because of his valour. He led a violent war against the gods, assisted by Prahlāda, Virocana, Kujambha, Jambha, Śaṅkukarṇa, Hayagrīva, Maya, Bali, Vṛtra and others and defeated the gods. After his conquest of the heaven he descended to the earth and extracted tribute from the kings (*Vāmana* 9-10). After the destruction of Tāraka and Mahiṣa, Andhaka again came to the forefront and this time he wanted Gaurī as his spouse. Disregarding Prahlada's advice he went to capture Gaurī and was repulsed by the goddess Śatarūpā who gave him a sound beating. Defeated and humiliated, he fled to the nether region (*Vāmana* 59.15-47). Prahlāda tried to dissuade him from the path of evil by telling him the account of his origin (*Vāmana* 63.4-19). The story of Andhaka's final battle with the gods as described in *Vāmana* (68-70) is based on the *Śiva* (7.40) account. Among the demons who were destroyed by the pramathas and gaṇas of Śiva we have references to Daṇḍa, Tuhaṇḍa, Rāhu, Duryodhana, Hastin, Kāntasvara, Viṣāṇa, Ayaḥśirā and Śambara, Jambha and Kujambha. Śukra, who used to restore the slain demons to life, was caught and devoured by Śiva. Andhaka was pierced by Śiva's trident and was kept hanging until he repented. But there are certain new features in the *Vāmana* in relation to the Andhakāsura episode. Andhaka for the purpose of enjoying Gaurī assumed the form of Śiva, and his assistant Sunda assumed the form of Nandī. The plan was, however, frustrated. The story of the creation of numerous Andhakas from each drop of blood of the original Andhaka is absent. Instead, we find that from the blood of Śiva appeared various Bhairavas such as Vidyārāja, Rudra, Caṇḍakapāla, Lalitarāja and Vighnarāja. From his sweat appeared a blood-stained goddess named Carcikā and a boy named Kuja who was empowered to determine the destiny of beings as a planet (*Vāmana* 70.31-47).

Prahlāda succeeded Hiraṇyakaśipu as the ruler of the Asuras in the netherworld. In his kingdom all the demons were virtuous. He learnt from the sage Cyavana that the three best places of pilgrimage were Naimiṣa on the earth, Puṣkara in the atmosphere, and Cakaratīrtha in the netherworld. Prahlāda with his followers made a pilgrimage to Puṣkara. On the way he met two ascetics engaged in meditation but carrying arms. There was a heated controversy between Prahlāda and the ascetics regarding the justification for their carrying arms, in consequence of which a battle ensued between the demons and the ascetics. Prahlāda, notwithstanding his best efforts, failed to win. Later he understood that they were Nara and Nārāyaṇa, and by appeasing them Prahalāda achieved spiritual merit (*Vāmana* 7.45-65; 8.1-72). When his grandson Bali refused to admit the supremacy of Viṣṇu, Prahlāda cursed him, foretelling his downfall. A repentant Bali begged to be excused, and Prahlāda assured him that if he became a devotee of Viṣṇu he would be protected by him (*Vāmana* 29.16-48; 30.1-11). In two other places we have Prahlāda-Bali discourses. When Bali was the lord of three worlds, at his request Prahlāda taught him the sciences of polity and ethics (*Vāmana* 74.19-50). In another place he explained to Bali the causes of the weakness of the demons, in which the story of his curse on Bali and the latter's repentance is retold (*Vāmana* 77.1-57). Though he was basically different from other Asuras in character and temperament, Prahlāda did not forsake his kinsmen during the battles of the demons against gods. He tried his best to bring the erring demons like Andhaka to the path of devotion and righteousness. The central theme of the *Vāmana Purāṇa* is the Bali-Vāmana episode. Bali's ascendency and the preconditions of Viṣṇu's assuming the dwarf (*vāmana*) form are described in *Vāmana* (24.1-38). In *Vāmana* (31.1-97), the story of Bali's granting of the three steps of land to Vāmana despite Śukra's warning, and his banishment to the netherworld is described. In *Vāmana* (75.1-52) the prosperity and greatness of Bali as well as the impending dangers of the gods from him have been discussed in detail. *Vāmana* (89.27-59) tells about the great sacrifice of Bali, his consecration, and the birth of Vāmana from the womb of Aditi; this is followed by a description of the various attributes of

Vāmana (90.1-48). The next chapter contains a discourse between Bali and Śukra regarding the causes of some omens and portents (91.1-119), followed by the well-known story of his gift of 'three steps' and capitivity in the nether region (92.1-66). The dramatic element of the story as found in the *Harivaṃśa* and other Purāṇas is absent here.

Regarding the origin of Mahiṣāsura, the *Vāmana* says that while two demons Rambha and Karambha were practising austerities, Karambha was killed by Indra and in order to average his brother's death Rambha received a boon from Agni that a son destined to conquer the three worlds would be born to him. Mahiṣa was the son of Rambha by a buffalo. They were all protected by the Yakṣas. Demons like Namara, and Raktavīja were also produced at the same time. Since in valour and might Mahiṣa surpassed all, great demons like Tāraka, Śambara, and others made him their king (*Vāmana* 17.39-73). Regarding the birth of the great goddess who was instrumental in slaying Mahiṣa, the *Vāmana* gives a different account. When Mahiṣa conquered the three worlds the gods became so angry that a mass of energy was produced from their face which was conserved and crystallized in the hermitage of Kātyāyana. The goddess thus produced came to be known as Kātyāyanī (*Vāmana* 18.1-13). As regards subsequent happenings, the *Vāmana* account differs from those of the *Mārkaṇḍeya* and *Varāha*. Two lieutenants of Mahiṣa, Caṇḍa and Muṇḍa, saw this goddess in the Vindhyas and reported to Mahiṣa that this paragon of beauty should be his wife. Dundubhi, the ambassador of Mahiṣa, went to her with a marriage proposal. The goddess replied that according to the custom of her lineage she would marry such a person who defeated her in battle (*Vāmana* 19.1-43). Then a terrible battle ensued, and among the generals of Mahiṣa Namara was the first to resist the goddess. We come across the name of this demon for the first time in the Vāmana, A contingent of Bhūtas came to assist the goddess. After Namara was slain, Cikṣura, Ugrakārmuka, Vāṣkala, Durjaya and Viḍālākṣa took the lead and they were all killed. Finally Mahiṣa was slain by the goddess (*Vāmana* 20.1-51).

The Śumbha-Niśumbha episode of the *Vāmana* is also different from the *Mārkaṇḍeya* version. Śumbha, Niśumbha and Namuci were sons of Danu by Kaśyapa. Indra killed Namuci in the same way as he previously killed Vṛtra, i.e. by using sea-foam. Śumbha and Niśumbha took its revenge by conquering heaven and earth. Raktavīja and Caṇḍa-Muṇḍa, who were previously ministers of Mahiṣa, joined them. The rest of the legend is the same as that of Mahiṣa—the same marriage proposal, the refusal by the goddess, commencement of the war and the extermination of the demons. Among the important demons belonging to Śumbha-Niśumbha's army, Dhūmralocana was reduced to ashes by the shouting of the goddess. When Caṇḍa-Muṇḍa came to fight, the goddess frowned as a result of which Kālī appeared with emaciated and blood-stained body. When the demon Ruru came to attack her she pulled out a tuft of hair from her head and from this sprang a terrible goddess. She came to be known as Caṇḍamārī and having killed Caṇḍa and Muṇḍa received the epithet Cāmuṇḍā. The supreme goddess has the following equation in the *Vāmana*: Pārvatī, Kātyāyani, Ambikā, Caṇḍikā, Kauśikī and Durgā. The next rank comprises Kālikā, Yogīśvarī, Śivā, Śarvā and the Mātṛkās. The Bhūtas and Piśācas were on the side of the goddess. After Caṇḍa and Muṇḍa were slain, Raktavīja came to fight. From the body of the goddess then appeared the Mātṛkās—Maheśvarī, Brahmāṇī, Kaumārī, Vaiṣṇavi, Nārasiṃhī, Aindrī and Śivadūtī. They fought against Raktavīja. Like Andhaka, each drop of Raktavīja's blood created another demon of his stature and Camuṇḍā alone drank all his blood. After Raktavīja was slain, came the turn of Niśumbha and Śumbha. Both of them were killed by the supreme goddess variously called as Kātyāyanī, Durgā, Ambikā, Caṇḍikā and Mṛḍaṇī (*Vāmana* 55-6).

The story of the slaying of the demon Dhundhu as described in the *Vāmana* differs substantially from that found in the *Mbh* (1.192-4) and *Hari* (11) in which it is stated that he was killed by the king Kuvalāśva of the Ikṣvāku line. According to the *Vāmana* version, Dhundhu, son of Danu by Kaśyapa, received the boon of immunity from the gods and made friendship with Hiraṇyakaśipu. The gods thereupon took shelter in the abode of Brahmā. Dhundhu thought of invading the abode of Brahmā, but did not know how to reach it. Dhundhu asked Śukra, the preceptor of the demons, and he replied that by performing the Aśvamedha ritual, Indra once found the place. Dhundhu also performed this sacrifice and the smell of the sacrificial *homa* smoke reached the abode of Brahmā. The gods learnt that Dhundhu had been consecrated in Aśvamedha, and fearing that he might invade the abode of Brahmā, resorted to Viṣṇu. The latter, knowing that Dhundhu could not be killed by the gods, assumed the form of a dwarf and fell on the river Devika on the bank of which Dhundhu was performing his sacrifice. The drowning dwarf was rescued by the demons, and Dhundhu, knowing him to be a poor Brāhmaṇa, wanted to make him a gift. The remaining part of the story is a poor imitation of the Bali-Vāmana legend (*Vāmana* 78.13-89). Among minor elements we have the legend of the demon Jalodbhava who was killed by Viṣṇu and Śiva. It is the story of an invincible and outrageous demon and it is interesting note that in dealing with this demon Śiva used Viṣṇu's *cakra*, and Viṣṇu used Śiva's *śula* (*Vāmana* 81.19-33). The story of the slaying of the demon Mura is narrated in connection with the Andhakāsura legend. This demon received the boon that anyone touched by him on the battlefield would perish. For the fear of his touch Indra left his kingdom. He challenged Yama to fight with him. Yama accepted defeat in advance and sent him to Viṣṇu. When Mura came to fight with Viṣṇu , the latter wanted to know the reason why his heart was trembling and why he was looking like a sick person. A bewildered Mura just pressed his own breast with his hands to make sure that he was all right. And by touching his own breast he perished instantly. Since then Viṣṇu has been known as Murāri (*Vāmana* 60-1).

The *Kurma Purāṇa* only deals with the dynasty of Hiraṇyakaśipu. The gods, being oppressed by Hiraṇyakaśipu, went to Viṣṇu and the latter sent a valiant giant made from his body to destroy the demon. The sons of Hiraṇyakaśipu—Prahlāda, Anuhrāda, and Hrāda as well as his brother Hiraṇyākṣa—offered stubborn resistance and hence Viṣṇu himself assumed the form of the man-lion and killed Hiraṇyakaśipu. Then Prahrāda (Prahlāda) installed Hiraṇyākṣa on the throne of the demon-kingdom. The latter was killed by Viṣṇu in his boar-form. Hiraṇyākṣa's son Andhaka fought against the gods and created thousands of Andhakas from his own body. This proved disastrous to the gods and Viṣṇu created a hundred special goddeses who destroyed all the newly born Andhakas. Then Śiva appeared on the spot and pierced Andhaka with his trident. After propitiating Śiva Andhaka became one of his Gāṇapatyas (*Kūrma* 1.16.21-241). After Andhaka, Prahlāda's son Virocana became the ruler of the demons. He was suceeded by his son Bali who was a devotee of Viṣṇu. Viṣṇu received his gift and he was sent to the netherworld (*Kūrma* 1.17.1-69). Among the hundred sons of Bali, Bāṇa was the chief. He used to oppress the gods and hence Śiva burnt his city. When he repented Śiva became his protector and offered him his Gāṇapatya. Then the Purāṇa goes on to say that among other sons of Danu, Tāra, Śambara, Kapila, Śaṅkara, Svarbhānu, and Vṛṣaparvā were prominent demons. From Surasā hundreds of Gandharvas were produced. From Ariṣṭā serpents were born. From Tāmrā were born six daughters who had begotten various kinds of mythical birds. Herbivorous animals and plants were born of Surabhi. From Khaśā were born the Yakṣas, from Muni the Apsarases, from Krodhavasā the Rākṣasas and from Vinatā, Garuḍa and Aruṇa (*Kūrma* 1.18.1-18).

CHAPTER VIII

Puranic Demonology–III

Among the third generation Purāṇas the *Agni* is a remarkable encyclopaedia of ancient knowledge in which we come across sections on geography, astronomy, astrology, marriage rules, death customs, omens and portents, house-building, various means of livelihood, usages of daily life, science of polity, art of war, civil and criminal laws (based on Yajñavalkya), medicine, metrics, poetry, grammar and even lexicography. It has no special demon lore, but the origins of the demons and their lineages are described in a nutshell in accordance with what is found in other Purāṇas. Apart from the genealogies of the offspring of Diti and Danu, those of Tāmrā, Krodhavasā, Khaśā, Muni and Ariṣṭā are also given (*Agni* 29.6-18). While dealing with the incarnations of Viṣṇu it presents glimpses of the established demon lore, e.g. in connection with the Kūrma (tortoise) incarnation it deals with the legend of the churning of the ocean, in which the Asuras were deceived; concerning the Varāha (boar) incarnation it describes the slaying of Hiraṇyākṣa; in that with Narasiṃha (man-lion) incarnation it tells about the slaying of Hiraṇyakaśipu; and about Vāmana, the dwarf it narrates how Bali was humbled (*Agni* 3.1-11). A summary of the *Rām* is given, in which we come across Rāvaṇa, Taḍakā, Mārīca, Śambara, Śūrpanakhā, Khara, Duṣana, Triśirā, Jaṭāyu, Aruṇa, Kumbhakarṇa, Indrajit, Kumbha, Nikumbha, Makarākṣa, Akampana, Mahodara, Mahāpārśva, Matta, Unmatta, Praghasa, Vaśakarṇa, Virūpākṣa, Devānta, Narānta, Atikāya, and other demon-like characters (*Agni* 5-11). The genealogy of the Rākṣasas, as given here, is as follows. From Brahmā was born Pulastya and from the latter Viśravā, who had two wives, Puṣpotkaṭā and Nikaṣā. From the former was born Kubera and from the latter Rāvaṇa, Kumbhakarṇa, and Vibhīṣana (*Agni* 11.1-4). The story of the *Mbh* is summarized in three chapters (13-16) in which, apart from Baka (13.13) no other demon is mentioned. The exploits of Kṛṣṇa, such as the slaying of Putanā, Ariṣṭā, Vṛṣabha, Keśi, Dhenuka, Gardhava, Cānura, Muṣṭika, Kaṃsa, and Kālayavana as well as the destruction of Śambara by Pradyumna, and Kṛṣṇa's fight with Bāṇa are mentioned (*Agni* 12.16-56).

The *Bhāgavata Purāṇa* is the most popular Purāṇa, regarded as the source of the medieval *bhakti* movement. In many parts of India, literature in regional languages begins with its translation. It may have originated at a comparatively late period, but it certainly utilized very ancient materials. Moreover, it is the one Purāṇa which, more than any one of others, bears the stamp of a unified composition. The myths agree on the whole with those of the *Viṣṇu*, but in some interesting details differ from it. The incarnations of Viṣṇu are described in detail. The legends which are told for the glorification of Viṣṇu are numerous. Those about Dhruva, Prahlāda and so on are already familiar to us from the *Viṣṇu*. With the *Mbh* too, the work has much in common. The demon lore as described in this Purāṇa can be classified under several categories: those which pertain to traditional ancient demons; those which pertain to the genealogies of the sons of Diti; those which pertain to the incarnations of Viṣṇu and those which pertain to the exploits of Kṛṣṇa. Among the legends of the first category those connected with the ancient demon Vṛtra are suggestive. The three-headed Viśvarūpa, son of Tvaṣṭṛ, offered a sacrificial share to the Asuras, because he was related to them on his mother's side. Having come to know of this, Indra severed his three heads. The same story is found in the *Mbh* in which the name of Viśvarūpa was Triśirā. The latter name also recurs in the *Devibhāgavata*. This was a *brahmāhatyā* (slaying of Brāhmaṇa) sin which he did not make any attempt to expiate, but distributed it among earth, water, trees, and women. After the death of Viśvarūpa, his father Tvaṣṭṛ performed a sacrifice for the purpose of killing Indra. From the sacrificial fire was produced an Asura whose name was Vṛtra, so called because he covered everything. Indra and other gods tried to kill him, but all their weapons were devoured by Vṛtra. The gods, finding themselves incapable of destroying Vṛtra, began to pray to the Supreme Being, who was no other than Viṣṇu or Hari, to protect them from Vṛtra's wrath. Viṣṇu agreed to help them provided they followed the path of true devotion (*Bhāgavata* 6.9.1-55).

Thereafter, in accordance with the desire of the Supreme Being, the gods went to the sage Dadhīci and begged of him his body, from which a deadly weapon was to be built for destroying Vṛtra. The gods tried to convince him with high-sounding words on religion and spirituality, but Dadhīci questioned whether the gods had the competence to impart spiritual knowledge. But he said that since the body made of the five material elements was bound to perish, it was better to sacrifice it for a noble purpose. He concentrated his mind to the lotus feet of Viṣṇu and gave up his mortal body. With his bones the divine craftsman Viśvakarman built the *vajra* or thunderbolt. Holding this weapon, Indra on his elephant Airāvata and surrounded by gods went to fight Vṛtra. The Asuras were not at first able to stand before the energy of the gods led by the Rudras, Vasus, Ādityas, Aśvins, Pitṛs, Vanhis, Maruts, Ṛbhus, Sādhyas and Viśvadevas. When they were running away Vṛtra encouraged them saying that it was better to die fighting with honour (*Bhāgavata* 6.10.1-33). Then Vṛtra alone gave a war-cry and rushed towards the gods who began to faint in fear. Indra hurled his club at him, but Vṛtra caught it and threw it at Airāvata, wounding him. Vṛtra fought with no ambition. He did not want heaven, the posts of Dhruva or Brahmā, or lordship of the world. His sole purpose was to receive the grace of Viṣṇu through pure devotion (*Bhāgavata* 6.11.1-27). In Vṛtra's counterattack, the *vajra* of Indra slipped down on the earth from his hand. Vṛtra did not kill Indra, but handed him the *vajra*. Indra was ashamed at this but Vṛtra consoled him saying that victory or defeat depended on the will of the Supreme Being, the controller of all. The fight was renewed and this time Vṛtra devoured Indra. But because Indra was protected by Nārāyaṇa's amulet, he was able to get out from his belly. Then by hurling the *vajra* Indra killed Vṛtra (*Bhāgavata* 6.12.1-35). The author of the *Bhāgavata* says that in reality Vṛtra was not killed. Humbling Indra, he thought that his purpose was achieved. He resorted to *yoga*. His soul left his body and went to the realm of Viṣṇu. It took 360 days to sever his head from the rest of his body.

Demon legends of the *Bhāgavata* pertaining to the genealogies of the incarnations of Viṣṇu are interrelated. While the Kūrma incarnation of Viṣṇu is connected with the churning of the ocean, the next three incarnations are directly connected with the lineage of Diti. One evening while Kaśyapa was offering oblations to the fire, his wife Diti having become sexually excited called her husband for union. Kaśyapa said that it was not the proper time. In the evening Śiva travelled on his bull in company of his ghostly attendants and nothing escaped his three eyes. But Diti, smitten by erotic passion (*manmathonmathitendriyā*), urged him repeatedly and had union with him at the most evil moment. Kaśyapa thereupon said that because the act was done at the wrong time, she would give birth to two evil minded sons. They were to be killed by Viṣṇu for their wickedness, but her grandson Prahlāda would be a pious and righteous person (*Bhāgavata* 3.14.1-51). Diti gave birth to twins, when the three worlds trembled in fear of an impending disaster. Hiraṇyakaśipu was born first and became the lord of the three worlds.

His brother Hiraṇyākṣa helped him in his conquests. He offended Varuṇa with his hot words. Varuṇa calmed his own anger and requested him politely to fight Viṣṇu (*Bhāgavata* 3.17.1-31). Hiraṇyākṣa went to the nether region and found Viṣṇu raising the earth high above in his boar form. He told Viṣṇu to desist since the earth was in his possession, and hurled his weapons at him. But Viṣṇu accomplished his task and placing the earth on the waters, determined to teach him a lesson. He challenged the demon to a fight and prolonged it for the sake of fun. But at the request of Brahmā, he killed Hiraṇyākṣa with his disc (*Bhāgavata* 3.18-19).

After the death of Hiraṇyākṣa, Hiraṇyakaśipu much aggrieved. He practised severe austerities to attain immortality, and received the boon that he could not be killed by any being in a covered or uncovered place, by day or night, with any weapon, on the earth or space or by conscious or unconscious entities. He also received eight *siddhis* (attainments) and overlordship of the three worlds. He became a sworn enemy of Viṣṇu and unleashed a reign of terror. The gods, sages and Brāhmaṇas prayed to Viṣṇu to get rid of this demon. Viṣṇu assured them that Hiraṇyakaśipu's doom would result from his dealing with his son Prahlāda. The *Bhāgavata* then narrates the *Viṣṇu Purāṇa* version of the Prahalāda legend. Two sons of Śukra, Ṣaṇḍa and Amarka, were appointed to teach Prahlāda, but they failed to dissuade him from the worship of Hari. Prahalāda advised Hiraṇyakaśipu to have recourse to Hari or Viṣṇu who was the driving force behind everything. At this an angry Hiraṇyakaśipu tried to kill Prahlāda by any means. But all his attempts were foiled. Prahalāda in his turn taught his follow-students about the greatness of Viṣṇu which he himself had learnt from Nārada when he was in the womb of his mother Kayādhu. Once an excited Hiraṇyakaśipu wanted to know of Prahalāda whether Hari could be within a pillar. Prahlāda answered that since he was everywhere he must be in the pillar as well. Hiraṇyakaśipu inflicted a blow on the pillar. It burst open and Viṣṇu in his man-lion form appeared at one. He killed Hiraṇyakaśipu with his sharp claws. Prahalāda appeased him by extolling his greatness (*Bhāgavata* 7.2-9).

The legend of Bali and Vāmana has been given a philosophical interpretation in the *Bhāgavata*. Aditi performed a *payovrata* ritual, in consequence of which Viṣṇu agreed to be born as her son. After he was born of her as Vāmana, he appeared at the sacrifice of Bali which was being held at Bhṛgukaccha on the Narmada. His lustrous presence made everyone happy and Bali requested him to accept his gift. Vāmana begged of him three steps of land, and Śukra tried to prevent Bali from making the gift since he understood that Viṣṇu himself came in the form of a dwarf. Bali also knew this, but did not dishonour his own commitment. The lord Vāmana then spread himself in heaven and earth by his two steps, but for the third he had no space. With the help of Garuḍa Bali was fettered by Viṣṇu. Even in that condition Bali wanted to know of the place where the third step of the lord could be placed. He said: 'O great one, if you think my commitment has proved false, I must rectify it into truth. I cannot break my promise. So please place your third foot on my head' (8.22.2). At this great self-sacrifice of Bali, Viṣṇu was highly pleased and fixed his residence in the pleasant Sutala world and presented him his own disc (*Bhāgavata* 8.15-22).

Among other legends, the struggle between the Devas and the Asuras is described in connection with the churning of the ocean. In the battle the illusory power of Bali was smashed by Viṣṇu while Indra killed Jambha, Vala, and Pāka. His *vajra*, however, failed to slay Namuci, and he was killed by the trick applied to Vṛtra in one of the *Mbh* stories, which was done by sea-foam (*Bhāgavata* 8.6-11). The stories of the slaying of the demons by Kṛṣṇa as described in the *Bhāgavata* are based on *Harivaṃśa* accounts. Here we shall refer to two stories, those of Tṛṇāvarta and Aghāsura. When Kṛṣṇa was still a child the former had stolen him by creating a whirlwind. But Kṛṣṇa pressed his neck so hard that he died of suffocation (*Bhāgavata* 10.7.1-37). When the boy Kṛṣṇa was enjoying a picnic with his friends the demon Aghāsura,in the form of a serpent came to devour him. But Kṛṣṇa entered his mouth and enlarged his body so that the demon died instantly (*Bhāgavata* 10.12.1-44).

The *Devībhāgavata* is the Śākta counterpart of the Vaiṣṇava *Bhāgavata,* which deals mainly with the slaying of various demons by the Devī. It begins with a Śākta version of the Madhu Kaiṭabha legend. Demons are said to be born from the ears of Viṣṇu. While moving through the waters they understood that their real origins were from the goddess, and with this realization they received the boon that they would remain invincible till the death of their own choice (1.6.19-44). The remaining part of the story is also in variance with what is found in other Purāṇas. Here Madhu and Kaiṭabha fought against Hari and tired him out. He began to contemplate the reason for his weariness and pray to the goddess to come to his rescue, because it was she who gave the demons the boon that they would have the death of their own choice. The goddess, Mahākālī, then assuming the form of a beautiful woman, came to them and made erotic gestures. Both Madhu and Kaiṭabha, smitten by lust, stared at her. Understanding their mental condition, Viṣṇu said to them that their valour had pleased him and he was willing to grant them any boon they desired. The proud demons replied that they had no desire for any boon. Instead, they could grant Viṣṇu a boon. Hari at once asked that they be killed by him (1.9.1-87).

The fourth *skandha* of the *Devībhāgavata* deals with the incarnations of Viṣṇu. The story of the cutting of Diti's embryo to forty-nine pieces, is told here from a different perspective. When Diti was carrying a son equal to Indra, her sister and co-wife Aditi was jealous of her. Aditi told her son Indra that his rival was developing in Diti's womb which he must destroy by any means. While other Purāṇas refer to certain ritualistic lapses of Diti (lying in a wrong position or forgetting to wash her feet), the *Devībhāgavata* does not refer to any such matter. Diti thereupon cursed Indra that he would repeatedly be kicked out from his lordship of heaven. She cursed Aditi that in her next birth she would have to stay in imprisonment and bear repeatedly the loss of her sons. In her next birth Aditi became Devakī, the mother of Kṛṣṇa, who had to remain in imprisonment and bear the loss of seven children (4.3.1-55). The Prahlāda legends have been narrated in the *Devībhāgavata*. After the death of Hiraṇyakaśipu, Prahalāda became the lord of the netherworld. From Cyavana he came to know that Naimiṣa was the greatest *tīrtha* and he went to visit it with his army. There he came in conflict with two sages who were carrying arms. In spite of his best efforts he could not conquer them. Later he understood that they were Nara and Nārāyaṇa. This story has been narrated in the preceding chapter (4.9.1-57). But the *Devībhāgavata* does not give the traditional account of Viṣṇu's subduing the demons in his different incarnations. A new story cycle is found here, glimpses of which are presented below.

Prahlāda fought for a period of a hundred years against Indra. Once defeated he installed his son Virocana on the throne and set out for the Gandhamādana hill for meditation. Virocana's successor Bali also fought against the gods, but he was also defeated and lost his kingdom. Thereupon the Daityas resorted to Śukrācārya and sought his protection. Śukra protected them and the gods left the war in despair. Then Śukra told the demons that his special power was declining. He would go to Mahādeva to have his original power restored. So long as he did not return, the demons should live a peaceful life. The Daityas agreed and approached Prahlāda who informed the gods that the demons had given up their arms and there was no need of conflict. There was a peace treaty. But the gods made a breach of trust. They invaded the kingdom of the demons. Since the demons had given up their arms they could not protect themselves. They went to Śukra's mother and took shelter in her hermitage. The gods followed and began to hit the demons. Thereupon Śukra's mother invoked the goddess of sleep, who overpowered the gods. Under her influence the gods lay fast asleep. At this Viṣṇu with the consent of Indra cut off the head of Sukra's mother with his disc. This act of Viṣṇu was unethical. Śukra's father Bhṛgu, knowing of this, cursed Viṣṇu that he would have to be reborn on earth many times and suffer the pain of mortals. He then restored his wife to life. During Śukra's absence, according to the plan of the gods, Bṛhaspati assumed the form of Śukra and misguided the demons by imparting to them the anti-Vedic Jain religion. When the real Śukra returned to the demons, they failed to recognize him as the real Śukra. Then an angry Śukrācārya cursed the demons and went away. The purpose of Bṛhaspati was achieved. He went back to the gods and asked them to prepare for war. This brought the demons to their senses. They understood that they were deceived by Bṛhaspati who in the form of Śukra had misguided them. Making Prahlāda their spokesman they went to Śukra and pleased him, admitting their fault. Śukra said there was nothing to despair, in the Sāvarṇi age the demons would regain their old position (4.8.15).

The Mahiṣāsura episode of the *Devībhāgavata* is based on the *Vāmana* (17.20) version which describes how he was born of a buffalo and fathered by Rambha, how through his austerities he received the boon that he was not to be killed by any male being,why and how the demons accepted his overlordship, how he fought against the Dikpālas and the gods, and how by defeating the gods he assumed the post of Indra and ruled over the three worlds (5.27). The stories of the conference of the defeated gods, their deputation to Viṣṇu, the creation of the goddess from their energies, and her embellishment with the weapons presented by the gods to her (5.8-9) are based on the *Devīmahātmya* account of the *Mārkaṇḍeya Purāṇa*. The *Varāha* and the *Vāmana* versions of the attraction of Mahiṣa towards the goddess and his marriage proposal to her is also found in the *Devībhāgavata* according to which, having heard the war-cry of the goddess the officers of Mahiṣa reported to him about the eighteen-armed goddess seated on the lion. Mahiṣa sent her a marriage proposal through his officers, but the goddess sternly refused and advised Mahiṣa through them to return to the netherworld. Mahiṣa then bade his officers bring her by force, in consequence of which there was a severe battle (5.10-12). The demons were routed and the commanders of Mahiṣa such as Vāṣkala, Durmukha, Cikṣurākhya and Tāmra were killed (5.13-15). Mahiṣa, assuming human form, went to the battlefield and tried to attract the goddess to him telling various stories about vainglorious women (5.16-17). But the goddess disregarded all his entreaties and threats and cut off his head with her disc (5.18). The story of the slaying of Śumbha and Niśumbha as given in the *Devībhāgavata* is an elaboration of the earlier Puranic accounts. It describes how Śumbha and Niśumbha humbled the gods (5.21), how on the advice of Bṛhaspati the gods invoked Ambikā or Caṇḍikā who was also known as Kauśikī because of her emergence from the black muscles of Pārvatī, how she along with Kālikā came to the city of Śumbha and Niśumbha, how she was seen by Caṇḍa-Muṇḍa and her details were reported to Śumbha and Niśumbha, and how the marriage proposal by Śumbha sent through Sugrīva was turned down by the goddess on the ground that she would marry only one who defeated her in battle (5.22-3). In the battle that ensued, in the first round Dhumralocana, in the second Caṇḍa and Muṇḍa, in the third Raktavīja, and in the fourth Niśumbha were killed. In the final round Śumbha was killed by the goddess (5.24-31).

Among other demon lore in the *Devībhāgavata*, the story of Vṛtra is given in detail. Here it is said that the three heads of Triśrā (Viśvarūpa of the *Bhāgavata*) son of Viśvakarman (Tvaṣṭṛ of the *Mbh* and *Bhāgavata*), were severed by Indra. Viśvakarman in anger performed a sacrifice from the fires of which Vṛtra was produced. Vṛtra fought against the gods and defeated them. Indra fled in fear, leaving his favourite elephant Airāvata to the mercy of Vṛtra. He told his father that by humbling Indra he had accomplished his mission and thereafter repaired to the forest to practise austerities. When Brahmā came to bestow on him a boon, Vṛtra wanted immunity from weapons made of hard and soft materials, during day and night, which was granted. The struggle of the gods and Asuras was renewed and the gods were again defeated. The gods then approached the great goddess and requested her to save them by enchanting Vṛtra by assuming the form of a very attractive woman. But the *Devībhāgavata* does not refer to any incident which proves that Vṛtra was attracted to the goddess or her erotic gestures. There was already a truce between the gods and the demons made at the behest of the gods to find time of respite. One evening Indra saw Vṛtra walking on the sea shore. He thought that evening was neither day nor night, and the froth of the waves neither hard nor soft. He took some foam, and remembering the great goddess, threw it at Vṛtra. By the grace of the goddess the thunderbolt of Indra, recharged with Viṣṇu's energy, entered the foam, and Vṛtra perished (6.1-6). The source of this legend is the *Mbh* and the goddess element has been grafted on to it.

The story of the demon Durgama occurs for the first time in the *Devībhāgavata* though his name is mentioned in the earlier Purāṇas as a potential future victim of the Devī. This demon happened to be the son of Ruru and belonged to the Hiraṇyākṣa lineage. The demons under his leadership captured heaven, for which the gods did not receive their sacrificial share. As a result of that there was no rain, and people were suffering from drought. At the request of the gods and people the great goddess, assuming the form of Śatākṣi, killed Durgama. The latter like Vṛtra was evidently the demon of drought (7.28.1-83). The legend of Tarākasura is not directly mentioned in the *Devībhāgavata* which, however, contains a prayer of the gods to the supreme goddess to become the wife of Śaṅkara, so that their son, who was destined to kill the demon, would save them from his torture (7.31.58-74). The *Devībhāgavata* also gives a sketchy description of Viṣṇu's in his boar form raising the earth and destroying the Asura Hiraṇyākṣa (8.2.1-38). It also describes the Devī's fight with the demons of the Vipracitti lineage, referred to in the earlier Purāṇas in the list of the Devī's future exploits. In this great war Indra fought against Vṛṣaparvā, Bhāskara against Vipracitti, Candra against Dambha, Kāla against Kālakeśvara, Kubera against Kālakeya, Viśvakarman against Maya, Mṛtyu against Bhayamkara, Yama against Śamhara, Varuṇa against Vikamkara, and other gods against various demons. The great goddess in the form of Kālī, accompanied by her attendants, created havoc among the demons. Rudra and Skanda also took part in this battle. The leader of the host of demons, Śankhacuḍa, eventually understood the greatness of the Devī and submitted to her. Under the influence of the Devī Viṣṇu showered his grace on him (9.22-3).

Like the *Devībhāgavata* the *Devī Purāṇa* also belongs to the Śakti cult. This Pūraṇa brings a new set of demon lore, most of the names being unknown in earlier tradition. It begins with the Ghorāsura cycle of legends. Ghora was the lord of demons and a devotee of Viṣṇu who granted him invincibility against all except the Devī. His son Vijradaṇḍa wanted to launch a career of conquest. Ghora was at first unwilling, but his minister Suṣena took up the cause of the prince and convinced Ghora that conquest of other kingdoms was a necessary function for a sovereign monarch. Ghora prayed to Viṣṇu and also received his consent. He conquered the four quarters, but his ambitions did not cease (*Devī* 2.36-104). He conquered the seven island-continents and his sons Vajradaṇḍa and Kāla invaded the nether regions and subdued the Nāgas, Asuras and Rākṣasas by applying *gāruḍī* and *bhairavī* illusions (3.1-22). Then they went to Bhṛgu's son Śukra to ask how they could conquer Indra and other gods. Śukra advised them not to invade heaven because the gods were powerful and firmly established by law. But they paid no heed and reached the Sumeru. Yamāntaka took up a position on the east, Ghora on the north, Vajradaṇḍa on the west, and Kāla on the south. A fierce battle began. The gods were defeated and went to Viṣṇu for help. Viṣṇu said that it was impossible to defeat Ghora. He then told the gods an ancient legend, relating to the former life of the demon (4.1.56). The legend is as follows:

There was once an Asura king known as Dundubhi who became invincible by the boon of Brahmā. He defeated the gods and drove them out of heaven. One day he saw on the top of a hill Umā with Śiva. He was sexually roused at the sight of Umā and tried to capture her. An angry Śiva stared at him and at once his body was reduced to ashes. From the ashes was created a miniature demon who also looked lustfully at Umā. At this Umā cursed him to be born on the earth with a terrible (*ghora*) figure. Śiva said that he was contemplating to kill the demon for ever, but Umā's curse gave him a fresh base of life in the earth. He rebuked Umā for lacking foresight. Umā also got angry with Śiva and said that this Asura would stay at Kuśadvipa and be invincible. Śiva gave a counter curse to Umā that she would also be reborn on the earth and that this Asura would strive to become her husband. Umā retorted that in such a case she would herself kill the demon. The same Dundubhi had become the invincible Ghorāsura in his subsequent birth. But since he had made no transgression of law and remained absolutely religious it was impossible to kill him (4.57-91).

Thereafter Viṣṇu and Bṛhaspati went to Brahmā to find ways and means to destroy Ghorāsura. They invoked the goddess because it was only she who could slay him. At their request the Devī went to reside on the Vindhya mountain along with her companions who were all paragons of beauty. At Viṣṇu's request Nārada went to Ghora and by various apparently attractive arguments misguided Ghora, deflected him from the Vedic way, and roused in him sensual and carnal desires (*Devī* 5-8). He succeeded in converting the entire Asura race to Digambara and Pāṣaṇḍa faith. He had drawn Ghora's attention to the goddess living in the Vindhyas with her beautiful companions. Induced by Nārada, he felt, the sexual attraction of the goddess and thus became devoid of all virtures. The Asura then marched with his army towards the Vindhyas. One of his commanders, Durmukha, saw Devī Vijayā and driven by lust tried to seize her. The goddess looked at him and he was burnt into ashes. Then the Asura army marched upwards and rushed towards the attendants of the great goddess. The demon Kāla was slain by Devi Jayā. Vajrāsura and Yamāntaka were also killed. Suṣena, minister of Ghora created an illusory elephant to fight the goddess. This elephant killed the lion of Jayā. The latter thereupon cut off the head of Suṣena with a disc. Among the companions of the great goddess Jayā, Vijayā, Sandhyā, Ajitā and others participated in the battle. Finally Ghora met his doom at the hand of the great goddess (*Devī* 13-20).

Next we have the story of one Mahādharmāsura. This demon was originally known as Kṛṣṇadharma. The great demon Tāraka pleased Viṣṇu, who told him that he would be immensely benefited by Mahādharmāsura. Accordingly Tāraka went to him and requested him to drive Indra and Brahmā out of heaven. Mahādharmāsura went to conquer them and a battle began between the gods and the demons. His general, the demon Ugrasena, terrorized the gods with his feats. Thereupon Brahmā invoked the supreme goddess, the primal energy, to save the gods. The goddess appeared at once and killed Ugrasena by putting him in fetters. Mahādharmāsura or Kṛṣṇadharma had the same fate (*Devī* 40-1). Another demon, known as Amaya or Amāra, who many times defeated Brahmā and other gods, tried to destroy Gaṇeśa. At this the goddess Kālikā became angry and cursed him. Being cursed, he went to the Jaṭākhya mountain and practised austerities. Viṣṇu granted him the boon that he would remain invincible in battle provided he did not cross thirty-five arrays (*vyūhas*). Following this principle he conquered the gods, the Pitṛs and others. Once he went to the Daṇḍaka forest. Gajānan (Gaṇeśa) was staying there with his friend Paraśūrama. Amaya demanded Sumati, the daughter of Agastya and lover of Gaṇeśa. Paraśurāma tried to dissuade him but Amaya began to shower arrows on him. Thereupon Gaṇeśa made thirty six arrays for battle and put Sumati at the rear. A terrible battle ensued between Gaṇeśa and Paraśurāma on the one side and Amaya and his army on the other. In the course of the war Amaya transgressed the limit of thirty-five arrays and was killed (*Devī* 43.1-66). Another story says that the demon Ruru by the grace of Brahmā became lord of the seven worlds. He invaded heaven and defeated all the powerful gods. Even Śiva failed to resist him. Thereupon Brahmā created from his own energy the goddess Brāhmāṇī who came to assist Śiva in the battle against Ruru. Then from Kārttikeyas's energy emerged Kāumarī. Thus came into existence the Mātṛkās who destroyed Ruru and his army and danced in the battlefield (*Devī* 83-8). These are all dull stories invented mostly for the glorification of the Devī. The story of Khaṭvāsura (111, 118) is a clear example of this. Once Śiva was travelling in the form of an elephant. He had a clash with Viṣṇu. From their wrath was produced Khaṭvāsura who had conquered the three worlds. He defeated the Devas, Dānavas and Nāgas but reinstalled them in their own positions and renounced the world to practise austerities.

In the *Kālikā Purāṇa* which seems to have been composed in the Brahmaputra valley, we have only one demon story about Narākasura, which has a bearing on the early history of Kāmarūpa. Naraka is mentioned in the earlier Purāṇas as one who fought and was slain by Viṣṇu. In the *Kālikā Purāṇa* details have been given. Naraka was the son of the earth, born of her union with Viṣṇu in his boar form. It is said that apprehending the birth of a mighty demon Brahmā and other gods made the womb of the earth so stiff that the delivery of the child was delayed. Viṣṇu consoled the earth, saying that the son would be born to her after destruction of Rāvaṇa by Rāma in the Tretā age. After Rāvaṇa's death the earth appeared before king Janaka and requested him in the presence of Nārada to bring up the child she bore. Jānaka readily agreed. Then she gave birth to Naraka when Viṣṇu came to her and said that this child would be the ruler of Prāgjyotiṣa country. Naraka excelled other princes in beauty, character and valour. When Nāraka was sixteen years old the earth took him to the bank of the Ganges and disclosed the secret of his birth. Viṣṇu was also present there. Then they took him to the Prāgjyotiṣa country which was inhabited by the Kirātas who had no regard for the Vedas and Vedic rites. Their king Ghaṭaka came with a huge army and fought Naraka. But the latter routed the Kirāta army. He drove away the hostile Kirātas beyond the Dikkaravāsinī river, and became king. The rivers Karatoyā and Lauhitya (Brahmāputra) flowed through his kingdom where was installed the great goddess Kāmākhya. Viṣṇu married Naraka to Māyā, daughter of the king of Vidarbha, installed him as the ruler of the land and advised him to pay respect to the sages and the Brāhmaṇas. Naraka proved himself to be a very wise and successful ruler (*Kālikā* 235-8).

The legend has evidently an historical attraction since the region in which Naraka was installed as king is a well known geographical region. It implies the introduction of Vedic culture to the north-eastern region of India. The remaining part of the Naraka legend, however, follows the earlier mythical tradition. Naraka was acquainted with the Asura Bāṇa (son of Bali) of Śoṇitapura who was a worshipper of Śiva (testified by earlier Puranic tradition). Under his influence Naraka had taken an anti-Brahmānical attitude. He did not even honour the goddess Kāmākhya. At this the sage Vasiṣṭha uttered a curse that he would be destroyed by the same Viṣṇu who was his father. Naraka then went to the temple of Kāmākhya on Nīlakūṭa mountain and found that the goddess had left. He remembered Viṣṇu and his mother Pṛthivī, but they did not appear before him. A frustrated Naraka then depended solely on his friend Bāṇa and invoked his own doom. Bāṇa advised him to worship Brahmā and Śiva. He practised austerities on the bank of the Lauhitya. When Brahmā came to grant him boons he asked for immunity from gods and demons, perpetuation of his lineage, invincibility, beautiful women as his wives, and prosperity. But he forgot about the curse of Vasiṣṭha. Hearing of the boons he received Bāṇa was not happy because the austerities of Naraka gave him a chance to redress Vasiṣṭha's curse. Naraka had four powerful sons—Bhagadatta, Mahāśīrsa, Madavān, and Sumālī. On Bāṇa's advice, he brought an Asura named Hayagrīva and appointed him as his general. Other demons joined Naraka's army. They defeated Indra and ravaged the heaven. The Earth went to Brahmā and Viṣṇu and said that she was overburdened with the demons and wanted to be relieved of them . The gods requested Mādhava (Viṣṇu) to relieve the Earth. In the final war Viṣṇu destroyed Hayagrīva and other demons (the Hayagrīva-Mādhava temple at Hajo near Gauhati is a remembrance of this event). While the battle was going on the goddess Kālikā appeared and encouraged the gods. Naraka was slain by Viṣṇu. The Earth did not lament because she knew that it would happen (*Kālikā* 37-40).

The *Brahmavaivarta Purāṇa* is basically Vaiṣṇavite and narrates the stories of Kṛṣṇa's slaying of the demons on the basis of the Harivaṃśa accounts. It deals with Kṛṣṇa's slaying of Putanā by sucking her breast (4.10) , destruction of Tṛṇāvarta (4.11), killing of Vaka, Keśi and Pralamba (4.16), the taming of Kāliyā (4.19), slaying of Dhenuka (4.22) and killing of Kaṃsa (4.72). It also describes the exploits of Kṛṣṇa's son Pradyumna or Kāmadeva and the story of his slaying the Asura Śambara (4.112). The love of the Asura Bāṇa's daughter Uṣā and Aniruddha, abduction of Aniruddha by Citralekhā, *gāndharva* marriage of Uṣā and Aniruddha which resulted in Bāṇa's fight with Aniruddha and his defeat (4.114-16) is narrated. The story of Siva's participation in the war in favour of the Asura Bāṇa against Kṛṣṇa and Yādava army has also been described (4.120). The legend of the demon Śaṅkhacūḍa and Tulasī is interesting. Tulasī, who was in her previous birth a *gopī* of Kṛṣṇa was reborn as a demon princess owing to a curse uttered by Rādhā. Once while she was resting in a garden at Badarika Tulasī met the demon lord Śaṅkhacūḍa and fell in love with him. Śaṅkhacūḍa in his previous birth was Sudāmā, one of the eight *gopa* associates of Kṛṣṇa. He was a *yogī* who received an amulet of invincibility from Brahmā. He was also granted the boon that so long as his wife remained chaste no one in the three worlds could kill him. They were married and lived a very happy life. For a whole *manvantara* Śaṅkhacūḍa remained lord of the Devas, Dānavas, Asuras, Gandharvas, Kinnaras and Rākṣasas. But the gods resented Śaṅkhacūḍa's sovereignty. They conspired against Śaṅkhacūḍa and went to Viṣṇu, who said he would do the needful. Thereupon Śiva sent the Gandharva Puṣpadanta as his envoy to Śaṅkhacūḍa, who carried the message to him that the gods had declared war against him. Tulasī was sad to receive the news of the invasion, but Śaṅkhacūḍa consoled her saying that he was invincible. He had a meeting with Śiva in which he said that he was unable to betray his tribe. He pointed out that the gods were basically selfish, ungrateful and unjust. He asked what the offence of Bali was, why his treasures were appropriated, why he was sent to the nether world. Why did the gods deceive the demons during the churning of the ocean? Then the war between the gods and the demons took place, but notwithstanding their best efforts the gods failed to conquer the demons. Kārttikeya was defeated by Śaṅkhacūḍa and so was Kālī. Then Viṣṇu in the disguise of an old Brāhmaṇa stole Śaṅkhacūḍa's amulet of invincibility. He also committed another heinous offence. Śaṅkhacūḍa was granted the boon that so long as his wife remained chaste he could not be killed. Assuming the form of Śaṅkhacūḍa he violated the chastity of Tulasī. Then Śiva was able to slay Śaṅkhacūḍa (2.15-21).

No demon lore is found in the *Bṛhaddharma Purāṇa* except the well known story of Bali and Vāmana. The account is in accordance with that of the earlier Purāṇas. Only one extra episode has been given explaining why the goddess Aditi agreed to conceive Viṣṇu in her womb. When the gods were repeatedly defeated by Bali, Aditi, their mother, for the sake of their welfare, began to practise austerities in a forest. In order to dissuade her, the Asuras assumed the forms of gods and entreated her with sweet words and appealing gestures to desist. But Aditi recognized them. The demons, being exposed, tried to kill her by creating a fire, but Viṣṇu protected her with his disc (2.15). The *Bṛhaddharma* also narrates the Rāma story in brief and refers to Rāma's Durgā worship in autumn for the purpose of destroying Rāvaṇa (1.18-22). The *Liṅga Purāṇa* describes the destruction of Tripura, the triple-cities of gold, silver and iron made by Maya for the Asuras Vidyunmālī, Tārakākṣa and Kamalākṣa, by Śiva with a single shaft (1.71-2). We have already had occasion to narrate the story. In the *Liṅga* a bare outline has been inserted with numerous verses in praise of Śiva. The Andhaka legend is also mentioned in which his antecedents have not been described. The story of creation of other demons from his blood is absent. Here he is only pierced by Śiva and becomes a changed personality (1.93). The story of the destruction of Hiraṇyākṣa by Viṣṇu in his boar form and that of Hiraṇyakaśipu by Viṣṇu in his man-lion form are also described in brief outline (1.94-5), but since the Purāṇa is devoted to Śiva, the story of a combat between Narasiṃha (man-lion) and Virūpākṣa (attendant of Śiva) is narrated in which the latter came out victorious (1.96). The Bali-Vāmana episode is narrated in the *Bṛhannāradīya Purāṇa* (10-11) in which the *Bṛhad-dharma* account of dissuading Aditi from performing austerities, the demons assuming the form of gods, and the futile attempt to burn Aditi and the conception of Viṣṇu in her womb is found.

In the third generation Purāṇas the earlier demon lores has been reviewed and restated with sectarian motives. The *Liṅga Purāṇa* is basically Śaivite and an extension of the earlier *Vāyu* and *Śiva Purāṇas* while the *Devībhāgavata*, *Devī* and *Kālika* Purāṇas, extolling the greatness of Śakti, have their roots in the *Devīmāhātmya* section of the *Mārkaṇḍeva Purāṇa*. The Vaiṣṇavite *Bhāgavata*, and *Brahmavaivarta* follow the tradition introduced by the *Harivaṃśa*, *Viṣṇu* and *Matsya Purāṇas*. The *Padma Purāṇa* is also a Vaiṣṇavite Purāṇa in which the cause of the discomfiture of the demons is attributed to their failure to recognize the greatness of Viṣṇu. In the Bhūmikhaṇḍa of the *Padma*, it is stated that Danu, the mother of the Dānavas, reported to her sister Diti, the mother of the Daityas, that their sons were victims of injustice, despite their best qualities, deprived of the heavenly kingdom and destroyed ruthlessly. Their husband Kaśyapa consoled them saying that what happened to the demons was due to their *karma* and incapability of appreciating the greatness of Viṣṇu who caused Aditi give birth to Vasudatta (Indra) as the exterminator of the demons (*Bhūmi* 6-7). Elsewhere in the same text we find that Hiraṇyakaśipu and other demons asked Kaśyapa the same question, and his answer was the same as was given to Diti (*Bhūmi* 10).

Apart from such observations the said section of the *Padma Purāṇa* presents a summary version of the earlier demonic tradition with *Viṣṇu* as the key person controlling everything. But this demon lore is somewhat different from the earlier accounts. Here it is said that after the destruction of Hiraṇyakaśipu and Hiraṇyākṣa along with their attendants by Viṣṇu, an aggrieved Diti prayed to Kaśyapa to bestow upon her a son who would surpass Indra in might and valour. Her prayer was granted and Diti gave birth to a son named Vala. In course of time Vala became powerful in knowledge, valour and virtue. Then Diti advised him to fight the gods and Danu advised him to have Indra as his principal rival. One day Indra found Vala meditating on the seashore and killed him quite unjustly. When Diti heard the news that her son was killed by Indra while he was engaged in prayer, she reported it to Kaśyapa who became furious. He tore out a tuft of his hair and threw it on the fire. From this emerged Vṛtra, and Kaśyapa bade him destroy Indra. Indra became afraid and sent the seven sages (Saptarṣi) to mediate. Vṛtra relented, provided that Indra would not resort to chicanery. But Indra, who was by nature deceitful, engaged Rambhā, the celestial nymph, to mislead him to the path of vice. Rambhā attracted him greatly and owing to her repeated request Vṛtra once drank wine and became intoxicated. Taking advantage of this situation Indra killed Vṛtra with his *vajra.* Being accused by the seven sages, who acted as intermediaries in the conclusion of the friendship treaty, of this act of knavery Indra said that it was pure politics in which nothing was improper. When Vala and Vṛtra were thus slain, at the request of Diti, Kaśyapa promised to give her a son. When Diti was carrying him Indra entered her womb and cut the embryo into pieces.

We come across a new demon called Huṇḍa in the *Padma Purāṇa.* A maid, Aśokasundarī, born of a tree and adopted by Śiva and Pārvatī, was destined to marry Nahuṣa, son of Āyus. The demon Huṇḍa of the Vipracitti lineage saw her and desired her as his wife. The maid said that the goddess Pārvatī had selected Nahuṣa as her husband and hence she could marry no other person. The demon said that Nahuṣa was yet to be born and so there was no need to waste her youth. But the maid was not convinced. The demon thus tried another trick. Assuming the form of another beautiful maid he made friends with her and invited her home; there he disclosed his identity and wanted to have her. The maid Aśokasundarī cursed Huṇḍa that he would be slain by Nahuṣa and then went to the Ganga and practised austerities in order to have Nahuṣa as her husband. The king Āyus, having pleased Dattātreya, received the boon of an invincible son. When the child was born, Huṇḍa stole it, assuming the form of a maid-servant, and gave it to his wife Vipulā, asking her to cut it into pieces and cook its flesh for him. Vipulā wanted to know the reason and Huṇḍa had to explain why he was cursed by Aśokasundarī. Vipulā, thinking that the child was destined to kill her husband, gave it to their cook. The cook and a female attendant had compassion on the child. It was sent to Vasiṣṭha's hermitage, and the cook served Huṇḍa the flesh of a deer. Huṇḍa knew that he had eaten the child and became fearless. Meanwhile Nārada came and consoled Āyus and Indumatī saying that a demon had stolen their child, but the child would return to them with the head of the demon. The child grew up and came to be known as Nahuṣa. Huṇḍa went to Aśokasundarī who was still practising austerities and told her that he had eaten up the son of Āyus and again entreated her to have union with him. Aśokasundarī did not believe in his words and turned him down. Meanwhile Nahuṣa came to know of everything and set out to punish Huṇḍa. The gods presented him various divine weapons. He seized the city of Huṇḍa and after a violent war killed him. He married Aśokasundarī and came back to his parents at Hastināpura with his newly-wedded wife (*Bhūmi* 103-17).

There is another legend, that of Huṇḍa's son Vihuṇḍa. In order to avenge his father's death he ravaged the heaven. Viṣṇu thereupon created an illusory maiden at whose appearance Vihuṇḍa was infatuated. The maiden, Māyā, said that she was ready to be his wife if he worshipped Śiva with seven crores of *kāmoda* flowers. When he went to Śukra for help to identify the flower, the latter said that there was no *kāmoda* tree. But there was a *kāmoda* woman from whose laughter thousands of fragrant yellow flowers were produced and from whose tears sprang forth red flowers, without any fragrance. The yellow ones were auspicious but the red ones were dangerous. The woman lived in the city of Kāmodākhya. Śukra advised Vihuṇḍa to find the woman and make her laugh by gentle means. But the wily Nārada, learning his intention, advised Vihuṇḍa not to go to the city of Kāmodākya since it was protected by Viṣṇu who could create problems. It would be far easier for him to collect the flowers coming afloat from their source down the Ganga. Then Nārada went to Kāmoda and by persuasion made her weep. From her tears were produced thousands of flowers with which the infatuated demon worshipped Śiva. When Śiva was worshipped with inauspicious flowers emanating from grief, he became angry. He also understood that Vihuṇḍa worshipped him not with any noble intention. Vihuṇḍa also failed to appease Śiva and this caused his ruin (*Bhūmi* 118-23).

The story of the destruction of Tripura is found in the *Padma Purāṇa*. Here it is stated that the triple city was in possession of the Asura Bāṇa. This Bāṇa seems to be different from the son of Bali and a favourite of Śiva. Or it is possible that the narrator of the *Padma Purāṇa* had not in his mind the earlier tradition, though this Bāṇa is described by him as a great soul and very religious in character. What provoked Śiva to destroy

Tripura is not clearly stated in the *Padma*. Śiva said that the male inhabitants of Tripura were godlike while the females were like the Apsarases. He directed Nārada to spoil the women of Tripura which Nārada did with misleading advice. The *Padma* says that the three cities were united and Śiva seated on a special chariot destroyed Tripura by 'three' shafts. But the background of this event has not been given (*Svarga* 7). The *Pātālakhaṇḍa* of the *Padma Purāṇa* is a restatement of the Uttarakāṇḍa of the *Rāmāyaṇa*. It has no demon lore except the birth-stories or Rāvaṇa, Kumbhakarṇa, Vibhīṣana and Kubera (*Pātāla* 4). While dealing with Rāma's horse sacrifice it refers to the slaying of the Rākṣasa Vidyunmālī who had stolen the wandering sacrificial horse (*Pātāla* 19).

In the *Skanda Purāṇa* the earlier demon lores has been restated with slight modification. It begins with the story of Dakṣa's sacrifice, to which Śiva was not invited. Śiva's wife Satī asked her father Dakṣa why he had not invited Śiva. At this Dakṣa made disparaging remarks on Śiva. The insulted Satī put an end to her life. Hearing this news an angry Śiva tore one of his matted locks and dashed it on the top of a hill. Vīrabhadra, Bhadrakālī and crores of Bhūtas thus came into existence. These Pramathas of Śiva destroyed the sacrifice of Dakṣa. The gods then came to fight Śiva. Virabhadra and his *gaṇas* defeated Indra, Viṣṇu and other gods. Dakṣa's head was cut off (*Kedāra* 3-5). In this episode we find that like any other demon chief, Śiva fought against the gods and his army comprised Bhūtas and demon-like beings. It is said that among the demons, the Vaiṣṇavas like Prahlāda, Rākṣasas like Vibhīṣana and Asuras Bali, Namuci, Hiraṇyakaśipu, Vṛṣaparavā, Saṃhrāda and Bāṇa were protected by Śiva. Among other famous Rākṣasa worshippers of Śiva mention is made of Heti, Praheti, Vighasa, Praghasa, Vidyujjihva, Dhumrākṣa, Mālī, Sumālī, Mālyavāna, Vidyutkeśa, Tātijjhva, Rāvaṇa and Kumbhakarṇa. Rāvaṇa, was the greatest worshipper of Śiva. It was due to Śiva's grace that Rāvaṇa surpassed the Devas, Ṛṣis and Pitṛs, defeated the Lokapālas, raised Kailāśa and subdued Indra. Rāvaṇa offered his ten heads to Śiva and when the latter came to grant him a boon he asked for nothing but unflinching devotion to him (*Kedāra* 7.26-54). Vast and varied are the contents of *Skanda* which deals with Śiva in his various capacities. But his association with the demons has been narrated in numerous passages. Eventually, however, his role was reversed.

The legend of Bali has been dealt with in the *Skanda* in a different perspective. It is stated that once Indra dishonoured Bṛhaspati and the latter left the company of gods. When their preceptor left them the gods became weak. Taking advantage of the weakness of the gods, Bali, the lord of the demons, came with his army from the netherworld, defeated the gods, and occupied the post of Indra. Thereupon Indra went to Viṣṇu who advised him to make friendship with the demons (of course with the ulterior motive of reconquest of their kingdom). Then Indra went to Bali with the Lokapālas and other gods and told him that since both Devas and Asuras were children of Kaśyapa, there was no need to maintain hostility. Great as he was, Bali made friendship with Indra. One day Indra proposed a joint churning of the ocean by gods and demons, in order to obtain various riches. Bali honestly agreed and the churning of the ocean began with Mandara as the pole and Vāsuki as the cord. In course of the churning arose deadly poison which covered the space. Then at the invocation of the gods Śiva appeared on the spot and consumed the poison. The churning started once again, from which emerged the moon, the wish-fulfilling cow, gems, and Lakṣmī who became Viṣṇu's spouse. The churning continued then out came Dhanvantari with the pot of *amṛta* in his hand. It was taken by the Dānava Vṛṣaparvā, but Viṣṇu assumed the form of a woman of unparalleled beauty, took the pot of *amṛta*, asked the gods and demons to sit in rows, but distributed it only to the gods. Then ensued the great fight between the demons and the gods. Under the leadership of Kālanemi the demons were victorious. But eventually Kālanemi was killed by Viṣṇu and the gods reconquered heaven. The defeated demons thereupon went to Śukra, who practised austerities for their success, and restored the dead demons to life (*Kedāra* 9-14).

When Bṛhaspati left Indra, Viśvarūpa (son of Viśvakarman), became the priest of the gods. But since he offered sacrificial oblations to the Asuras, Indra pierced his head with his *vajra*. In order to avenge the killing of his son, Viśvakarman practised austerities and received Vṛtra as his son. Hearing of the emergence of Vṛtra the demons of the nether world received him as their lord and came to fight the gods. Directed by Brahmā, the gods begged Dadhīci for his bones with which the deadly weapon *vajra* was produced. The war with the demons was renewed. When Vṛtra proved himself to be more powerful, the gods at the command of Bṛhaspati began to worship Śiva and perform the *sanipradoṣa* ritual. In his previous birth Vṛtra was the Gandharva Citraratha who incurred the wrath of Śiva for his straight words and was cursed to be born as an Asura. By the grace of Śiva Indra was revitalized but he was again defeated by Vṛtra. Advised by Śiva, Indra made friendship with Vṛtra but killed him by unfair means. The head of Vṛtra fell on the Mālava country and his body on Antarvedī, the region between the Ganga and Yamuna. It took six months to sever the head of the dead Vṛtra. When the news of Vṛtra's slaughter reached the nether region Bali was angry. At the command of Śukra he performed a sacrifice and obtained a special chariot. Then he set out to fight the gods and conquer heaven (*Kedāra* 15-17).

Hearing the news of Bali's arrival Indra and other gods assumed the form of birds and ran away from heaven. They went to the hermitage of Kaśyapa and informed their mother Aditi of the impending danger. Aditi performed the vow of *srāvaṇadvādasī* to invoke Viṣṇu. Meanwhile Śukra consecrated Bali on the throne of Indra. Bali donated the property of Indra to the Brāhmaṇas and thus acquired great merit. The *Skanda* narrates a peculiar story with regard to the origin of Bali. Once a debauch was carrying flowers and betels for his favourite courtesan. But these articles fell from his hands and the debauch uttered *śivārnavamestu* and thus received Śiva's grace. For a very limited period he obtained Indra's post and in his limited tenure performed some pious acts. That debauch then entered the womb of Suruci, the wife of Virocana, and was born as Bali. Bali conquered heaven, but, advised by Śukra, left and settled at Gurukula *tīrtha* on the bank of Narmadā, where he performed the Aśvamedha sacrifice. Meanwhile Aditi gave birth to Viṣṇu as Vāmana (dwarf) who came to the place of Bali's sacrifice and begged of him 'three steps' of land. The remaining part of the story is well known (*Kedāra* 18-19).

The legend of the slaying of Tarakāsura is narrated in the *Skanda* on the basis of the earlier accounts. The story of the burning of Madana has been slightly fabricated. After Madana was burnt, and his wife Rati was lamenting, Pārvatī consoled her saying that Madana would be reborn. Nārada went to the Asura Śambara and instigated him to abduct Rati. This is the precursor of the legend of Madana's rebirth as Pradyumna or Kāmadeva, son of Rukminī, his slaying of the Asura Śambara, and winning back his beloved Rati, narrated above. The story of the austerity of Pārvatī, Śiva's marriage with her, the birth of Kumāra or Skanda-Kārttikeya and the slaying of Tarakāsura has been narrated in the *Skanda* in accordance with the accounts given in the *Kumārasambhava* and earlier Purāṇas (*Kedāra* 20-30). These are also described in another section in detail (*Kumārikā* 22-32). The story of the birth of Tāraka is also mentioned in connection with which the birth of Vajrānga as the son of Diti, his capture of Indra, his austerities, his wife Varāṅgī's suffering at the hands of Indra, the development of the spirit of vengence in him, etc., have been described in detail. The severe austerities of Tāraka on the Pāriyātra hill and Brahmā's boon of immunity from everyone save a seven-year old child, are also given (*Kumārikā* 14-15).

In connection with the Tārakāsura legend a detailed account of the struggle between the gods and the demons is furnished in the *Skanda*. Among the generals of Tāraka, Grasana defeated Yama and his troops. Kubera was, however, able to defeat the Asura Jambha, but he was defeated by Kujambha. Then Nirṛti came to fight Kujambha, but was defeated. Thereupon Varuṇa by his illusory power fettered Kujambha. The Asura Mahiṣa then came to devour Nirṛti and Varuṇa Candra imposed a severe winter upon the Asuras, but Kalanemi prevented that with his fire weapon. Sūrya by his special power created an illusion before Kālanemi who was puzzled. But his son Nemi dispelled the illusion and Kālanemi brought the situation in his favour. At last Viṣṇu himself came to fight, seated on Garuḍa. He defeated Kālanemi and killed many demons. But the Asura Jambha advanced with his forces and Viṣṇu had to run away. Indra also fought bravely and killed Jambha. The demons won the battle. Indra, Viṣṇu, and other gods were given the form of apes and brought before Tarakāsura. The victorious Tarakāsura heroically freed the gods and reinstated them at the posts they previously held (*Kumārikā* 16-21). Chapters 22-30 of the *Kumārikā-Khaṇḍa* of the *Skanda* deal with the marriage of Śiva and Pārvati and the birth and consecration of Kārttikeya. Making him leader the gods again attacked the Asuras. In the battle Kārttikeya was unwilling to kill Tāraka because he was a devotee of Śiva. But for the sake of the welfare of the gods, he had to do so (*Kumārikā* 31-2).

The *Skanda* relates a legend about Ghaṭotkaca and his son Barbarika. Ghaṭotkaca's wife was Kāmakaṭankaṭā. Kṛṣṇa advised Barbarika to worship the goddess Siddhāyikā. He became a favourite of the goddess and stayed with her at Dagdhathalī. Once Bhīma came there and entered the spring of the goddess without permission. Barbarika gave him a sound beating and was about to throw him on the sea, but Rudra appeared and told Barbarika that Bhīma was his grandfather. Barbarika was repentant. He became an ally of the Pāṇḍavas. Before the Kurukṣetra war he boasted, not without reason, that he could alone exterminate the Kaurava army. As proof of his ability he shot an arrow which showered ashes. Particles of ash fell on the limbs of the heroes, creating burn-spots on vulnerable parts of their bodies. Thus the ashes fell on the pores of Bhīṣma's skin, the necks of Droṇa, Karṇa, Śakuni, Bhagadatta, Drupada and Virāṭa, the thigh of Duryodhana, the breast of Śalya, the abdomen of Śikhaṇḍī, and the feet of Kṛṣṇa. At this every one was spellbound. But

Kṛṣṇa instantly beheaded him with his disc. Seeing him dead the Pāṇḍavas began to weep and Ghaṭotkaca began to lament loudly. Then the goddess Siddhāyikā appeared and consoled them saying that in his previous birth Barbarika was the Yakṣa king Sūryavarcā. When the Earth requested Viṣṇu that she was overburdened with people and that she wanted relief, this Sūryavarcā boasted that he could do it alone. Thereupon Brahmā cursed him that he would be slain by Viṣṇu in his next birth. But since he was pious and devoted he had always been protected by the goddess herself and notwithstanding his death he was still protected. Kṛṣṇa then anointed the severed head of Barbarika with *amṛta*, placed it on the top of a mountain, and declared that this head would remain immortal through the ages (*Kumārikā* 68.1-80).

The story of Devī's slaying of Asura Mahiṣa is told twice in the *Skanda*. The version is, however, different from the *Mārkaṇḍeya* account. While the goddess was practising austerities at Aruṇācala, Mahiṣa arrived on a hunt . The Vaṭukas who were the guards of Devī's resort, dissuaded him to enter there. Mahiṣa assumed the form of an old man, entered as a guest, disclosed his identity and proposed marriage to the goddess. The goddess challenged him in war, and assuming the form of Durgā, attacked Mahiṣa. From her body came out numerous Bhūtas, Vetālas, Mātṛkās and Yoginīs who fought the demon army. After a fierce battle Mahiṣa was slain, but since he was a devotee of Śiva, the goddess was touched by sin. At Aruṇācala she created Khaḍgatīrtha and had a bath there. She asked the sage Gautama how her sin would be expiated. Gautama advised her to make penance on the full-moon day of Kārttika at Aruṇācala until the flame of Śiva was seen by her. When the Devī performed all the rituals Śiva appeared before her and said that by slaying Mahiṣa she had done the right thing (*Aruṇācala, Pūrva* 10-11; *Uttara* 19-20).

The Purāṇas deal with numerous subjects, demon lore being one of them. In this the greatest emphasis has been laid upon the demons of the Asura category, that is, the Daityas and the Dānavas. The Rākṣasas are there, but they are less prominent. In fact with the destruction of Rāvaṇa, the importance of the Rākṣasa race was lost. After Rāvaṇa no charismatic personality developed among the Rākṣasas. The Purāṇas deal with the origins of the Gandharvas, Yakṣas, Apsarases, Nāgas, and various demonic birds and beasts, but in constrast with the Daityas and Dānavas, they are colourless and insignificant. True, there is Kubera, but he is ranked with the gods and fights against the demons on their behalf. While in the epics we come across many of his exploits, in the Purāṇas he is almost a passive spectator. The Apsarases in certain cases are more active, because they were often employed by Indra to delude the demons and sages. The Bhūtas, Piśācas, Pitrs, and Pramathas are conspicious but they have no special role. By nature demons, were with the gods because of their association with Śiva. In fact in order to drive all demons out, Śiva himself became eighty per cent demon. The Asuras are not described as cannibals, but the Rākṣasas are. The blood of Andhaka and Raktavīja was consumed by Mātṛkās. That the Puranic demon-lore had great impact on popular imagination is attested to by sculptural representations all over India. There are numerous representations of the incarnations of Viṣṇu, even though the Vaiṣṇava devotees do not seem to have been inclined to depict his terrible demon killing form. The Śaivas, however, did not hesitate to depict the *saṃhāra-mūrtis*, demon-slaying forms, of Śiva. This held good also in the case of the Śaktas as is attested by the numerous depictions of the Mahiṣamardinī images. Representations of other terrible forms of the goddess and her associates are frequently found.

NOTES AND REFERENCES

Traditionally there are eighteen Mahā-Purāṇas and eighteen Upa-Purāṇas. The list of the Mahā-Purāṇas is given in almost all the Purāṇas, mostly in the same order, and is uniform except for a couple of changes. However, there is no uniformity in the enumeration of the Upa-Purāṇas. Texts of the major Purāṇas were published by the Ānandāśrama Sanskrit Series of Poona and the Veṅkateśvara Press, Bombay. Edited texts of the Purāṇas were published by the Asiatic Society of Bengal in the Bibliotheca Indica Series. In the absence of a Critical Edition, the most dependable Puranic texts were published by the Vaṅgavāsī Press, Calcutta. The volumes were edited by the renowned Sanskrit scholar Panchanan Tarkaratna (1887ff.) by comparing various unprinted and printed manuscripts. Some of the Purāṇas have been translated into English and other European languages. There is no specific work on Puranic demonology, but the following works are important—H.H. Wilson, *Purāṇas: An Account of Their Contents and Nature*, Calcutta, 1897; F.E. Pargiter, *The Puranic Texts of the Dynasties of the Kali Age*, London, 1913; *Ancient Indian Historical Tradition*, Oxford, 1922; J.N. Farquhar, *Outline of Indian Religious Literature*, London, 1990; E. Abegg, *Der Pretakalpa des Garuḍa Purāṇa*, Leipzig, 1921; H.D. Sarma, *Padma Purāṇa and Kālidāsa*, Calcutta, 1925; W. Kirfel, *Das Purāṇa Pañcalakṣaṇa*, Leiden, 1927; H. Mainhard, *Beiträge zur Kenntnis des Śivaismus nach den Purāṇen*, Berlin, 1928; V.R.R. Dikshitar, *Some Aspects of the Vāyu Purāṇa*, Madras, 1933; *Matsya Purāṇa: A Study*, Madras, 1935; *The Purana Index*, 3 vols., Madras, 1951-5; R.C. Hazra, *Studies in the Puranic Records on Hindu Rites and Customs*, Dacca, 1940; D.R. Patil, *Cultural History from the Vāyu Purāṇa*, Poona, 1946; Y. Tandon, *Concordance of Purāṇa Contents*, Hoshiarpur, 1952; A.B.L. Awasthi, *Studies in the Skanda Purāṇa*; V.S. Agrawala, *Matsya Purāṇa: A Study*,

Varanasi, 1963; *Vāmana Purāṇa: A Study,* Varanasi, 1964; N.Y. Desai, *Ancient Indian Society, Religion and Mythology as depicted in the Mārkaṇḍeya Purāṇa,* Baroda, 1968; Vettam Mani, *Puranic Encyclopaedia,* Delhi, 1978; P.G. Lalye, *Studies in the Devibhagavata,* Bombay, 1973; C.M. Brown, *God as Mother: An Historical and Theological Study of the Brahmavaivarta Purāṇa,* Hartfort, 1974; P. Solis, *The Kṛṣṇa Cycle in the Purāṇas: Themes and Motives in a Heroic Saga,* Delhi, 1984; Sindhu S. Dange, *The Bhagavata Purāṇa—Mytho-Social Study*, Delhi, 1984; Clifford Hospital, *The Righteous Demons,* University of British Columbia Press, 1984; T.B. Coburn, *Devīmāhātmya,* Delhi, 1984; Ariel Glucklich, *The Sense of Adharma,* New York, 1944; N.N. Bhattacharyya, *The Indian Mother Goddess,* 2nd edn., New Delhi, 1999; *Indian Religious Historiography,* New Delhi, 1996; *History of the Śakta Religion,* 2nd edn., New Delhi, 1996.

Abbreviations and Bibliography

AA — *Aitareya Āraṇyaka*, ed. by R.L. Mitra, Bib. Ind., Calcutta, 1876; ed. with Eng. trans. by A.B. Keith, Oxford, 1909.

AB — *Aitareya Brāhmaṇa*, ed. with com. of Sāyaṇa by Satyavrata Samasrami, Bib. Ind., Calcutta, 1894-1906; Eng. trans. by A.B. Keith, HOS, Cambridge Mass, XXV, 1920.

ADV — *Advayayajrasaṃgraha*, ed. by M.M. Haraprasad Sastri, GOS, XL, Baroda, 1927.

Agni — *Agni Purāṇa*, ed. by R.L. Mitra, Bib. Ind., Calcutta, 1873-79; ed. by Panchanan Tarkaratna, Vaṅgavāsī Press, Calcutta, 1897, rpt. Calcutta, 1992; Ānandāśrama edn., Poona, 1957; Eng. trans. by M.N. Dutt, Calcutta, 1901.

AGS — *Āśvalāyana Gṛhyasūtra*, ed. with the com. of Gārgyanārāyaṇa by R.N. Vidyāratna and A.C. Vedāntavāgīśa, Bib. Ind., Calcutta, 1866-69; ed. with com. of Haradatta by T. Ganapati Sastri, TSS no. 78, Trivandrum, 1923; Eng. trans. by H. Oldenberg, SBE XXIX.

AN — *Aṅguttara Nikāya*, ed. by R. Morris and E. Hardy with Index by E. Hunt, London, 1885-1900, PTS rpt. by A.K. Warder with Eng. trans., London, 1961; Eng. trans. by F.L. Woodward and E.M. Hare, *The Book of Gradual Sayings*, PTS, London, 1935-36.

Anta — *Antagaḍadasāo*, ed. with Abhayadeva's com., Āgamodaya Samiti, Bombay, 1920; Eng. trans. by L.D. Barnett, London 1907.

ApDS — *Āpastamba Dharmasūtra*, ed. by G. Bühler, Bombay Sanskrit Series, 1892, 1894; ed. with Haradatta's *Ujjvala*, com. by Mahādeva Sastri and K. Rangacharya, Mysore 1898; Eng. trans. by G. Bühler in SBE II, Oxford, 1897.

ApGS — *Āpastamba Gṛhyasūtra*, ed. by M. Winternitz, Vienna, 1887; Eng. trans. by H. Oldenberg in SBE XXX.

AU	*Aitareya Upaniṣad*, Eng. trans. in R.E. Hume, *Thirteen Principal Upaniṣads*, Oxford, 1921; S. Radhakrishnan, *Principal Upaniṣads*, London, 1953.
AV	*Atharvaveda*, Eng. trans. in part by M. Bloomfield in SBE XLII, Oxford, 1897; by W.D. Whitney, Cambridge Mass, 1905.
Āva Cū	*Āvaśyaka Cūrṇi* by Jinadāsagani Mahottara, Ratlam, 1928.
Avadāna	*Avadānaśataka*, ed. by J.S. Speyer, Bibliotheca Buddhica III, St. Petersburg, 1902-1909.
Āva Nir	*Niryukti* of Bhadrabāhu on *Āvaśyaka Sūtra*, with the com. of Malayagiri, Āgamodaya Samiti 56, Bombay, 1928.
BDS	*Baudhāyana Dharmasūtra*, Eng. trans. by G. Bühler, SBE XIV, Oxford, 1882.
BGS	*Baudhāyana Gṛhasūtra*, ed. by R. Shamasastry, Mysore, 1920.
BhGS	*Bhāradvāja Gṛhyasūtra*, ed. by J. Solomon, Leiden, 1913.
Bib. Bud	Bibliotheca Buddhica, St. Petersburg.
Bib. Ind.	Bibliotheca Indica, Asiatic Society, Calcutta.
BKSS	*Bṛhatkathāślokasaṃgraha* of Buddhasvāmin, ed. with notes by V.S. Agrawala, Varanasi, 1974; with Eng. trans. by R.P. Poddar, Varanasi, 1986.
BM	*Buddhist Monuments*, by Debala Mitra, Calcutta, 1971.
Bhāgavata	*Bhāgavata Purāṇa*, text with Bengali trans. and com. by A.C. Bhaktivedāntasvāmī, 12 vols., Mayapur, 1996; Eng. trans. by J.M. Sanyal, 5 vols., Calcutta, 1930-34.
Brahmāṇḍa	*Brahmāṇḍa Purāṇa*, Venkateśvara Press, Bombay, 1913; ed. by Panchanan Tarkaratna, rpt. Vaṅgavāsī Press, Calcutta, 1989.
Brahmavaivarta	*Brahmavaivarta Purāṇa*, ed. by Panchanan Tarkaratna, Vaṅgavāsī Press, Calcutta, 1904; rpt. Calcutta, 1984.
Bṛhaddharma	*Bṛhaddharma Purāṇa*, ed. by M.M. Haraprasad Sastri, Bib. Ind., Calcutta, 1886-97; by Panchanan Tarkaratna, Vaṅgavāsī Press, rpt. Calcutta, 1989.
Bṛhannāradīya	*Bṛhannāradīya Purāṇa*, ed. by Hrishikesh Sastri, Bib. Ind., Calcutta, 1886-91; by Panchanan Tarkaratna, Vaṅgavāsī Press, rpt. Calcutta, 1996.
BST	Buddhist Sanskrit Texts, Mithila Institute, Darbhanga.

BT	*Buddhism in Tibet or Lamaism*, London, 1895.
BU	*Bṛhadaraṇyaka Upaniṣad*, Eng. trans. in R.E. Hume, *Thirteen Principal Upaniṣads*, Oxford, 1921; S. Radhakrishnan, *Principal Upaniṣads*, London, 1953.
CU	*Chāndogya Upaniṣad*, Eng. trans. in R.E. Hume, *Thirteen Principal Upaniṣads*, Oxford, 1921; S. Radhakrishnan, *Principal Upaniṣads*, London, 1953.
CV	*Culavaṃsa*, ed. by W. Geiger, PTS, London, 1925.
Devī	*Devī Purāṇa*, ed. Panchanan Tarkaratna, Vaṅgavāsī Press, 1895, rpt. Calcutta, 1993.
Devī Bh	*Devībhāgavata Purāṇa*, ed. Panchanan Tarkaratna, Vaṅgavāsī Press, 1910, rpt. Calcutta, 1917.
Dhamma	*Dhammapada*, ed. by S.S. Thera, PTS, London, 1914; Eng. trans. by F. Max Müller, SBE, Oxford, 1898.
Divyā	*Divyāvadāna*, ed. by E.B. Cowell and R.A. Neil, Cambridge, 1886.
DN	*Dīghā Nikāya*, ed. by T.W. Rhys Davids and J.E. Carpenter, 3 vols., PTS, London, 1890, 1903, 1911; Eng. trans. *Dialogues of the Buddha* by T.W. Rhys Davids, 3 vols., SBB, London, 1899, 1910, 1921.
DS	*Dravyasaṃgraha* of Nemicandra, ed. Intro., Eng. trans., notes and *Vṛtti* by S.C. Ghoshal, Arrah, 1917.
EI	*Epigraphia Indica*.
ERE	*Encyclopaedia of Religion and Ethics*, ed. by J. Hastings.
Garuḍa	*Garuḍa Purāṇa*, ed. P. Tarkaratna, Vaṅgavāsī Press, Calcutta, 1907, rpt. Calcutta, 1995; Eng. trans. by M.N. Dutta, Calcutta, 1908.
GB	*Gopatha Brāhmaṇa*, ed. by R. Mitra and H.C. Vidyabhushan, Bib. Ind., Calcutta, 1910.
GDS	*Gautama Dharmasūtra*, Eng. trans. by G. Bühler in SBE II, 1897.
GGS	*Gobhila Gṛhyasūtra*, ed. by C. Tarkalankar, Bib. Ind., Calcutta, 1907-8, Eng. trans. by H. Oldenberg in SBE XXX.
GOS	Gaekwad Oriental Series, Baroda.
Hari	*Harivaṃśa* with com. of Nīlakaṇṭha, pub. by Gopal Narayan, Bombay, 1895; ed. by R. Kinjawadekar, Poona, 1936; Eng. trans. by M.N. Dutta, Calcutta, 1897.

HOS Harvard Oriental Series, Cambridge Mass.

IBI *Indian Buddhist Iconograhy,* by Benoytosh Bhattacharyya, Calcutta, 1958.

ITV *Itivuttaka*, Eng. trans. by J.H. Moore, *Sayings of Buddha*, New York, 1908.

Jambu *Jambuddīvapaññatti* with Śānticandra's com. Devchand Lalbhai, Bombay, 1920.

JAOS *Journal of the American Oriental Society.*

Jāt. *Jātaka*, ed. by V. Fausböll, 7 vols., Index by D. Anderson, PTS, London, 1877-97; rpt. 1962-64; Eng. trans. ed. by E.B. Cowell, 7 vols., Cambridge, 1895-1913.

JB *Jaiminīya Brāhmaṇa*, ed. by Raghu Vira and L. Chandra, Delhi, 1954.

JUB *Jaiminīya Upaniṣad Brāhmaṇa*, text, trans. and notes by Hanus Oertel in *JAOS*, XVI, 1896.

Kālikā *Kālikā Purāṇa*, ed. by P. Tarkaratna, Vaṅgavāsī Press, rpt. Calcutta, 1977.

Kau Sū *Kauśika Sūtra*, ed. by M. Bloomfield, New Haven, 1890.

KB *Kauṣītaki Brāhmaṇa*, ed. by E.B. Cowell, Calcutta, 1861; Eng. trans. by A.B. Keith, HOS, XXV, Cambridge Mass, 1920.

KhGS *Khadira Gṛhyasūtra*, ed. by A. Mahadeva Sastri and L. Srinivasacarya, Mysore, 1913; Eng. trans. by H. Oldenberg, SBE XXIX.

KS *Kāthaka Saṃhita*, ed. by L. Von Schroeder, Leipzig, 1900-1910; A.B. Keith, in *JRAS*, 1910, 517ff; 1912, 1095ff.

KU *Kaṭha Upaniṣad*, S. Radhakrishnan, *Principal Upaniṣads*, London, 1953.

Kūrma *Kūrma Purāṇa*, ed. by Nilmani Mukhopadhyay, Bib. Ind., Calcutta, 1890, ed. by P. Tarkaratna, Vaṅgavāsī Press, Calcutta, 1914, rpt. Calcutta, 1988.

KV *Kathāvatthu*, ed. by A.C. Taylor, PTS, London, 1894; Eng. trans. *Points of Controversy or Subject of Discourse*, by S.J. Aung and C.A.F. Rhys Devids, PTS, London, 1915.

KVLM *Kuvalayamālā* by Udyotanasuri, ed. by A.N. Upadhye, Bombay, 1959, 1970.

Lalita *Lalitavistara*, ed. and Eng. trans. by R.L. Mitra, Bib. Ind.

Calcutta, 1877, 1886, rpt. by P.L. Vaidya in BST series, Darbhanga, 1958.

Liṅga — *Liṅga Purāṇa*, ed. by Jivananda Vidyasagara, Bib. Ind., Calcutta, 1885; ed. by P. Tarkaratna, Vaṅgavāsī Press, rpt. Calcutta, 1989.

Mārkaṇḍeya — *Mārkaṇḍeya Purāṇa*, ed. by K.M. Banerjee, Bib. Ind., Calcutta, 1862; Eng. trans. by F.E. Pargiter, Calcutta, 1904; ed. by P. Tarkaratna, Vaṅgavāsī Press, Calcutta, 1910.

Matsya — *Matsya Purāṇa*, pub. by Ānandāśrama Press, Poona, 1907; Eng. trans. by A. Taluqdar of Oudh in SBH series, 2 vols., Allahabad, 1916-17; ed. by P. Tarkaratna, Vaṅgavāsī Press, Calcutta, 1890, rpt Calcutta, 1988.

Mbh — *Mahābhārata*, Critical Edition, Poona, 1927ff; Eng. trans. by K.M. Ganguly, Calcutta, 1894-96, rpt. Calcutta, 1936; and New Delhi, 1993.

MBV — *Mahābodhivaṃsa*, ed. by S.A. Strong, PTS, London, 1891.

MGS — *Mānava Gṛhyasūtra*, ed. by F. Knauer, St. Petersburg, 1897; pub. with com. of Aṣṭāvakra in GOS, Baroda, 1926.

Milinda — *Milindapañho*, ed. by V. Trenckner, London, 1880; Eng. trans. by T.W. Rhys Davids in SBE, Oxford, 1890 94.

MN — *Majjhima Nikāya*, ed. by V. Trenckner and R. Chalmers in 3 vols., PTS, London, 1888-99, rpt. 1948-51; Eng. trans. by I.B. Horner, *Middle Length Sayings*, PTS, London, 1954-59.

MNid — *Mahāniddesa*, ed. by Louis de la Vallée Poussin and E.J. Thomas, PTS, London, 1916-17.

MS — *Maitrāyaṇī Saṃhita*, ed. by L.V. Schroeder, Leipzig, 1881-86.

MV — *Mahāvamsa*, Eng. trans. *The Great Chronicle of Ceylon*, by W. Geiger, London, 1912.

Nāyā — Nāyādhammakahāo, ed. by N.V. Vaidya, Poona, 1940.

Nir — *Nirukta* of Yāska, ed. by S.V. Samasrami, Bib. Ind., Calcutta, 1891; rev. edn. H.V. Samasrami, Calcutta, 1912; ed. with Eng. trans. by Laksman Sarup, 2 vols., Lahore, 1922.

Piṇḍa Nir — *Piṇḍa Niryukti* with Malayagiri's com. pub. from Surat, 1918.

PTS — Pali Text Society, London.

PTSMS — *Pañcastikāyasamayasāra*, ed. and trans. by Appaswamy Chakrabarti, SBJ, Arrah, 1920; pub. in Sanatana Jain Granthamala, Benares, 1914.

PU — *Praśna Upaniṣad*, S. Radhakrishnan, *Principal Upaniṣads*, London, 1953.

Rām — *Rāmāyaṇa*, Eng. trans. by M.N. Dutta, Calcutta, 1893-94; by R.T.H. Griffith, Benares, 1915; by M.L. Sen, rpt., New Delhi, 1994.

RV — *Ṛgveda*, Critical Edition by Vaidika Samsodhana Maṇḍala, 4 vols., Poona, 1933ff; Eng. trans by F. Max Müller in SBE, XXXII, 1891; by H. Oldenberg in SBE XLVI, Oxford, 1897; by R.T.H. Griffith, Benares, 1896-97.

Saddharma — *Saddharmapuṇḍarīka*, Sanskrit edn. by H. Kern and B. Nanjio, Bib. Bud., Leningrad, 1908-12; Eng. trans. by H. Kern in SBE, 1909.

Samādhi — *Samādhirājasūtra*, ed. by P.L. Vaidya, BST, Darbhanga, 1961.

SDM — *Sādhanamālā*, ed. by B.T. Bhattacharyya, 2 vols., GOS, Baroda, 1925-28.

SB — *Śatapatha Brāhmaṇa*, ed. S. Samasrami, Eng. trans. by J. Eggeling in SBE XII, XXVI, XLI, XLIII, XLIV, Oxford, 1882-1900.

SBB — Sacred Books of the Buddhists, London.

SBE — Sacred Books of the East, Oxford.

SBH — Sacred Books of the Hindus, Allahabad.

SBJ — Sacred Books of the Jains, Arrah.

SDS — *Sarvadarśanasaṃgraha* of Mādhavācārya, ed. by Isvara Chandra Vidyasagar, Bib. Ind., Calcutta, 1906; ed. by K.V. Abhayankar, Poona, 1950; Eng. trans. by E.B. Cowell and A.E. Gough, London, 1899.

SDSC — *Ṣaḍdarśanasamuccaya* of Haribhadra, ed. with Guṇaratna's *Tarkarahasvadīpikā* by L. Suali, Bib. Ind., Calcutta, 1914.

SGS — *Śāṅkhyāyana Gṛhasūtra*, Eng. trans. by H. Oldenberg in SBE XXIX.

Śiva — *Śiva Purāṇa*, pub. by Venkateśvara Press, Bombay, ed. by P. Tarkaratna, Vaṅgavāsī Press, Calcutta, 1907, rpt. Calcutta, 1994.

Skanda — *Skanda Purāṇa,* ed. by G.P. Raverkar, Venkateśvara Press, Bombay, 1909-11; ed. by Panchanan Tarkaratna, Vaṅgavāsī Press, rpt. Calcutta, 1990.

SN — *Saṃyutta Nikāya,* ed. by L. Feer, 5 vols., PTS, London, 1884-91; Eng. trans. *Book of the Kindred Sayings,* by C.A.F. Rhys Davids and F.L. Woodward, PTS, London, 1917-30.

Sum. Vil — *Sumaṅgalavilāsinī,* ed. by T.W. Rhys Davids et al., PTS, London, 1931.

Suttani — *Suttanipāta,* ed. by V. Fausböll, PTS, London, 1885, 1893, Eng. trans in SBE X(2), Oxford, 1881; *Woven Cadences of the Early Buddhists,* by E.M. Hare, SBB, London, 1944.

TĀ — *Taittirīya Āraṇyaka,* ed. by R.L. Mitra, Bib. Ind., Calcutta, 1872.

TB — *Taittirīya Brāhmaṇa,* ed. by R.L. Mitra, Bib. Ind., Calcutta, 1890.

Ṭhān — *Ṭhānāṅga,* ed. in Āgama Saṃgraha III, Benares, 1880; with Abhayadeva's com., Bombay, 1918-20.

Thera/Therī — *Theragāthā/Therīgāthā,* ed. by H. Oldenberg and R. Pischel, PTS, London, 1883; Eng. trans. by C.A.F. Rhys Davids, PTS, 1909, 1913.

Triṣaṣṭi — *Trisaṣṭiśalākāpuruṣacarita* of Hemacandra, Eng. trans. by H.M. Johnson, 6 vols., Baroda, 1913-62.

TS — *Taittirīya Saṃhita,* ed. with com. of Madhava by E.B. Cowell, Bib. Ind., Calcutta, 1899; Eng. trans. by A.B. Keith, Cambridge, 1914.

TTDS — *Tattvārthādhigama-sūtra* of Umāsvāti, ed. by M.K. Premchand, Bib. Ind., Calcutta, 1903-5, with intro., trans., notes and com. in Eng. by J.L. Jaini in SBJ series II, Arrah.

TU — *Taittirīya Upaniṣad,* S. Radhakrishnan, *Principal Upaniṣads,* London, 1953.

Uttara — *Uttarādhyayana-sūtra,* ed. with intro., notes and com. by Jarl Charpentier, Upsala, 1922; Eng. trans. by H. Jacobi in SBE XLV.

Uvav — *Uvavāiya,* pub. by Āgamodaya Samiti, 1921.

Vāmana — *Vāmana Purāṇa,* pub. by Venkateśvara Press, Bombay, 1908; ed. by P. Tarkaratna, Vaṅgavāsī Press, Calcutta, 1908, rpt. Calcutta, 1989.

Varāha — *Varāha Purāṇa,* ed. by H.P. Sastri, Bib. Ind., Calcutta,

1887; ed. by P. Tarkratna, Vaṅgavāsī Press, rpt. Calcutta, 1994.

Vāyu — *Vāyu Purāṇa*, pub. by Ānandāśrama, Poona, 1905; ed. by P. Tarkaratna, Vaṅgavāsī Press, Calcutta, 1921, rpt. Calcutta, 1990.

VH — *Vasudevahiṇḍi* by Saṅghadāsagani Vācaka, ed. by Muni Caturvijaya and Puṇyavijaya, Bhavnagar, 1930-31; J.C. Jain, *Vasudevahiṇḍi: An Authentic version of the Bṛhatkathā*, Ahmedabad, 1977.

VI — *Vedic Index* by A.A. Macdonell and A.B. Keith, London, 1912.

Vibh — *Vibhaṅga*, ed. by C.A.F. Rhys Davids, PTS, London, 1904.

Vim — *Vimānavatthu*, ed. by E.R. Gonaratne, PTS, London, 1886.

Vis — *Visuddhimagga*, ed. by C.A.F. Rhys Davids, PTS, London, 1920-21; Eng. trans. as *Path of Purity* by P. Mungtin, PTS, London, 1922-31.

Viṣṇu — *Viṣṇu Purāṇa*, ed. by B.L. Sarkar, Vaṅgavāsī Press, Calcutta, 1887; Eng. trans. by H.H. Wilson, London, 1840, rpt. Calcutta, 1961.

Viy — *Viyāhapaññati* (Bhagavatī Sūtra) with com. of Abhayadeva, Bombay, 1921, Ratlam, 1937.

VS — *Vājasaneyi Saṃhitā*, ed. with Mahīdhara's com. by A. Weber, London, 1852.

YT — *Yast*, J. Darmesteter, *The Zend Avesta*, in SBE IV, XXIII, XXXI.

YV — *Yajurveda*, see *Kāṭhaka*, *Maitrāyaṇīya*, *Taittirīya* and *Vājasaneyi Saṃhitās*.

Index